Lafcadio Hearn's
Creole Cook Book

Lafcadio Hearn's

CREOLE COOK BOOK

With the addition of a collection of drawings
and writings by Lafcadio Hearn during his
sojourn in New Orleans from 1877 to 1887.

A Literary and Culinary Adventure

Pelican Publishing Company
Gretna 1990

First printing, 1967
Second printing, 1990

Library of Congress Cataloging-in-Publication Data

Hearn, Lafcadio, 1850-1904.
   [Creole cook book]
   Lafcadio Hearn's Creole cook book : with the addition of a
collection of drawings and writings by Lafcadio Hearn during his
sojourn in New Orleans from 1877 to 1887 : a literary and culinary
adventure.
     p.   cm.
   ISBN 0-88289-788-8
   1. Cookery, Creole. I. Title. II. Title: Creole cook book.
TX715.H397   1990
641.59763--dc20
                                        89-26575
                                            CIP

This edition was reproduced from a copy in the Lafcadio Hearn collection of
Tulane University.

Manufactured in the United States of America
Published by Pelican Publishing Company, Inc.
1101 Monroe Street, Gretna, Louisiana 70053

FOREWORD

His name was Lafcadio Hearn. He was bulbous eyed and myopic to the point of blindness and all his life he knew a waif's sense of insecurity and often the hunger that is frequently a waif's lot. Of all places on this earth of his loneliness he loved New Orleans most, and there is irony in his creation of this classic, which has to do with the food and drink and some of the foibles of his beloved adopted city, for it can be said that it was written by a hungry man out of hunger, a physical hunger that seldom was far away.

He was at home with the Creole city's food from the day he stepped off the *Thompson Dean* as she landed at New Orleans in November 1877 but frequently he could afford barely enough of such food to keep himself alive.

He found his way to the boarding house of Mary Bustillos, 228 Baronne Street and paid over to her his small amount of cash for several weeks room and board. For several months he wandered in the New Orleans streets, often near starving, as the *Cincinnati Commercial* did not pay him for his articles on New Orleans.

Eventually he found work with the *Democrat* and made the acquaintance of Major William M. Robinson, editor of the New Orleans *Republican*. He was welcomed in the Robinsons' home and perhaps here began his acquaintance with better New Orleans American and Creole cooking. He also developed a lasting friendship with Dr. Rudolph Matas and his family. Hearn said Mrs. Matas supplied a good deal of the material for his cookbook.

After his first six lean months, Major Robertson introduced Hearn to Mark Bigney who together with Edwin L. Jewel had started a modest newspaper called the *Item*. He became a member of their staff—an assistant editor with a salary of $10.00 a week. Hearn's contributions to the *Item* were to make him a noted regional literary figure of his day. His descriptions of the New Orleans scene, his broad literary interest and criticisms and his advanced ideas on psychology and the creative instinct were a sensation in his day. The self-taught little literary figure developed for himself during this period a polished writing style.

In 1879 Hearn learned that the *Item* was in precarious financial circumstances. In this extremity he suggested that illustrations on the front page of the *Item* might increase its circulation. Wandering through the Vieux Carre, he sketched the Negro vendors, tramps, gentlemen and dozens of other habitants. Each day a wooden block cut was fixed at the head of an article. The paper was printed directly from this combination of metal type and wood blocks. All in all, Hearn published about 175 cartoons in two years, 1879 and 1880. Taken as a whole, the columns and pictures present a sensitive illustrated description of life in New Orleans in 1880.

In the meantime, Hearn had moved to the French Quarter where he lived in a number of houses, always seeking cleanliness and comfort. For a while he lived at 105 Bourbon Street (now 516). This almost faced the old French Opera. For a while he lived in a particularly shabby room in the northern end of the French Quarter where by doing his own cooking he could cut down his food expense to $2.00 a week.

He was saving his money for the special purpose of starting a cheap restaurant. He wrote to his friend Henry Watkins in Cincinnatti in June of 1778, saying "Money can be made here out of the poor. The people are so poor nothing pays except that which appeals to poverty—now one can make 30 milk bisquits for 5¢ and 8 cups of coffee for 5¢." He horded $100.00 and opened a little restaurant in a sordid back street building at 160 Dryades. Yellow hand bills were printed which read:

"THE 5-CENT RESTAURANT,

160 DRYADES,

This is the cheapest eating house in the South. It is neat, orderly and respectable as any other in New Orleans. You can get a good meal for a couple of nickels. All dishes 5 cents. Everything half the price of the markets."

This name did not appeal to him so he changed to an even stranger one. On the 2nd of March 1879 *The Hard Times* opened for business and a little advertisement appeared in the *Item*. In spite of advertising in the *Item* full of the flavor and quaintness of Hearn's style, his business hopes collapsed on March the 22nd. His "partner" disappeared with the little cash and the cook, leaving Hearn to shoulder the debts.

His most comfortable period during his New Orleans days came when he began to take his meals at the boarding house 68 Gasquet Street of Mrs. Courtney, a genial Irishwoman. She and her family adopted Hearn, nursed and fed him for a number of years, and his grateful letters reflect his appreciation of their kindness.

In 1881 Hearn went to work for the *Times-Democrat* under its new editor, Page Baker. Very probably many of the recipes Hearn used in this book came from the Baker family and those of others he visited. He was viewed with mixed feelings because of his strange and exotic tastes in literature. He had an intense interest in the Negro lore in the Creole countries of the world, and his notebooks were full of quaint Negro proverbs in Gombo French. These he arranged and translated first into correct French and then into English.

He persuaded his friend, William H. Coleman who had opened a second-hand book shop in the old Astor Hotel in New York to publish this book of sayings by offering to submit a second book of the Creole recipes he had gathered in the many New Orleans homes in which he visited. He had already said in the columns of the *Item* that he would like to edit a cookbook. Coleman published these two works—*Gombo Zhèbes* and *La Cuisine Creole* —and a third book, the *Historical Sketch Book and Guide to New Orleans* to which Hearn also contributed.

The books were to be on the market by the time of the Cotton Centennial Exposition which opened in 1884 and were to attract a sale among the hordes of tourists expected to attend. But printing delays occurred and they did not appear until April 1885 and the books sold badly. However, *La Cuisine Creole* did better than either of the others.

This Pelican edition of *La Cuisine Creole* is a reproduction of the original by photo offset process, including the original cover—to which we have added, for the first time, the name of the author. We have also added other Hearn material.

The original numbering of the pages persists. We have inserted sketches reproduced from Hearn's cartoons in the *Item,* among the first used by a Southern newspaper, some of Hearn's other work in the *Item,* and selections from *Gombo Zhèbes.*

For much of the information used in this sketch of Hearn I am indebted to the pioneer research of Edward Larocque Tinker whose *Lafcadio Hearn's American Days* published by Dodd, Mead and Co. in 1924 is the basic Hearn bibliography of that period in his life. Our thanks to the staff of the Lafcadio Hearn Collection of Tulane University for their invaluable assistance.

The raven we have used on the end sheets was the symbol Hearn often used as a rebus in letters to friends.

HODDING CARTER

INTRODUCTION.

"La Cuisine Créole" (Créole cookery) partakes of the nature of its birthplace—New Orleans—which is cosmopolitan in its nature, blending the characteristics of the American, French, Spanish, Italian, West Indian and Mexican. In this compilation will be found many original recipes and other valuable ones heretofore unpublished, notably those of Gombo filé, Bouille-abaisse, Courtbouillon, Jambolaya, Salade à la Russe, Bisque of Cray-fish à la Créole, Pousse Café, Café brulé, Brûlot, together with many confections and delicacies for the sick, including a number of mixed drinks. Much domestic contentment depends upon the successful preparation of the meal; and as food rendered indigestible through ignorance in cooking often creates discord and unhappiness, it behooves the young housekeeper to learn the art of cooking.

It is the author's endeavor to present to her a number of recipes all thoroughly tested by experience, and embracing the entire field of the "Cuisine," set forth in such clear, concise terms, as to be readily understood and easily made practicable, thereby unveiling the mysteries which surround her, upon the *entrée* into the kitchen. Economy and simplicity govern " La Cuisine Créole ; " and its many savory dishes are rendered palatable more as the result of care in their preparation, than any great skill or expensive outlay in the selection of materials. The Créole housewife often makes delicious *morceaux* from things usually thrown away by the extravagant servant. She is proud of her art, and deservedly receives the compliments of her friends. This volume will be found quite different from the average cook-book in its treatment of recipes, and is the only one in print containing dishes peculiar to " la Cuisine Créole."

ULTRA-CANAL.

VOICES OF DAWN [1]

A dreadful sound is in his ears.—Job xv, 21.

There have never been so many fruit-peddlers and viand-peddlers of all sorts as at the present time—an encouraging sign of prosperity and the active circulation of money.

With the first glow of sunlight the street resounds with their cries; and, really, the famous "Book of London Cries" contains nothing more curious than some of these vocal advertisements—these musical announcements, sung by Italians, negroes, Frenchmen, and Spaniards. The vendor of fowls pokes in his head at every open window with cries of "Chick-EN, Madamma, Chick-EN!" and the seller of "Lem-ONS—fine Lem-ONS!" follows in his footsteps. The peddlers of "Ap-PULLS!" of Straw-BARE-eries!" and "Black-Brees!"—all own sonorous voices. There is a handsome Italian with a somewhat ferocious pair of black eyes, who sells various oddities, and has adopted the word "lagniappe" for his war-cry—pronouncing it Italianwise.

He advances noiselessly to open windows and doors, plunges his blazing black glance into the interior, and suddenly queries in a deep bass, like a clap of thunder, "LAGNIAPPA, Madam-a!—lagniap-PA!" Then there is the Cantelope Man, whose cry is being imitated by all the children:

"Cantel-lope-ah!
Fresh and fine,
Jus from the vine,
Only a dime!"

There are also two peddlers, the precise meaning of whose cries we have never been able to determine. One shouts, or seems to shout, "A-a-a-a-ah! SHE got." Just what "SHE got" we gave not yet been able to determine; but we fancy it must be disagreeable, as the crier's rival always shouts—"I-I-I!—I want nothing!" with a tremendous emphasis on the I. There is another fellow who seems to shout something which is not exactly proper for modest ears to hear; but he is really only announcing that he has fine potatoes for sale. Then there is the Clothespole Man, whose musical, quavering cry is heard at the distance of miles on a clear day, "Clo-ho-ho-ho-ho-ho-ho-ho-se-poles!" As a trilling tenor he is simply marvelous. The "Coaly-coaly" Man, a merry little Gascon, is too well known as a singer to need any criticism; but he is almost ubiquitous. There is also the fig-seller, who crieth in such a manner that his "Fresh figs!" seems to be "Ice crags!" And the fan-sellers, who intend to call, "Cheap fans!" but who really seem to yell "Jap-ans!" and "Chapped hand!" Then there is the seller of "Towwells" and the sellers of "Ochre-A" who appear to deal in but one first-class quality of paint, if we dare believe the mendacious sounds which reach our ears; neither must we forget the vendors of "Tom-ate-toes!" Whose toes? we should like to know.

These are new cries, with perhaps three exceptions;—with the old cries added to the list—the "calas" and the "plaisir" and other Creole calls, we might "spread out" over another column. If any one has a little leisure and a little turn for amusement, he can certainly have plenty of fun while listening to the voices of the peddlers entering his room together with the first liquid gold of sunrise.

[1] *Item*, July 22, 1881.

LITTLE DICTIONARY OF CREOLE PROVERBS

In old days the Creole story-teller would always announce his intention of beginning a tale by the exclamation *"Tim-tim!"* whereupon the audience would shout in reply *"Bois sec;"* and the story-teller would cry again, *"Cassez-li,"* to which the chorus would add *"....dans tchu* (bonda) *macaque."* Thus the story-teller intimated that he had no intention of merely *"joking,"* but intended to tell the whole truth and nothing else—"a real good story"—*tois fois bonne conte!*

316. Tout bois cé bois:
      Main mapou
      Pas 'cajou.
   (Tout bois c'est du bois;
      Mais le mapou
      N'est pas de l'acajou.)
   "All wood is wood; but mapou wood isn't mahogany (cedar)"[1]— [*Trinidad.*]

317. *Tout ça c'est commerce Man Lison. (Tout ça c'est affaire de Maman Lison.)
   "All that's like Mammy Lison's doings."[2]—[*Louisiana.*]

318. Tout ça qui poté zépron pas maquignon. (Tout homme qui porte éperons n'est pas maquignon.)
   "Everybody who wears spurs isn't a jockey." All is not gold that glitters.—[*Martinique.*]

321. *Toutt jour c'est pas dimanche. (Tous les jours ne sont pas le dimanche.)
   "Every day isn't Sunday."—*Louisiana.*

77. C'est cuiller qui allé lacail[3] gamelle; gamelle pas jamain allé lacail cuiller . (C'est la cuille qui va à la maison de la gamelle; jamais la gamelle ne va à la maison de la cuiller.)
   "Spoon goes to bowl's house; bowl never goes to spoon's house."— [*Hayti.*]

74. Causer cé manger zoreîes. (Causer, c'est le manger des oreilles.)
   "Conversation is the food of the ears."—[*Trinidad.*]

47. Ça qui gagné piti mil dehors, veillé laplie. (Celui qui a un peu de mil dehors veille la pluie.)
   "He who has [would raise] a little millet out of doors, watches for rain."—[*Hayti.*]

48. Ça qui gagne zoli fille gagne coudeçapeau. (Celui qui a une jolie fille reçoit des coups de chapeau.)
   "He who has a pretty daughter receives plenty of salutes."— [*Mauritius.*]

Gombo Zhèbes 1885

Item 1880

325. *Toutt mounn save ça qui ka bouï nens canari yo. (Toute personne sait ce qui bout dans son canari [marmite].)

"Everybody knows what boils in his own pot"—i. e., knows his own business best.[1]—[*Martinique.*]

332. *Vie cannari ka fé bon bouillon. (Les vieux pots font les bonnes soupes.)

"It's the old pot that makes the good soup."—[*Martinique.*]

[1] In Thomas's Trinidad version: *"Tout moune connaite ça qui ka bouï nans canari yeaux."* In Louisiana Creole: *"Chakin connin ça kapé bouilli dans so chodière."* Canari is sometimes used in our Creole, but rarely. I have only heard it in old songs. The iron pot (*chodière*) or tin utensil has superseded the *canari*

147. *Jadin loin, gombo gaté. (Jardin loin, gombo gâté.)
   "When the garden is far, the gombo is spoiled."[4]—[*Martinique*.]
299. Si moin té gagnin moussa, moin té mangé gombo. (Si j'avais du moussa, je mangerais du gombo).
   "If I had some *moussa*[3] I would eat some gombo." If I had the necessary I could enjoy the superfluous."—[*Martinique*.]

   [4] This appears to be a universal Creole proverb. If you want anything to be well done, you must look after it yourself: to absent oneself from one's business is unwise, etc.
   [3] *Mousse* is a word used in *Martinique* for hominy, or a sort of corn-mush which is used to thicken gombo-soup. In Louisiana boiled rice is similarly used.

Gombo Zhèbes 1885

LA CUISINE CREOLE.

SOUP.

Soup being the first course served at all ordinary dinners, we make it the basis for preliminary remarks. Nothing is more palatable than good, well-made soup, and nothing less appetising than poor soup. Now to attain perfection in any line, care and attention are requisite, careful study a necessity, and application the moving force. Hence, cooking in all its branches should be studied as a science, and not be looked upon as a haphazard mode of getting through life. Cooking is in a great measure a chemical process, and the ingredients of certain dishes should be as carefully weighed and tested as though emanating from the laboratory. Few female cooks think of this, but men with their superior instinctive reasoning power are more governed by law and abide more closely to rule; therefore, are better cooks, and command higher prices for services.

Now with regard to soup making, the first care is to have the fire brisk, the vessel in which it is cooked thoroughly cleaned and free from odor. To insure this, keep one vessel sacred to soup as nearly as possible; and after serving, wash the pot with potash water, or take a piece of washing soda the size of a nutmeg, dissolve in hot water and then cleanse the vessel.   A good workman is known by his tools, so also a good cook will look well to the utensils before commencing operations.   Good results follow carefulness.

Soup must have time to cook, and should always boil gently, that the meat may become tender, and give out its juices. Allow a quart of water and a teaspoonful of salt for each pound of meat.   Soup meat must always be put down in cold water.   Skim well before it comes to the boiling point, and again skim off superfluous fat before putting in the vegetables.   The vegetables most used in soups are carrots, leeks, parsley, turnip, celery, tomatoes, okras, cabbage, cauliflower, peas and potatoes.

One large leek, two carrots, one bunch of parsley, two turnips and a potato, will be enough for one pot of soup.   One head of celery, two leeks, two turnips, and five or six small potatoes will be enough another time.

Six tomatoes skinned, the juice strained from the seeds, a leek, a bunch of parsley, and six potatoes will answer for another style ; a carrot, some cabbage, tomatoes, and potatoes will do another time.   Okra alone is vegetable enough for a gombo, unless onion is liked with it.   Green peas, lettuce, and new potatoes are enough for spring lamb soup.   Vermicelli and macaroni are for chicken, lamb or veal soup, with the addition of onion if liked.

It is well to prepare the vegetables when the meat is put over the fire to boil; allow a quart of water to a pound of meat.   Trim and scrape carrots, then cut or grate them.   Wash parsley and cut it small.   Pare turnips and cut them in slices a quarter of an inch thick.   Cut leeks in thick slices.

Cut celery in half lengths; the delicate green leaves give a fine flavor to the soup.

Pour boiling water on tomatoes, which will cause the skins to peel off easily; when cool, squeeze out the seeds, and reserve the juice for use in soup.

Shave cabbage in thin slices. Slice okra for gombo or ochra soup. Pare the potatoes, shell the peas, and cut off green corn from the cob, for all these add fine flavor to soup.

To color soup brown, use browned flour or a little burnt sugar. Spinach leaves give a fine green color. Pound the leaves, tie them in a cloth, and squeeze out all the juice, which, add to the soup five minutes before serving. This is also used to give color to mock-turtle soup.

You may color soup red by putting in the strained juice of tomatoes, or the whole tomato, if it is run through a sieve; grated carrot gives a fine amber color; okra gives a pale green.

For white soups, which are made of veal, lamb, and chicken, white vegetables are best, such as rice, pearl barley, vermicelli, and macaroni; the thickening should then be made of unbrowned flour.

STOCK FOR SOUP.

Stock in its composition is not confined to any set rules or any particular proportions. All cook-books give particular, as well as general, directions for its manufacture; but all cooks know that the most economical plan is to have a general stock-pot, where, or into which, you can throw any pieces of beef or any piece of meat from which gravy can be extracted—bones, skin, brisket or tops of ribs, ox-cheek, ham, trimmings of turkey and other fowls, pieces of mutton, bacon, veal, game, etc., etc. In fact, anything that will become a jelly will assist in making stock. To this medley of ingredients add pepper, salt, spices, herbs, carrots cut small, onions, and curry, if wished, etc., and stew all to a rich consistency over a slow fire, and then remove to cool. When cool, or rather cold, every particle of fat must be removed and stock poured clear of all sediment; it is now ready for use. When very rich soup is desired, the jelly from a cow-heel, or a lump of butter rolled in flour, must be added to the stock.

TO CLARIFY STOCKS OR SOUPS.

The whites of two eggs to about four quarts of stock or soup; two pints and a half of cold water.

Whisk the whites of two fresh eggs with half a pint of water for ten minutes; then pour in very gently the four quarts of boiling stock or soup, stirring it all the time. Place the stewpan over the fire, and skim the mixture till clear before allowing it to boil. When on the point of boiling, stir rapidly; then place it a little back from the fire, and let it settle till the whites of the eggs become separated. Strain it through a fine cloth placed over a sieve, and it will be clear and good.

STOCK FOR GRAVIES.

Cut the meat from a knuckle of veal, and put it, with a pound of lean beef, into two quarts of water; add one table-spoonful of salt and a teaspoonful of pepper; cover it close, and let it stew until the meat is very tender; then strain it and keep it for rich soups or gravies, as thinning them with

water spoils them. Always keep a pot or stewpan in which
to throw all nice pieces of meat left from dinner, also any
steak, bones, chicken-wings, etc., etc. This makes a reserve
of stock with very little fresh meat. It is useful and economical, and, being without vegetables, never sours. In
making oyster soup use a pint or so of this stock to the
usual quart of oysters and a pint of milk.

PLAIN BEEF SOUP.

Five pounds of the leg or shin of beef; one gallon of
water; a teaspoonful of salt; two heads of celery; five carrots; three onions; four turnips; two tomatoes, and a bunch
of sweet herbs. Boil four hours and a half.

Cut the meat in two or three pieces, and put them into a
pot with a gallon of cold water, which gradually soaks out
the juices of the meat before coming to the boil. Salt well,
then skim as the soup heats. Boil slowly with a regular heat
for about four hours; then add two heads of celery, five carrots cut small, two tomatoes, three onions sliced and fried,
and the sweet herbs tied up in muslin. The turnips should
be added half an hour before serving. If any portion of the
meat is required for the table, take it from the soup about
two hours before dinner. Let the remainder be left in the
soup, which must be strained through a hair sieve before it
is served.

SOUPE ET BOUILLI.

Six or eight pounds of a brisket of beef; three carrots;
four turnips; two onions; six cloves; two heads of celery;
one clove of garlic; a bunch of sweet herbs; a little salt; a

piece of butter; a little flour; one French roll; a table-spoonful of French mustard.

Put the beef into a pot and cover it with water, and when it boils take off the scum as it rises; then draw it to the side of the fire to stew slowly for five or six hours, with the carrots, turnips, celery, garlic, bunch of sweet herbs, and the onions stuck with cloves. When done lay the bouilli on a hot dish, and strew over it some carrots, turnips and the stalks of celery, previously boiled and cut into shapes. Add to it a sauce made of a little of the soup, thickened with flour fried in butter, and seasoned with pepper and salt. Strain the soup over a French roll placed at the bottom of the tureen and serve. The bouilli may have a spoonful of French mustard added to the soup sauce.

BROTH IN HASTE.

Cut some rare roast meat or broiled steak very fine. To a teacupful of the cut meat put a pint and a half of boiling water; cover it, and set it on the fire for ten minutes; season to taste. Roll a cracker fine, and put in with the meat. This broth is both excellent and convenient for invalids or children.

PLAIN CHICKEN-BROTH FOR AN INVALID.

Cut a young fowl into four parts, wash well in cold water, put the pieces in a stewpan with one quart of cold water and a little salt; let it boil gently, skim it well; add the white heart of a head of lettuce and a handful of chervil. Boil the broth for an hour, then strain it into a bowl. Two tablespoonfuls of pearl barley added to the broth when first put on makes it quite nourishing for an invalid.

CRAYFISH-BROTH FOR PURIFYING THE BLOOD.

Take two pounds of the lean part of very white veal, chop it very fine; add to it three dozen crayfish and a handful of green chervil; pound them together to thoroughly bruise the crayfish; then put the whole into a stewpan, and pour upon it three pints of cold spring water; add a little salt, and place the stewpan on the stove to boil. After half an hour, set it back on the stove, and let it simmer very gently for an hour, then strain. It should be taken fasting to insure its best effect.

SOUPE MAIGRE, WITHOUT MEAT, FOR LENT.

Melt half a pound of butter in a stewpan, put in six onions sliced; add two heads of celery cut small, one-half a head of white cabbage, and a bunch of chopped parsley; let them boil twonty minutes, then stir in three rolled crackers; pour in two quarts of boiling milk, or milk and water; let this boil up gently for half an hour, and just before serving stir in two well-beaten eggs.

CHICKEN SOUP. YELLOW AND VERY RICH.

Take two pounds of veal, half as much beef or lamb, and one small chicken cut up; boil them in three quarts of water, skim off all the scum as it rises; slice a leek or two onions, grate a large carrot or two small ones; put all these to the soup; add two tablespoonfuls of salt and one of pepper. Let it boil gently for two hours, then add a spoonful of butter worked in flour; cover this for fifteen minutes, and serve in a tureen. Take the chicken into a deep dish, put over it butter, pepper, and sprigs of parsley; or you may chop the chicken up, season with pepper, salt, butter, and an egg; form into balls, roll them in flour, and drop them in a few minutes before serving.

VEAL GRAVY SOUP.

Throw into a stewpan one pound veal cutlet, three slices of ham, two tablespoonfuls of lard, and let them fry gently; then, before browning, add three sliced onions, two carrots, two parsnips, a head of celery, and a few cloves. Let them cook slowly till lightly browned, then add a pint and a half of boiling broth or water; let this cook for an hour, and then put in a cup of mushrooms; skim and strain for use.

SCOTCH BARLEY BROTH. CHEAP AND SUBSTANTIAL.

Wash half a pound of Scotch barley in cold water; put it in a pot with four or five pounds of shin beef sawed into small pieces, cover it with cold water and set it on the fire. When it boils skim it well, and then add three onions. Set it near the fire to simmer gently for two hours. If much fat rises skim again; then add two heads of celery and a couple of turnips cut into thin pieces. Season with salt, and let it boil for an hour and a half. Take out the meat on a platter and cover to keep warm; then pour the soup in a tureen and serve.

CONSOMME OF BEEF AND FOWL.

Take two pounds of lean beef and a fowl half roasted and cut in pieces, put into a saucepan, which must be filled with stock or plain broth; skim it well, salt it to taste, and add two carrots, two onions, a head of celery or a pinch of celery seed, also a little thyme, a whole pepper, mace, and a bay leaf. Let it simmer gently for three or four hours, then strain through a coarse cloth; free it entirely from fat, and clarify it with the white of an egg.

WHITE CONSOMME OF FOWL.

Take one or two fowls, old or young. Let them lie half an hour in cold water to cleanse from the blood, then drain and put them in a pot; fill it with water, let it boil, then skim it. Add one large carrot, or two small ones, two turnips, one onion, one head of celery, two cloves, a piece of mace, and a little salt. Let it boil gently for two hours if the chickens are young; if old, three hours. When they are tender, skim off the fat and pass the consommé through a sieve. This consommé may be considered a basis for all white soups, as well as white sauces, and should be used instead of water for filling them up.

PLAIN VERMICELLI SOUP, No. 1.

Put a soup-bone, weighing from two to three pounds, or a brisket of beef, into four quarts of water; add two onions, two carrots, and two turnips; salt to taste, and place over the fire to boil for three hours; then remove and strain; put back on the stove, and add a quarter of a pound of vermicelli, and let it boil till tender; serve with tomatoes.

VERMICELLI SOUP, No. 2.

Cut about four pounds of knuckle of veal, one pound and a half of the scrag of mutton, and a few slices of ham into small pieces; put them into a saucepan with one onion stuck with cloves, and four ounces of butter; then add the carrots, mace, bunch of sweet herbs, one anchovy, and the celery. Mix all together, cover it close, and set it over the fire till all the gravy has been extracted from the meat; pour the liquor into a bowl, let the meat brown in the pan, and add to it four quarts of water; boil it slowly till it is reduced to three pints, strain it, and stir in the gravy drawn from the meat. Set it over the fire, add the vermicelli, one head of celery cut fine, a little cayenne, and salt; boil it up for ten minutes. Lay a French roll in the tureen, pour the soup over it, and strew some vermicelli on the top.

BAKED SOUP.

Cut the beef or mutton and the vegetables in pieces, season them with salt and pepper, and put them into a jar with a pint of peas and the Patna rice. Pour in four quarts of water, cover the jar very closely, and set it in the oven to bake. When done, strain it through a sieve, and serve it very hot.

VERMICELLI OR MACARONI SOUP.

Swell a quarter of a pound of vermicelli or macaroni (whichever is preferred) in a quart of warm water for one hour; then add it to some good stock or plain veal, chicken, or beef soup; add a spoonful of butter and half a pint of stewed tomatoes just before the soup is served. This is a very fine soup, and is especially nourishing for delicate stomachs.

GREEN PEA SOUP, WITHOUT MEAT, FOR LENT.

Put two pints of green peas in two quarts of water, boil until the peas are very soft; then add three or four onions, two heads of celery, a carrot, and a turnip, all cut small; season with salt to taste, add a little butter, and boil for two hours. If it becomes too thick, add one pint of boiling water. The peas may be boiled the day before, and kept over for convenience, if desired. This receipt is intended for green peas, but it may be made with dried peas also, and the longer they boil, the better the soup will be. Do not add the vegetables until the day it is wanted.

TOMATO SOUP WITH VEGETABLES. VERY FINE.

Cut small, three carrots, three heads of celery, four onions and two turnips; put them into a saucepan with a table-spoonful of butter, a slice of ham and a half cup of water; let them simmer gently for an hour; then if a very rich soup is desired add to the vegetables two or three quarts of good soup stock, made by boiling a beef bone in three quarts of water until the meat is tender. Let all boil together for half an hour, and then add ten or twelve ripe tomatoes and a half-dozen whole peppers. It should cook for another hour or so. It must then be strained through a sieve or coarse cloth. Serve with toasted or fried bread cut in bits in the tureen. This is an elegant family soup, particularly nice in summer when the vegetables are fresh.

CHEAP WHITE SOUP.

Chop up any remains you may have of cold veal, chicken, game or rabbit roasted dry. Grate them, beat them in a mortar, and rub them through a sieve. Than add to the panada a quart of stock, put it into a saucepan and cook. Pay great attention to skimming as it boils.

QUEEN VICTORIA'S FAVORITE GREEN PEA SOUP.

Take two quarts of green peas, a double-handful of parsley, four stalks of green mint, and a good handful of green onions. Have ready two quarts of veal or beef stock, place it on the fire, throw in the above peas, mint and onions. Let all boil; when they are thoroughly done take them out, drain them and pound them well together. Put them in the stewpan again with the liquor; warm it and run it through a sieve. Add at the last moment a half pound of butter and a spoonful of sugar. Serve with fried bread.

ECONOMICAL GREEN PEA FAMILY SOUP WITH EGG DUMPLINGS.

Take a quart of shelled English peas for a large family, but if for a small family a pint will do. Put on the fire a veal bone or half a chicken; if a pint only of peas is used add any broiled steak, bones, nice scraps, or a small beef marrow bone; set it on the fire with a gallon of water and let it boil two hours. Then tie up in a muslin bag, one coffeecupful of the green peas; let the others stand in a cool place until wanted. Put this bag of peas into the pot with the beef and chicken stock, and let them boil till the peas are perfectly done. Skim out the peas, meat and bones, and add the rest of the peas, and let them boil gently. While these are cooking pour the peas in the bag into a pan and mash them smoothly; then add to them a batter made with two eggs, a spoonful of milk and flour. Add to the boiling peas a spoonful of butter and a little eschalot, if the flavor of onion is liked; then drop the batter in gently, a little at a time, in small round dumplings, and when they boil up your soup is ready to serve. This is an excellent spring soup, and is improved by adding lettuce heads, but they must be taken out before the dumplings are put in, as they give a dark color if left in too long.

CLEAR PEA SOUP.

Take two quarts of good beef or veal soup stock—which is better for being boiled the day before; into this put a quart of young green peas, two heads of lettuce, and a sprig of mint; add salt and pepper to taste.

DRIED SPLIT-PEA SOUP.

Take a good beef marrow-bone of one or two pounds weight, or the remains of roast beef-bones and gravy; add a slice of ham. Put these in a pot with a gallon of cold water; throw in the pot two cups of split peas or small white beans, two carrots, two turnips, two large onions or three small ones, a stalk of celery cut in pieces, a bunch of thyme, and a teaspoonful of mixed black and red pepper. When the vegetables are quite soft, which will be in about two hours, take the soup from the fire, strain it through a sieve or coarse cloth; add salt, and put on the fire again and boil for a few moments; then pour it over toasted bread.

GREEN CORN SOUP. VERY DELICATE.

Cut corn from the cob until you have at least a pint; cover it with a quart of sweet milk. Let it boil half an hour, add a teaspoonful of salt, skim it carefully, then throw into it a piece of butter the size of a hen's-egg and pepper to suit your taste. Serve with rolls or toasted bread.

OYSTER SOUP. DELICATE.

Take the oysters from their liquor. To every quart of the liquor add a pint of water or milk (milk is preferable); season with salt, pepper, butter, and toasted bread-crumbs that have been toasted and pounded. When this has boiled, put in a quart of oysters to two quarts of the liquor. Let all boil a few minutes, aud serve.

ANOTHER OYSTER SOUP. VERY STRENGTHENING.

Take a knuckle of veal or a piece of lamb; allow a quart of water and a teaspoonful of salt to each pound; set it over the fire, let it come to a boil, skim it well, and then set it back on the stove. Let it simmer for two hours. This will form a fine, strong, nourishing stock for the soup. Take out the meat, and skim the stock clear; put in half a pound of rolled crackers and a quart of nice oysters. Let it boil up, and finish by putting in a large tablespoonful of butter, and pepper and salt to taste. Macaroni or vermicelli can be substituted for the crackers, if preferred.

TURTLE SOUP FOR A LARGE COMPANY, No. 1.

Cut the head off the turtle the day before you dress it, and drain the blood thoroughly from the body. Then cut it up in the following manner: Divide the back, belly, head and fins from the intestines and lean parts. Be careful not to cut the gall bag. Scald in boiling water to remove the skin and shell. Cut up in neat pieces and throw into cold water. Boil the back and belly in a little water long enough to extract the bones easily. If for a large company a leg of veal will also be required, and a slice of ham, which must be stewed with the lean parts till well browned; then add boiling water, and the liquor and bones of the boiled turtle. Season with sliced lemon, whole pepper, a bunch of parsley, two leeks sliced, and salt to taste. Let this all boil slowly for four hours, then strain. Add the pieces of back, belly, head and fins (take the bones from the fins), pour in half a pint of Madeira wine and a quarter of a pound of good sweet butter, with a tablespoonful of flour worked in it; also, a lemon sliced thin. Let it boil gently for two hours, then serve.

In cutting up the turtle great care should be taken of the fat, which should be separated, cut up neatly, and stewed till tender in a little of the liquor, and put into the tureen when ready to serve. Garnish with the eggs, if any; if not, use hard-boiled eggs of fowls.

TURTLE SOUP, No. 2.

Put on, at an early hour in the morning, eight pounds of beef or veal, one pound of ham or bacon, eight onions, with pepper, salt, and sweet herbs to taste. Make a rich soup of this, and add to it the liquor of a boiled turtle; season very high with wine, spice, cayenne, and catsup. Put in the flesh of the turtle, prepared as in receipt No. 1—do not use the eyes or tongue. Let this boil up till tender, and serve with force-meat balls in tureen. Curry powder will give a higher flavor to soups than spice.

PLAIN MOCK-TURTLE SOUP.

Boil a calf's-head until very tender; take out the head, strain the liquor, and skim off the fat when cold, and keep till following day. Cut up the meat of the head and brain, and add to the liquor; place over the fire, after seasoning to taste with pepper, salt, mace, cloves, sweet herbs, and onions. Let it stew an hour, then add a tumbler of white wine, and it is ready for the force-meat balls. For the balls, chop a pound of lean veal with half a pound of salt pork; add the brains of the calf's-head, seasoned with pepper, salt, mace, cloves, sweet herbs, or curry powder. Make into balls the size of the yolk of an egg; boil part in the soup, fry the rest for a separate dish.

MOCK TURTLE SOUP, No. 2.

Put into a pot a knuckle of veal, two calfs' feet, two onions, a few cloves, pepper, allspice, mace and sweet herbs; cover them with water; tie a thick paper over the pot, or cover it close. Let it stew four hours. Remove from the fire and let it cool. When cold take off the fat very nicely, cut the meat and feet into bits an inch square, remove the bones and coarse parts; then place over the fire again to warm. Add a large spoonful of walnut catsup, one of mushroom catsup, a little mushroom powder, or a few mushrooms, and the jelly of the meat. When hot, serve with hard eggs, forcemeat balls, and the juice of one lemon.

MOCK TURTLE SOUP. EXCELLENT, No. 3.

Clean a calf's *head* nicely, split it and take out the brains; put the head into considerably more water than will cover it. Let it boil gently, and skim it carefully; when very tender take it out and cut in small pieces. Put into the boiling soup three pounds of beef and a knuckle of veal with all the bones broken fine. Add to this four or five onions, a carrot and turnip sliced, and a bunch of sweet herbs. Let it boil gently for three hours. Parboil the tongue and brains of the calf's head, and add them when the soup is nearly done. Let it cool and take off the fat.

To finish it for the table, melt a quarter of a pound of nice fresh butter, add a handful of flour and stir over the fire till the butter and flour are brown; add to this a little of the soup, a few sprigs of parsley and sweet basil; boil it for fifteen minutes and add it to the soup, together with two tablespoonfuls of catsup, the juice of a lemon, and salt to taste. It is usual to add a pint of sherry. When dished in the tureen, put in two dozen egg balls.

EGG BALLS FOR MOCK TURTLE SOUP.

Make a paste of the yolks of four hard-boiled eggs and the white of two raw ones; season with salt and cayenne pepper. Take bits of the paste the size of small marbles, rub them in flour and roll into balls; fry carefully in butter and drop into the soup.

OX-TAIL SOUP.

Cut each joint of two ox-tails with a meat-saw, steep them in water for two hours; then place them in a stewpan with three carrots, three turnips, three onions, two heads of celery, four cloves, and a blade of mace.

Fill up the stewpan from the boiling stock-pot; boil this over a slow fire until done and the joints quite tender. Take them out, cool them, and clarify the broth. Strain this into a soup-pot, put with it the pieces of ox-tail, some olive-shaped pieces of carrot and turnip which have been boiled in a little of the broth; add to this when it has boiled half an hour a small lump of sugar and a little red pepper. This soup is excellent, and may be served with any kind of vegetables strained in it, such as purée of peas, carrots, turnips, or celery.

RABBIT SOUP.

Cut one or two rabbits into joints; lay them for an hour in cold water; dry and fry them in butter until they are half done; place the meat in a saucepan with four or five onions and a head of celery cut small; add to these three quarts of cold water and a cup of peas, either green or dry; season with pepper and salt, then strain and serve it. Some like it unstrained.

REMARKS ON GOMBOS OF OKRA OR FILEE.

This is a most excellent form of soup, and is an economical way of using up the remains of any cold roasted chicken, turkey, game, or other meats. Cut up and season the chicken, meat, or other material to make the soup; fry to a light brown in a pot, and add boiling water in proportion to your meat. Two pounds of meat or chicken (bones and all), with half a pound of ham, or less of breakfast-bacon, will flavor a gallon of soup, which, when boiled down, will make gombo for six people. When the boiling water is added to the meat, let it simmer for at least two hours. Take the large bones from the pot, and add okra or a preparation of dried and pounded sassafras-leaves, called filée. This makes the difference in gombo. For gombo for six people use one quart of sliced okra; if filée be used, put in a coffeecupful. Either gives the smoothness so desirable in this soup. Oysters, crabs, and shrimp may be added when in season, as all improve the gombo. Never strain gombo. Add green corn, tomatoes, etc., etc., if desired. Serve gombo with plain-boiled rice.

GOMBO WITH CRABS, OR SHRIMP.

To a pound of beef add half a pound knuckle of ham; chop up both in inch pieces and fry them brown in two table-spoonfuls of boiling lard; add to them four large crabs cut up, or a pound of peeled shrimps, or both if desired; cut into this four dozen small young okra pods, one large onion, a little red pepper, and salt to taste. Let all simmer on a slow fire for about twenty minutes; then fill up with warm water, enough to cover the contents two inches deep. Let this boil for two hours. If it becomes too thick, add as much water as required. If preferred, a chicken can be used instead of the beef.

SIMPLE OKRA GOMBO.

Chop a pound of beef and half a pound of veal brisket into squares an inch thick; slice three dozen okra pods, one onion, a pod of red pepper, and fry all together. When brown, pour in half a gallon of water; add more as it boils away. Serve with rice as usual.

OYSTER GOMBO WITH FILEE, No. 1.

Take a grown chicken, fifty oysters, and a half-pound of ham to flavor the gombo. Cut up two onions fine, fry them in lard and thicken the gravy with flour; a teaspoonful will be enough. Cut up the chicken and ham, and put them to fry with the onions. Let all cook gently till brown, then put

LA CUISINE CREOLE.

in a pint of boiling water and boil the chicken until it is almost in pieces. Half-an-hour before dinner pour in the oysters and their liquor. When ready for the table take a large spoonful of fresh powdered sassafras leaves or filée, wet it with a little of the soup, and stir it into the soup. If not thick or ropy enough, stir in another spoonful. Do not let the soup boil after the filée is put in, but remove it from the fire, or serve it immediately.

GOMBO FILEE WITH OYSTERS, No. 2.

Fry a tablespoonful of flour in a tablespoonful of lard. Let it brown slowly so as not to scorch. Boil the liquor of two quarts of oysters, and when it is boiling throw in a cupful of cut leeks or onions, a large slice of ham, some parsley, and stir in the browned flour. Let this cook fifteen minutes; then pour in two quarts of oysters. Let them boil a few minutes, season with salt and pepper; take out the parsley and sift in half a cup of dried and pounded fresh filée; if not fresh more will be required.

CHICKEN GOMBO WITH OYSTERS.

Take a young chicken, or the half of a grown one; cut it up, roll it in salt, pepper and flour, and fry it a nice brown, using lard or drippings, as if for fricassee. Cut up a quart of fresh green okras, and take out the chicken and fry the okra in the same lard. When well browned return the chicken to the pot and boil. Add to it a large slice of ham; a quarter of a pound will be about right for this gombo. Pour on to the chicken, ham and okra, half a gallon of boiling water, and let it boil down to three pints. Ten minutes before serving pour into the boiling soup two dozen fine oysters with half a pint of their liquor. Let it come to a good boil, and serve it with well-boiled rice.

MAIGRE OYSTER GOMBO.

Take 100 oysters with their juice, and one large onion; slice the onion into hot lard and fry it brown, adding when brown a tablespoonful of flour and red pepper. When thick enough pour in the oysters. Boil together twenty minutes. Stir in a large spoonful of butter and one or two tablespoonfuls of filée, then take the soup from the fire and serve with rice.

MAIGRE SHRIMP GOMBO FOR LENT.

Boil a pint of shrimps in a quart of water; give them only one boil up; then set them to drain and cool, reserving the water they were boiled in. Chop up three dozen okra pods, two onions, a pod of pepper, and a little parsley, and fry them brown in a little lard or butter; add to the okra the shrimps and the strained water in which they were boiled. Let all boil for an hour, and season with salt and pepper to taste. When shrimp and crabs cannot be procured, half a pound of dry codfish, soaked an hour or two, and chopped fine, will do very well. All gombo should be thickened with a little flour—browned if preferred—and stirred in just before adding the water; then boil an hour.

CRAB GOMBO, WITH OKRA.

Take six large crabs, throw them in cold water for a few moments. When cool cut off the limbs—while they are living if possible, as this renders them more delicate; clean

them, and put them to fry, shells and all, in a pot containing a cup of lard, a cup of cut onions, a small bunch of
parsley, and two tablespoonfuls of browned flour.   Let them
cook about fifteen minutes, and then pour on them two pints
of boiling water and a quart of sliced okra; let it all stew
gently for half an hour, and add a slice of lean ham and a
quart of good veal or beef stock (made by boiling two
pounds of veal or beef in two quarts of water until reduced
to a quart); season with a teaspoonful of salt, and same
of black and red pepper, and let all boil for half an hour.
This soup can be made in the oyster season by putting in a
quart of oysters and two quarts of their liquor instead of
the boiled beef stock.

CRAYFISH BISQUE.   A CREOLE DISH.

Parboil the fish, pick out the meat, and mince or pound it
in a mortar until very fine; it will require about fifty crayfish.   Add to the fish one-third the quantity of bread soaked
in milk, and a quarter of a pound of butter, also salt to
taste, a bunch of thyme, two leaves of sage, a small piece of
garlic and a chopped onion. Mix all well and cook ten minutes, stirring all the time to keep it from growing hard.
Clean the heads of the fish, throw them in strong salt and
water for a few minutes and then drain them.   Fill each one
with the above stuffing, flour them, and fry a light brown.
Set a clean stewpan over a slow fire, put into it three spoonfuls of lard or butter, a slice of ham or bacon, two onions
chopped fine; dredge over it enough flour to absorb the grease,
then add a pint and a-half of boiling water, or better still,

plain beef stock. Season this with a bunch of thyme, a bay leaf, and salt and pepper to taste. Let it cook slowly for half an hour, then put the heads of the crayfish in and let them boil fifteen minutes. Serve rice with it.

AN ARTFUL DODGER.

WHY CRABS ARE BOILED ALIVE[1]

And for why you not have of crab? Because one must dem boil 'live? It is all vat is of most beast to tell so. How you make for dem kill so you not dem boil? You not can cut dem de head off, for dat dey have not of head. You not can break to dem de back, for dat dey not be only all back. You not can dem bleed until dey die, for dat dey not have blood. You not can stick to dem troo de brain, for dat dey be same like you—dey not have of brain.

Item, October 5, 1879.

75. C'est bon khé crâbe qui lacause li pas tini tête. (C'est à cause de son bon cœur que le crabe n'a pas de tête.)
   "It is because of his good heart that the crab has no head."[1]— [*Martinique.*]

210. Moin ainmein plis yon balaou jòdi là qu'taza dimain. (J'aime mieux un balaou aujourd'hui qu'un tazard demain.)
   "I'd rather have horn-fish to-day, than mackerel to-morrow."[1]— [*Martinique.*]

295. *Si lamèr té bouilli, poissons sré tchuite. (Si la mer bouillait, les poissons seraient cuits).
   "If the sea were to boil, the fishes would be cooked."—[*Louisiana.*]

[1] "A bird in the hand is worth two in the bush." The translation is not literal. The *tazard* or *thazard,* although belonging to the scomber family, is not a true mackerel. *Balaou* is one Creole name for *l'aiguillette de mer,* hornfish [?].

Gombo Zhèbes 1885

FISH

FRICASSEE OF FISH.

All large fish make nice fricassee. Cut the fish into slices and lay it in a gravy made of fried onions, parsley, tomatoes and a little garlic; fry in butter and serve. Add catsup if liked.

TO FRY FISH.

The fat from bacon, or salt pork, is much nicer to fry fish in, than lard. After the fish is cleaned, wash it and wipe it dry, and let it lie on a cloth till all the moisture is absorbed; then roll it in flour. No salt is required if fried in bacon or pork fat. There must be fat enough to float the fish or they will not fry nicely, but instead soak fat and be soft to the touch.

TO STUFF AND BAKE FISH.

Choose any of the many dressings in this book. Take either plain bread stuffing, veal stuffing, or forcemeat; fill the fish and sew it up; put a tea-cup of water in the baking pan, with a spoonful of butter, and bake, according to the size of the fish, from thirty minutes to an hour. Season with pepper and salt, and bake brown.

CROAKERS AND MULLETS FRIED.

Have them perfectly cleaned; trim the fins, wipe the fish with a clean cloth, salt and pepper each one, and roll it in flour or fine corn meal, and then drop it into a pot of boiling lard and bacon grease mixed. When brown, pile up on a hot dish and serve, with any desired sauce or catsup.

FILLETS OR SLICED FISH, FRIED.

When the fish is too large to fry whole, cut into slices and place them in a crock; season with pepper, salt, oil, lemon juice, and chopped parsley. Turn the fish in this mixture so that all parts may become well saturated with the seasoning. When wanted, drain, wipe dry and dip each piece separately in flour; drop into boiling lard; take it up as it browns, and ornament the dish with a border of fried parsley. Send to table with sauce to suit the taste.

TROUT STUFFED AND BAKED.

Stuff one or more fish, with any stuffing desired; score them well and put in a buttered pan to bake; season with pepper, salt and chopped parsley, moisten them with a little essence of mushrooms, or catsup and butter. Baste every five minutes until they are done; remove the fish to a hot dish. Throw a little wine or vinegar into the pan, and stir it to detach the crust from the pan; boil this sauce down, add a little more butter and pour over the fish. Mushrooms are an improvement to the sauce; but if not convenient, tomato sauce will answer.

TROUT À LA VENITIENNE.

After well-cleaning your trout, make slashes in the back, and insert butter rolled in parsley, lemon, thyme, basil, chives, all minced very fine; pour some salad oil over it, and let it lie for half an hour; cover it with bread crumbs and chopped sweet herbs, boil it over a clear fire which is not too quick, and serve it with sauce No. 13.

BROILED SPANISH MACKEREL.

Split the mackerel down the back; season with pepper and salt, rub it over with oil, place it on a gridiron over a moderate fire, and, when browned on one side, turn. If it is a very large fish, divide it and broil one half at a time. When done, place it on a dish, and put butter, parsley and lemon juice over it. Serve with sauce No. 13.

BROILED FLOUNDER.

This is cooked just as the Spanish mackerel in the preceding receipt; and may be sent to table with the same sauce, or sauce à l'Aurore No. 14.

FLOUNDERS AND MULLETS FRIED.

These fish are very fine when fresh from the waters of Lake Pontchartrain. Flounder is better broiled, but still is very nice fried. Clean and dry the fish. Do not cut them in pieces, but score them across if very large. Have lard or bacon fat very hot; roll the fish in flour and drop into the boiling fat. Let them cook until brown, and serve with sauce No. 15.

PLAIN BOILED RED FISH OR RED SNAPPER.

Wash the fish; when cleaned, wipe it dry and rub it over with lemon juice and salt. Put it in a fish kettle or other vessel to boil, cover it with soft water and throw in a handful of salt. As soon as it begins to boil, skim it and let it simmer; **hard** boiling breaks the flesh before it is cooked thoroughly. When done, lift it out of the water with a drainer, slip it carefully on a dish and send to table with sauces No. 13 and No. 3.

RED FISH À LA PROVENÇALE.

Have properly cleaned, a medium sized fish; score it deep, then put it in a large dish and cover with a pickle or marinade made of two sliced carrots, two onions, some parsley and bay-leaves, three cloves of garlic, pepper and salt, the juice of two lemons, and a gill of salad oil. When thoroughly flavored, remove the fish from the marinade and bake three quarters of an hour, basting frequently **with** wine and butter. When done, put it on a platter and keep hot. Add half a bottle of wine and some cayenne pepper to the marinade; stew well and strain over the fish. Garnish with cut lemon, sprigs of parsley and capers.

BAKED AND STEWED CODFISH.

Scald for ten minutes some soaked codfish, it should soak all night); then scrape it white, pick it in flakes, and put it in a stewpan with a tablespoonful of nice butter worked into as much flour, and milk enough to moisten it. Let it stew gently ten minutes; add pepper to taste, and serve hot. Slice hard-boiled eggs over it, and sprigs of parsley around the dish.

If the fish is to be baked you must put it on to scald, as above, after soaking all night; you must then put on double as much Irish potatoes as the quantity of codfish. Boil them, mash them, and then pick up the codfish fine, seasoning it with butter and pepper; moisten it with two beaten eggs, a little chopped onion, and milk if necessary; make it all into a large soft pat, or cake, smooth it with a knife blade and put it in the stove to be browned lightly.

CODFISH CAKES.

Soak the codfish all night, then scald for ten minutes; put to it an equal quantity of potatoes boiled and mashed; moisten it with beaten eggs, a bit of butter and a little pepper; form it into round cakes, about half an inch thick, roll them each one in flour, and fry in hot lard until they are a delicate brown. The lard must be boiling, and the cakes fried gently.

COD AU BEURRE ROUX.

Cod; a little browned butter; a little flour; sugar; one onion; tablespoonful of vinegar.

For cod au beurre roux, boil a piece of cod and separate it into flakes; brown some butter, dredge in a little flour, and a little sugar in powder, and in this fry some slices of onion a fine brown; throw in the vinegar, boil it up, pour it over the fish, and serve it with crisped parsley.

OYSTER STUFFING FOR TURKEY.

Take three or four dozen nice plump oysters, wash and beard them, add to them a tumblerful of bread crumbs; chop up a tumblerful of nice beef suet; mix together, and moisten with three eggs; season with salt, pepper, a little butter, a teaspoonful of mace, and some cayenne pepper. Roll forcemeat into cakes, and fry them. They are pretty laid around a turkey or chicken.

OYSTERS STEWED WITH CHAMPAGNE.

Put into a silver chafing dish, a quarter of a pound of butter; lay in a quart of oysters; strew over them grated bread which has been toasted, beaten and sifted, some cut parsley and a little pepper and salt; cover the top with bits of butter cut thin; pour on a pint of champagne, cover and cook. This may be done in a pan or oven.

OYSTERS STEWED WITH MILK.

Take a pint of fine oysters, one half pint of their own liquor and half a pint of milk; boil the liquor, take off the scum; put in a quarter of a pound of butter, pepper and salt, to taste, and serve crackers and dressed celery with them.

STEWED OYSTERS ON TOAST.

Take the oysters from their liquor, let it settle; then strain and add some whole pepper, two blades of mace, and three cloves, and put over a moderate fire in a block-tin covered sauce-pan; mix a little flour with a piece of butter, as large as a hen's egg for two dozen oysters, and stir in the boiling liquor; remove any scum which may rise, then put in the oysters and let them cook for five minutes. Line a hot oyster dish with toasted, well-buttered bread, and pour over it the boiling oysters. Only rich juicy oysters will stew to advantage. Milk is always an improvement, but in this receipt it can be dispensed with; if, however, it is convenient, pour in half a pint just as the oysters are put in to boil, as earlier it might curdle.

OYSTER TOAST.

A nice little dish for a luncheon or late supper. Scald a quart of oysters in their own liquor, take them out and pound or chop them to a paste; add a little cream or fresh butter, and some pepper and salt. Get ready some thin slices of toast moistened with boiling water, and spread with fresh butter; then, spread over the butter the oyster paste. Put a thin slice of fresh cut lemon on each piece, and lay parsley on the platter. Serve this very hot or it will not be good.

SCALLOPED OYSTERS.—No. 1.

Lay the oysters in a shallow pan or dish with a little of their own liquor, some pepper, salt, chopped parsley, butter, and grated bread crumbs. Have a layer of bread crumbs on top of the pan, and set it in the oven to bake a light brown. They should be served hot with tomato or walnut catsup poured over them.

SCALLOPED OYSTERS.—No. 2.

Procure any quantity of oysters desired, and place in a baking dish; put alternate layers of oysters and pounded crackers; season each layer with salt, pepper and butter. When filled, pour on enough milk to soak the cracker, and bake forty minutes. Serve hot.

OYSTERS FRIED.

Take large oysters from their own liquor; dry and lay them in a towel till you heat, very hot, a cup of lard in a thick-bottomed pan. Dip each oyster in wheat flour, or rolled cracker, until it will hold no more; then lay it in the pan. The fire must be moderate, or the oysters will scorch before cooking through. They will brown on one side in five minutes, then turn them. Oysters may be dipped in beaten egg and rolled cracker, and then fried.

OYSTER PICKLE.   VERY EASY AND NICE.

Wash four dozen oysters; let them be fine and large, with plenty of their own liquor.   Pick them carefully, strain their liquor and to it add a dessertspoonful of pepper, two blades of mace, a tablespoonful of salt, and a cup of strong wine vinegar.   Simmer the oysters in this five minutes, then put them in small jars.   Boil the pickle again, and when cold add a cup of fresh vinegar; and fill up the jars, cork them, and set away for use.

VEAL SWEETBREAD AND OYSTER PIE.

The sweetbread of veal is the most delicate part of the animal.   Boil it tender, season with pepper, salt and butter; put in two dozen oysters; thicken their juice with a cup of cream, a tablespoonful of butter, the yolks of two hard-boiled eggs, and a tablespoonful of flour.   Pour all in a deep pan, and cover with paste and bake.   If there is too much liquid, keep it to serve with the pie, if necessary, when baked. After baking, the pie is sometimes too dry.

BEEFSTEAK AND OYSTER PIE.

Cut three pounds of lean beefsteak.   Salt, pepper, and fry quickly so as to brown without cooking through; then place in a deep dish.   Get four dozen oysters, beard them, and lay them in the pan over the beef; season with salt and pepper. Take the gravy in which the steaks were fried, pour out some of the grease; dredge in a tablespoonful of flour, let it brown, and add to it a pint of good beef broth, then put in a wineglassful of mushroom catsup, some of Harvey's or Worcestershire sauce; heat it, and let it boil up a few times, then pour

it over the oysters and steak. When the gravy has become
cool, cover the pie with a good puff paste, and bake it for an
hour and a half.

FRICASSEE OF CRABS.

Take six nice fat crabs, wash them, and while *alive* chop
off the claws; then clean the rest of the crabs carefully and
lay them in a dish. Chop up two onions fine, fry them in a
tablespoonful of butter, or butter and lard mixed; when
brown and soft stir in a large spoonful of flour, which must
also brown nicely; throw in some chopped parsley and a
little green onion, and when they are cooked pour on a
quart of boiling water—this is the gravy. Now put in the
crabs without parboiling. Let them simmer in the gravy
for half an hour, and serve with boiled rice. Parboiling
crabs destroys their flavor; they should be alive to the last
moment.

SOFT-SHELL CRABS, FRIED.

Clean the crabs properly, dip them into rolled cracker, and
fry them in hot lard salted. They must be dried carefully
before frying, or they will not brown well. Serve with any
favorite sauce.

TO DRESS A TURTLE.

Cut off the head and let it bleed well. Separate the bottom shell from the top with care, for fear of breaking the
gall bag. Throw the liver and eggs, if any, into a bowl of
water. Slice off all the meat from the under-shell and put
in water also; break the shell in pieces, wash carefully and
place it in a pot; cover it with water, and add one pound of
middling or flitch of bacon with four chopped onions. Set

this on the fire to boil. (If preferred, open and clean the chitterlings or intestines also—some use them.) Let this boil gently for four hours; keep the liver to fry. While the undershell is boiling, wash the top-shell neatly, cut all the meat out, cover it up and set it by. Parboil the fins, clean them perfectly; take off the black skin and throw them into water. Now cut the flesh removed from both shells, into small pieces; cut the fins up; sprinkle with salt, cover and set them by. When the pot containing the shells, etc., has boiled four hours, take out the bacon, scrape the shell, clean and strain the liquor, pour back in the pot about one quart, and put the rest by for the soup (Turtle Soup No. 2). Pick out the nice pieces strained out, and put with the fins in the gravy. Add to the meat one bottle of wine, one gill mushroom catsup, one gill of lemon pickle, cloves, nutmeg, salt, pepper, and one pound fresh butter rolled in flour. Stew together; take out the herbs, thicken with flour and put in the shell to bake with a puff paste around it. Trim with eggs.

"GRENOUILLES FRITES," OR FRIED FROGS.

Use only the hind quarters of the frogs. After washing them in warm water, soak well; then put them into cold vinegar with a little salt, and let them remain one or two hours, after which, throw them into scalding water, and remove the skin without tearing the flesh. Wipe them dry, dust flour on them and fry in butter or sweet oil, with plenty of chopped parsley. When brown, dust pepper and a little salt over them, and garnish with crisped parsley. Stewed frogs are seasoned with butter, wine, beaten eggs and parsley chopped fine.

TERRAPIN.

Like crabs and lobsters, terrapins are thrown alive into boiling water and let boil till the outer shell and toe-nails can be removed. Then wash and boil them in salted water till the fleshy part of the leg is tender. Put them in a bowl or deep dish, take off the second shell, remove the sand bag and gall bladder, and cut off the spongy part. Cut up the meat, season it with salt, pepper, cayenne and mace, thicken with butter and flour, and cook. Just before serving, put in a gill of sherry wine for every terrapin, and pour all over hot buttered toast.

137.   *Faut pas marré tayau[1] avec saucisse. (Il ne faut pas attacher le chien-courant (taïant) avec des saucisses.)

"Musn't tie up the hound with a string of sausages."—[*Louisiana.*]

Item 1880

11.   Babiez mouche, babiez viande. (Grondez les mouches, grondez la viande.)

"Scold the flies, scold the meat."—[*Hayti.*]

[1] Adopted from old French *"taïaut"* (tally-ho!) the cry of the huntsman to his hounds. The Creoles have thus curiously, but forcibly, named the hound itself.

Gombo Zhèbes 1885

COLD MEATS AND HOW TO SERVE THEM.

TO SERVE PICKLED OYSTERS.

Take them from the pickle jar, put them into a glass dish, and ornament it with the tender delicate leaves of celery and parsley. Serve with bread and butter sandwiches.

TO SERVE MEAT OR CHICKEN PIE.

Lay a fringed napkin in a waiter or plate larger than the dish in which the pie is baked; set the pie on it; turn up the edges of the napkin against it, and put sprigs of parsley or delicate green leaves of celery on the edge of the plate to keep the napkin in place.

A NICE WAY TO SERVE COLD MEAT.

Cut cold roast beef in slices, put gravy enough to cover them, add two tablespoonfuls of wine or catsup. If there is not enough gravy, make more by putting hot water and a good bit of butter, with a spoonful of browned flour. Let it stew gently. If liked, a sliced leek and a bunch of parsley may be added. Serve mashed potatoes with it. This is equal to beef à-la-mode.

GLAZING FOR TONGUES, HAMS, ETC.

Boil a shin of beef and a knuckle of veal for twelve hours in three or four quarts of water. Put in spices, herbs, and vegetables, the same as for soup; keep it boiling till it is

reduced to a quart, then strain through a sieve and put away
for use. This makes fine gravies, and is extremely useful to
finish off baked hams, tongues, and cold roasts.

BRAISED TONGUE WITH ASPIC JELLY.

Boil the tongue until tender, then place it in a stew-pan
with two onions, a head of celery, four cloves, and salt and
pepper; cover it with the liquor it was boiled in; add to it a
glass of brandy, a tablespoonful of sugar, a blade of mace,
a bunch of thyme, and a bunch of parsley. Let it simmer
gently for two hours. Take out the tongue, strain the liquor
it was boiled in, and add to it a box of Cox's gelatine which
has been soaked in a goblet of cold water. Heat it and pour
over the tongue. Serve cold.

SEASONING FOR SAUSAGE MEAT.

Chop up and run your sausage meat through the cutter,
and to every pound of the ground meat, allow a tablespoonful of salt, a teaspoonful of mixed black and red pepper, a
quarter of a teaspoonful of saltpetre, and a half cup of sage
and sweet marjoram. If you prefer it you may substitute for
the sage some thyme and summer savory.

SEASONING FOR STUFFING VEAL, PIG OR TURKEY.

When much seasoning is required it is well to keep it prepared on hand. It should always be kept well stopped. Dry
a pound of salt; grind an ounce of white or black pepper;
dry and powder two ounces of thyme and one of sweet
marjoram; grate one ounce of nutmeg, and mix with half a

pound of bread crumbs dried in a slow oven, three eggs, a quarter of a pound of butter or suet, and a cup of finely chopped parsley.

LIVER AND HAM FORCEMEAT FOR STUFFING.

Take a calf's liver, or the livers of three or four turkeys, or geese; lay them in cold water, till ready to use them; cut with them the same quantity of fat ham or bacon; throw them into a saucepan, and let them fry a good brown; season with salt, pepper, spices, chopped mushrooms, parsley and three shallots. When soft, chop them fine, or else pass them through a sausage grinder. This receipt can be used for raised pies, or, as an addition to turkey stuffing.

AROMATIC SPICES FOR SEASONING MEAT PIES, ETC.

Take an ounce each of mace and nutmeg, two ounces of cloves, two of pepper corns (whole pepper will do), marjoram and thyme, each one ounce, bay leaves half an ounce. Dry the herbs well first; put the spices and herbs in a paper, closely folded, to keep in the aroma, and place them in a slow oven to dry for an hour, or two; then pound and sift them, through a sieve. Cork tightly.

TRUFFLES AND CHESTNUT STUFFING FOR A PIG.

Many persons like truffles for stuffing for a roast pig; they should be mixed with fat bacon, livers of veal or fowl, sweet herbs, pepper, salt and butter. Chestnut stuffing is prepared by roasting sixty chestnuts. Remove their hulls while hot, and pound them fine, add four ounces of butter, run this through a sieve, and add to it a few green onions, or chives, sweet basil, parsley and thyme; grate in a nutmeg, put in pepper and salt, and bind it, with three eggs.　Stuff the pig with it and serve with tomato sauce.

LIVER AND TRUFFLE STUFFING FOR A PIG OR TURKEY.

Pare and cut into small pieces a pound of truffles, put them into a stew pan with a large spoonful of butter, one half pound of fat bacon, chopped very fine; add a spoonful of black pepper, a clove of garlic, a little salt, a bunch of sweet basil, and thyme, dried and powdered; add also half a pound of nice veal liver, boiled and grated.　Set this all on the fire, let it cook until the truffles are soft, then mash with a wooden spoon; take it off to cool it, and stuff the pig with the forcemeat.　Baste the pig with sweet oil, which is better than butter.　It is supposed the pig comes from the butchers all ready for stuffing and baking.　If the stuffing is desired for a turkey, add a quarter of a pound of bread crumbs and two beaten eggs, and baste the turkey with butter, instead of oil.

NICE FORCEMEAT, FOR STUFFINGS, ETC.

Take equal quantities of cold chicken, veal and beef; shred small and mix together; season with pepper, salt, sweet herbs, and a little nutmeg, *i. e.* if intended for white meat or anything delicately flavored, but if meant for a savory dish add a little minced ham, and garlic; pound or chop this very fine (it is well, and saves trouble, to run it through a sausage chopper), and make it in a paste with two raw eggs, some butter, marrow or drippings; stuff your joint, or poultry, and if there is some not used, roll it it round balls, flour them and fry in boiling lard.　This is a nice garnish for a side dish.

THE NURSE MAID.

Item 1880

ILLUSTRATED LETTERS FROM THE PEOPLE—NO. 8.

Item 1880

HOW TO MAKE TARTAR SAUCE

There are two good ways in which a Tartar sauce may be made. You can try whichever you please; but if you are in a hurry the second will suit your purpose better than the first. 1st:—Catch a *young Tartar*: for the old ones are very tough and devoid of juice. To catch a Tartar is generally a very unpleasant and at all times a difficult undertaking. A young Tartar will probably cost you at least $10,000—and perhaps your life—before you get through with him: but if you must have Tartar sauce you must be ready to take all risks. Having procured your Tartar you must kill him privately, taking care that the act shall escape the observation of the police authorities, who would probably in such a case be strongly prejudiced in favor of the Tartar. Having killed, skinned and cleaned the Tartar, cut off the tenderest part of the hams and thighs; boil three hours, and then hash up with Mexican pepper, aloes and spices. Add a quart of mulled wine and slowly boil to the consistency of honey. You will probably find the Tartar sauce very palatable; and if hermetically sealed in bottles with the addition of a little Santa Cruz rum, will serve for a long time. The rest of the Tartar will not keep, and must be disposed of judiciously. 2nd:—Take the yolk of a hardboiled egg, a teaspoonful of mustard, a tablespoonful of olive oil, a little vinegar, a little parsley and pickled cucumber, and hash up very fine.

[1] *Item*, November 16, 1879.

270. Quand ou mangé evec guiabe, quimbé cuillè ou longue. (Quand vous mangez avec le diable, tenez votre cuillère longue.)
    "When you eat with the devil, see that your spoon is long."— [*Martinique.*]

Gombo Zhèbes 1885

SAUCES FOR MEATS AND GAME.

No. 1.—DUCK SAUCE.

Boil six large onions; change the water two or three times while it is boiling, which takes away the strong taste. When soft, chop and put them in a saucepan, with two large spoonfuls of butter, a little pepper and salt; now add either mushroom catsup, a cup of vinegar or a cup of wine, whichever is preferred.

No. 2.—BROWN ONION SAUCE FOR POULTRY, ETC.

Slice three onions after peeling them; fry them a bright brown in a spoonful of butter; sprinkle a little flour in, and let it brown also; add salt, pepper, and also sage, if for goose or duck, and parsley and thyme if for chickens or roast meat; add a cup of the liquor in which the fowl was cooked, let it boil up and add a tablespoonful of catsup.

No. 3.—MUSHROOM SAUCE.

Peel and wash the mushrooms, cut them in small pieces, and put them in a sauce-pan; cover them with water, and let them boil soft; then stir in butter, mixed in flour, until it is thick enough to form a nice sauce; add pepper and salt.

No. 4.—MINT SAUCE FOR SPRING LAMB.

Wash carefully a cup of tender green spear mint, chop it fine, and mix with it half a cup of sugar and a cup of good vinegar.

No. 5.—WHITE ONION SAUCE.

Peel and boil six white onions, and when tender pour off the water; chop the onions small, and add to them a cup of hot milk, a large spoonful of butter, and pepper and salt to taste. Thicken with a little flour if preferred.

No. 6.—TOMATO SAUCE, PLAIN.

Peel and slice twelve tomatoes, pick out the seeds; add three pounded crackers, salt and pepper; stir twenty minutes and serve.

No. 7.—CRANBERRY SAUCE.

Stew cranberries till soft; when soft, stir in sugar; scald a few minutes and strain, or not, just as you please; it is good either way.

No. 8.—SALAD SAUCE OR DRESSING FOR LETTUCE.

Take the yolks of two hard-boiled eggs, rub them to a paste in a bowl with a tablespoonful of mustard and one of sweet cream; add gradually two tablespoonfuls of sweet oil; when well mixed add the yolk of a raw egg, to give the paste a delicate smoothness; a little salt, a spoonful of sugar, and one tablespoon and a half of fine vinegar.

No. 9.—SAUCE PIQUANTE FOR COLD MEAT.

Slice two onions, fry them in butter; put them in a stew-pan with a carrot, some sweet herbs, such as dried thyme or marjoram, two eschalots, some parsley and a clove of garlic; dredge in a spoonful of flour. When the carrot is perfectly done, mash it in the stewpan with a wooden spoon, and when smooth add to it a cup of soup stock. When this boils up, throw in a cup of strong vinegar. Add salt and pepper, and strain.

No. **10.**—BUTTER AND FLOUR SAUCE (OR WHITE SAUCE).

Mix a tablespoonful of butter and one of flour; mix over the fire, with a cup of cold water, stirring all the time. When this boils, take a quarter of a pound of fresh butter, if for a number of guests, and stir in the butter quickly, adding a cup of cold water by degrees, to keep the butter from oiling; finish with the juice of a lemon, and strain. It must be served hot, and made only a few moments before it is wanted. It gets oily if kept long. Add a spoonful of chopped parsley.

No. **11.**—CAPER SAUCE FOR BOILED MUTTON, ETC., ETC.

Take half a pint of butter sauce and add two tablespoonfuls of capers and a little salt.

No. **12.**—PARSLEY AND BUTTER SAUCE.

Take half a pint of butter sauce No. 10, and add half a cup of chopped parsley and the juice of one lemon. Pour hot water on the parsley before chopping.

No. **13.**—LEMON SAUCE FOR FISH.

To half a pint of butter sauce No. 10, add the juice of a lemon and another lemon sliced; take out the seeds, and let all boil together. This is good with broiled Spanish mackerel or pompano, also with broiled fish.

No. **14.**—SAUCE À L'AURORE, FOR FISH.

Pound the spawn of a lobster very smooth, with a small piece of fresh butter, and press it through a sieve into a stewpan ; season it with salt and cayenne ; pour in the white sauce and a large spoonful of lemon juice, and set it over a clear fire to simmer for a minute or two, taking care it does not boil.

No. **15.**—SAUCE FROIDE.

Mince quite fine, some parsley, chervil, tarragon, chives and burnet ; mix them in five or six tablespoonfuls of oil, or three yolks of hard-boiled eggs rubbed down smooth ; add two tablespoonfuls of vinegar, some made mustard, salt and pepper ; beat altogether until it is smooth and thick, and serve in a sauce-boat. A good sauce for fish.

No. **16.**—CHESTNUT SAUCE FOR TURKEY OR FOWLS.

Take half a pint of veal stock ; half a pound of chestnuts ; peel of half a lemon ; a cupful of cream or milk ; a very little cayenne and salt.

Remove the dark shell of the chestnuts, and scald them until the inner skin can be taken off. Then put them into the saucepan with the stock, the lemon peel cut very thin, some cayenne and salt. Let it simmer till the chestnuts are quite soft. Rub it through a sieve ; add the seasoning and cream, and let it simmer for a few minutes, taking care it does not boil, and stirring constantly.

No. **17.**—WHITE CELERY SAUCE FOR BOILED POULTRY.

Take six heads of celery, cut off the green tops, slice the remainder into small bits and boil in half a pint of water until it is tender ; mix three teaspoonfuls of flour smoothly, with a little milk. Add six spoonfuls more of milk, stir it in ; add a little salt and a small piece of butter. On boiling take off.

No. 17½.—CELERY PURÉE FOR TURKEY.

Chop up six or eight heads of celery, boil them a few minutes; drain and put them in a saucepan, with half a pound of butter, some white soup stock, a little sugar, pepper and salt ; cook till soft, then strain it through a sieve, heat it again and add a cup of milk or cream.

No. 18.—WHITE CUCUMBER SAUCE FOR MEATS.

Take four or five cucumbers; three-quarters of a pint of veal stock ; the yolks of three eggs; a little cayenne pepper and salt.

Peel and take out the seeds from the cucumbers, cut them into very small pieces and put them into a saucepan with the stock and seasoning, and simmer it slowly until they are tender. Then stir in the yolks of the eggs well beaten. Make it very hot, but do not let it boil ; and serve it up quickly.

No. 19.—EGGS AND BUTTER SAUCE.

Boil six eggs hard ; when cold, peel them and put them into a cup of butter, melted ; mix with a little flour, make it hot, stir in pepper and salt. Some people like lemon, and many require walnut catsup. This is left to personal taste.

No. 20.—WINE SAUCE FOR VENISON OR MUTTON.

Take from the stock pot a pint of the soup; let it boil down to half a pint ; season with a dozen cloves, a teaspoon of salt, and a little pepper ; then stir in a cup of wine, or of currant jelly.

No. **21.**—SAVORY JELLY FOR COLD TURKEY OR MEAT.

Put in the pot two pounds of beef; if you have veal or beef bones, break them and throw them in also, but they require longer boiling to dissolve the gelatine. Put in half a pound of sweet ham or bacon, add all the sweet herbs, such as thyme, basil, parsley and marjoram; last of all, salt and pepper to taste. Boil for three or four hours. When it is sufficiently boiled, take off, strain, and put away to cool. Take off all the fat and sediment, and clarify by throwing into it the whites and shells of three eggs; add three blades of mace and a cup of wine or lemon juice. Place it again on the fire, let it boil a few times, and strain it through a jelly-bag. When well made it is delicious with cold turkey, and under the name of " aspic jelly," figures in the finest French cooking.

No. **22.**—TOMATO SAUCE, RICH AND VERY FINE.

Take a dozen large ripe tomatoes, pick off the stalks; extract the seeds and watery juice by squeezing them in the hand. Place the pulp in a stewpan with four ounces, or a quarter of a pound, of raw ham, cut into cubes; a dozen small eschalots and a bunch of thyme or parsley. Throw in a little butter, and fry all gently until the tomatoes soften sufficiently to be passed through a strainer. Mix this *purée* with a cupful of good soup-stock or other soup; add the strained juice of the tomatoes and let boil fifteen minutes, then set it by to clarify. Serve it hot. When canned tomatoes are used, omit the first directions.

No. **23.**—BROWN OYSTER SAUCE.

Prepare this just as white oyster sauce (No 24); only you use brown gravy instead of cream, as in white oyster sauce.

No. **24**.—WHITE OYSTER SAUCE.

Put three dozen oysters in a stewpan, without their juice, which save; mix with the oysters, half a pound of butter, thickened with flour (work it well with a spoon); season with cayenne pepper and salt, and thin with a cup of milk or cream, and a cup of the oyster juice. Boil altogether for ten minutes.

No. **25**.—OYSTER SAUCE FOR BOILED TURKEY.

Put three dozen oysters in a stewpan; save their liquor in a bowl; mix with the oysters half a pound of butter and flour, worked together, and season with cayenne pepper and salt; thin this now with the liquor from the oysters and a cup of cream. Let it boil ten minutes and serve on the turkey.

No. **26**.—SAUCE PIQUANTE.

Put a large spoonful of sweet butter in a stew-pan, slice into it two onions, two carrots, a little thyme, two cloves, two eschalots and a bunch of parsley; add, if liked, a clove of garlic. Let them cook until the carrot is soft, then shake in a little flour; let it cook five minutes more, and add a cup of beef or veal stock, and half a cup of strong vinegar; skim and strain through a sieve. Add salt and pepper when boiling. This is nice on cold meat.

No. **27**.—STOCK FOR SOUPS OR GRAVIES.

Break the bones of a knuckle of veal, add to it a pound of lean beef and a half pound of lean ham; stew in two quarts of water until it is reduced to one. If for gravy, add to it

two carrots, two turnips and two heads of celery. When
the vegetables are soft, strain and keep for use. Water
added to gravies spoils them.

No. 28.—EGG SAUCE WITH LEMON.

Boil six eggs; when cold, take off the shells, and slice them
into a cup of melted butter; add pepper and salt, and stir
constantly while heating. Add the juice of a lemon, or vinegar, or catsup as preferred. This sauce is equally good for
boiled fish or poultry.

No. 29.—HORSE RADISH SAUCE.

To a spoonful of mustard add three tablespoonfuls of
vinegar and a little salt; if you have it, put in two spoonfuls
of cream. Grate into this as much horse radish as will
thicken it; then mash a clove of garlic, and your sauce is
ready.

No. 30.—TO KEEP HORSE RADISH.

Grate the root, and pour strong vinegar over it, and bottle.
This is fine for roast meat.

No. 31.—SAUCE ROBERT.

Cut into small pieces four large onions; brown them with
three ounces of butter and a spoonful of flour. When yellow-
brown, pour on them half a pint of veal, or beef gravy, or
soup; let all simmer for half an hour; season with salt and
pepper, and at the moment of serving, add a dessert spoonful
of made mustard.

No. 32.—PIQUANT TOMATO SAUCE.

Mash half a dozen ripe tomatoes (pick out the seeds), put
them in a stewpan with sliced onions, and a little meat

gravy; let them simmer, till nearly dry, then add half a pint
of brown gravy, left of cold meat, and let it cook twenty
minutes. Strain and season with cayenne pepper, salt and
lemon juice. Tarragon vinegar may be used instead of the
lemon juice.

No. 33.—CREAM SAUCE.

Put a quarter of a pound of butter in a stew-pan, with a
small tablespoonful of wheat flour, a teaspoonful of chopped
parsley, and the same of young onions, or eschalots, chopped
fine; add a saltspoonful of salt, and the same of pepper, and
a grated nutmeg. Mix these well together, then add a glass
of cream, or rich milk, set it over the fire, and stir it with
a silver spoon until it is ready to boil; if it is too thick, add
more milk. This sauce should be stirred for fifteen minutes.
Extract of celery improves it. Serve with boiled rabbits,
meat or poultry.

No. 34.—APPLE SAUCE.

Peel, quarter, and core some rich, tart apples; add a very
little water, cover and set them over the fire; when tender,
mash them smooth, and serve with roasted pork, goose, or
any other gross meat.

No. 35.—CRANBERRY SAUCE.

Wash and pick a quart of cranberries; put them into a
stew-pan, with a teacupful of water, and the same of brown
sugar; cover the pan, and let them stew gently for one hour;
then mash them smooth with a silver spoon; dip a quart-
bowl in cold water, pour in the stewed cranberries, and leave
till cold. Serve with roast pork, ham, turkey or goose.

No. **36.**—SAVORY SAUCE FOR A ROAST GOOSE.

A tablespoonful of made mustard, half a teaspoonful of cayenne pepper, and three spoonfuls of port wine. When mixed, pour this (hot) into the body of the goose before sending it up. It wonderfully improves the sage and onions.

No. **37.**—FRIED PEACHES FOR SAUCE.

Take peaches, not fully ripe, wash and wipe them; then cut them in slices a quarter of an inch thick, and fry in the pan, after pork. Serve with the meat. This is a South Carolina dish.

No. **38.**—FRIED APPLES, AS A RELISH.

Wash fine, fair apples without paring; cut them in slices an eighth of an inch thick, and fry in hot lard, or pork fat. Serve with fried pork.

No. **39.**—RICH LEMON SAUCE, FOR PUDDINGS.

Boil a fresh lemon in plenty of water, until a straw will penetrate it, then cut it in slices, and each slice in quarters; add a teacupful of sugar, and the same of butter, with a large teaspoonful of wheat flour worked into it; put all together into a stew-pan, and stir in gradually half a pint of boiling water; keep it over the fire for ten minutes, stirring it all the time, then serve with half a nutmeg grated over.

No. **40.**—HARD SAUCE.

Beat a quarter of a pound of butter to a cream, then stir into it half a pound of pulverized white sugar, and beat it until it is light. A wineglass of wine or brandy may be added. Grate nutmeg over it. Put it on ice if the weather is warm.

No. **41.**—TO KEEP HORSE-RADISH FOR SAUCE.

Grate a quantity when in season, and keep it in bottles filled with strong vinegar. A clove of garlic added to each bottle is an improvement.

No. **42.**—TO MAKE GOOD VINEGAR; No. 1.

Mix a quart of molasses in three gallons of rain water; add to this, one pint of sharp yeast. Let it ferment and stand four weeks; you will then have good vinegar.

No. **43.**—ANOTHER WAY TO MAKE VINEGAR; No. 2.

To make good pickles or sauces of several kinds, good vinegar is required. To a gallon of water put two pounds of coarse brown sugar; boil and skim it for half an hour. Put it in a tub or jar, to ferment; add to it in the tub a slice of raised wheat-bread soaked in yeast. It can be bottled off or put in a cask in a week or two, but must be left unstopped, and the bung covered with muslin to keep out insects.

No. **44.**—TO MAKE GOOD VINEGAR FOR PICKLES.

To a gallon of whiskey add four pounds of brown sugar, a cup of yeast, and seven gallons of water. Put it into a demijohn or keg. If you set the vinegar in April, it will be good in November to pickle with. Cover the mouth of the vessel with muslin, to keep out flies or insects, which trouble, and sometimes ruin vinegar while making. When sharp and clear, bottle it.

No. **45.**—TO MAKE GOOD AND CHEAP VINEGAR.

Take three quarts of molasses, add to it eight gallons of
rain water; turn the mixture into a clean cask, shake it well
two or three times, throw in a few spoonfuls of good yeast,
or, two yeast cakes; place the cask in a warm place, and in
ten days throw in it a sheet of common brown paper, smeared
with molasses; it should be torn into narrow strips. This
paper seems necessary to form mother, in making vinegar,
unless you use whiskey to commence the fermentation; then
paper is not necessary.

THE KNIFE GRINDER.

Item 1880

337. Yo ka quimbé[1] chritiens pa langue yo, bef pa còne yo. (On prend les Chrétiens par la langue, les bœufs par les cornes.)
"Christians are known by their tongues, oxen by their horns." (Literally, are taken by or caught by.)—[*Martinique.*]

[1] *Quimbé* is a verb of African origin. It survives in Louisiana Creole as *tchombé* or *chombo:*

> *Caroline, zolie femme,*
> *Chombo moin dans collet.*

["Caroline, pretty woman; put your arm about my neck!"—lit.: "take me by the neck."]

There are other African words used by the older colored women, such as *macayé*, meaning to eat at all hours; and *Ouendé*, of which the sense is dubious. But the Congo verb *fifa*, to kiss; and the verbs *souyé*, to flatter; *pougalé*, to abuse violently; and such nouns as *saff* (glutton), *yche* or *iche* (baby), which are preserved in other Creole dialects, are apparently unknown in Louisiana to-day.

In Chas. Jeannest's work, *Quatre Années au Congo* [Paris: Charpentier, 1883], I find a scanty vocabulary of words in the Fiot dialect, the native dialect of many slaves imported into Louisiana and the West Indies. In this vocabularly the word *ouenda* is translated by "partir pour." I fancy it also signifies "to be absent, and that it is synonymous with our Louisiana African-Creole *ouendé*, preserved in the song:

> *Ouendé, ouendé, macaya;*
> Mo pas, 'barassé, *macaya!*
> *Ouendé, ouendé, macaya;*
> Mo bois bon divin, *macaya!*
> *Ouendé, ouendé, macaya;*
> Mo mangé bon poulé, *macaya!*
> *Ouendé, ouendé, macaya;* .. etc.

This is one of the very few songs with a purely African refrain still sung in New Orleans. The theme seems to be that, the master and mistress of a house being absent, some slave is encouraging a slave-friend to eat excessively, to "stuff himself" with wine, chicken, etc. "They are gone, friend: eat, fill yourself; *I'm* not a bit ashamed; stuff yourself!—I'm drinking good wine; stuff yourself!—I'm eating good chicken; gorge yourself," etc. Here *ouendé* seems to mean "they are out; they are gone away,"—therefore there is no danger.

There is another Creole song with the same kind of double refrain, but the meaning of the African words I have not been able to discover.

> Nicolas, Nicolas, Nicolas, ou dindin;
> Nicolas, Nicolas, Nicolas marché ouaminon:
> Quand li marché
> *Ouarasi, ouarasa!*
> Quand li marché
> *Ouarasi, ouarasa!*

["Nicholas, etc., you are a turkey-cock! Nicholas walks *ouaminon:* when he walks, it is *ourasi, ouarasa.*"] The idea is obvious enough; viz.: that Nicholas struts like a turkey-cock; but the precise signification of the three italicised words I have failed to learn.

Gombo Zhèbes 1885

ENTREES.

KIDNEY AND MUSHROOM STEW.

Cut the kidneys into slices, wash and dry them carefully; pepper and salt them, roll them in flour, and fry in butter till of a delicate brown color. Pour some plain beef stock, or beef gravy, in the pan; add a chopped onion, and stew for half an hour; then put in a cupful of mushrooms, and cook for fifteen minutes. Mushroom catsup will serve as a substitute. Use one-half the quantity of catsup.

STEWED LAMB CHOPS WITH GREEN PEAS.

Season the chops with pepper and salt; roll in flour and fry to a pale brown. When done, if the chops are very fat, pour some of it into the stock-pot and cover the chops with boiling water. Parboil a pint of green peas; add them to the chops, together with a large spoonful of sweet butter. Dredge in a spoonful of flour, and let all stew gently for half an hour.

IRISH STEW.

Take from one to three pounds of loin of mutton, or ribs of beef; cut it into chops; add by weight as many white potatoes, sliced, as there is beef. Throw in from two to six chopped onions, according to size, some pepper and salt, and a large spoonful of butter to each pound of meat. Let all stew gently for two hours and serve with boiled rice or macaroni.

PIGEON STEW.

Pick and wash the pigeons, stuff them with bread crumbs, parsley, pepper, salt and butter mixed; dust with flour, and put into a pan to brown. Add butter and a little soup-stock or gravy. Stew gently until tender. Before dishing add a glass of wine if approved, if not, a little more stock, if the gravy has become too thick.

TRIPE WITH MUSHROOMS.

Clean and parboil tripe before cooking. When it is white and tender, cut it into pieces suitable to fry; pepper and salt it, and dip it in flour or rolled cracker, then drop it into hot bacon fat. When browned on both sides, take up and make a gravy of some of the fat in which it was fried, a little flour, and a wineglass of good vinegar. Pour this around the tripe and serve with mushrooms.

STEWED TRIPE, PLAIN.

Cut a pound of tripe in long narrow pieces, lay it in a stew-pan and add a cup of milk, or milk and water, a piece of butter as large as a hen's egg, a tablespoonful of flour sifted in, a bunch of parsley, and a green onion, if desired. Cook slowly for nearly two hours.

TO FRY TRIPE BROWN.

It must be thoroughly boiled and tender, or no frying will make it good. Let it be perfectly cold, cut it in pieces, roll each piece in salt, pepper and flour, and fry brown in bacon grease. Frying tripe in lard makes it tasteless. When nicely brown take it up, dredge a little flour in the gravy, and put in a half cup of vinegar. Serve in a sauceboat, or pour over the tripe as preferred.

SCALLOPS OF MUTTON, WITH MUSHROOMS.

"Sautez," or fry the scallops brown, then pour off the fat, add a glass of wine, a dozen button mushrooms, three ounces of truffles cut in pieces, and a cup of broth, or the stock of plain soup without vegetables. Simmer gently, and finish by adding the juice of a lemon.

HASHED BEEF, PLAIN.

Slice some beef in very thin pieces, season with pepper and salt, and shake a little flour over it. Next, chop a medium sized onion and put it (without the beef) into a stew pan with a tablespoonful of mushroom or tomato catsup. Boil for a few minutes, then add a pint of broth, stock, or gravy-soup; boil it down to half the quantity. Five minutes before serving, throw in the cold sliced beef; let it boil five minutes and serve on toasted bread.

SANDWICHES. VERY FINE.

Take half a pound of nice sweet butter, three tablespoonfuls of mixed mustard, the same of sweet oil, a little salt, pepper and the yoke of an egg. Put it over the fire and stir till it thickens; set it by to cool and chop fine some tongue or boiled ham. Cut the bread thin, then spread on the dressing and over it put a layer of ham or tongue. Press the slices of bread hard together, trim the edges and garnish with curled parsley.

SANDWICHES OF VARIOUS KINDS, FOR PIC-NICS.

Home-made bread cuts better for sandwiches than baker's bread, so if you wish the sandwiches very nice, it is better to make a loaf at home. For bread and butter sandwiches, cut the bread very thin, spread it evenly with sweet butter, and lay the buttered sides together. Lay them in circles on a plate, and put parsley on top of them. Sandwiches may be made with cheese sliced and placed between the buttered bread, or with hard-boiled eggs sliced or chopped, and put between. The best are made with boiled smoked tongue or ham, with French mustard spread over the butter.

TO MAKE FRENCH MUSTARD.

Put on a plate an ounce of the best mustard, add to it salt, a clove of garlic or a few tarragon leaves. Mince the garlic, stir it in, and pour on vinegar till it is of the proper thickness for use.

VEAL HASH FOR BREAKFAST. VERY NICE.

Take a pint cup of cold veal cut small, dredge it with a spoonful of flour, and add a piece of butter the size of a hen's egg. Put all in a stewpan with half a pint of water; cover up and put it on the stove; let it simmer for an hour at least, stir it occasionally and add to it some parsley and sweet herbs. Just before serving add a teacup of milk, and serve on toasted bread.

PLAIN VEAL AND HAM PIE. EASILY MADE.

Cut a pound of veal and a pound of ham into slices, salt them slightly; chop a cupful of mushrooms, a bunch of parsley and some eschalots, and fry them lightly; add to them a pint of soup-stock, boil it together for five minutes and pour it into the piepan where you have placed your ham and veal. Put a dozen hard-boiled yolks of eggs in among the contents of the pie, cover it with a nice paste and bake it one hour and a half.

FRICANDELLONS OF COLD VEAL OR MUTTON.

Mince the meat very fine, soak a thick slice of bread in boiling milk, mash it, and mix it with the cold meat ; add a beaten egg (or two if you have more than a quarter of a pound of meat), some chopped parsley and thyme, a little grated lemon peel, pepper and salt; make this into cakes, and fry in butter or lard. Serve them dry on a serviette, accompanied with a gravy made from the bones of the minced meat which must be cooked with an onion, a little butter and flour, and milk; when brown it is ready.

VEAL AND HAM RAISED PIE, OR TIMBALE.

Lard two pounds of lean veal well with strips of fat bacon, and add two pounds of ham. Line a deep pan or mould with rich paste ; lay in the bottom of this a layer of liver forcemeat, then the veal and ham, and so on, in alternate layers, till the dish is full. Season between each layer with thyme, bay leaf, marjoram, or any dried and pounded sweet herbs; fill up the hollow places, and cover the pan with paste. Decorate the top of the pie with cut dough leaves; make a hole in the top to pour in the gravy, and let out the steam. Egg the top of the pie and bake it for three hours; withdraw it from the oven, and place the point of a funnel in the hole in the top, and pour in about a pint of good gravy or veal consommé. This should be eaten cold. It will be jellied all through if cooked enough.

VEAL SALAD FOR LUNCH.

To a pint of minced veal add three heads of celery. Pour over this a dressing made of the yolks of four hard-boiled eggs, a tablespoonful of dry mustard, and a large spoonful of olive oil. When this dressing is well beaten and perfectly smooth, add to it slowly (to keep from curdling) four tablespoonfuls of good wine vinegar, a little cayenne and salt. Garnish the dish with parsley and celery leaves.

VEAL SWEETBREADS WITH TOMATOES.

Set over the fire two quarts of ripe tomatoes; stew slowly, and strain through a coarse sieve. Add to them four or five sweetbreads, well trimmed and soaked in warm water; season with salt and cayenne pepper. Thicken with three spoonfuls of flour and a quarter of a pound of butter, mixed; cook slowly till done, and just before serving stir in the beaten yolks of three eggs.

VEAL LOAF FOR LUNCH OR TEA.

Mince cold roast veal as fine as possible; add a fourth part as much fat ham, a cup of grated bread, or cracker crumbs, and two well-beaten eggs to bind the crumbs together; season with salt, and pepper (black and red), mix and form it into a loaf. Glaze the outside with yolk of egg, and sprinkle over it fine cracker crumbs. Bake half an hour, and serve with gravy made from the bones, etc., of the veal. Serve the gravy hot.

MINCED VEAL AND POACHED EGGS.

One pound of cold veal chopped very fine. Boil half a pint of sauce till it begins to thicken or glaze; then add a cup of cream and the minced veal; season with pepper and salt. When dished put six poached eggs around it, alternately with slices of red tongue or ham. This is a nice breakfast dish, and uses to advantage the cold meats from the day previous.

CALF OR PIG BRAINS FRIED.

Wash the brains in salt and water, wipe dry and dip in wheat flour or in beaten egg and then in bread crumbs. Fry in butter or lard, and season with pepper, salt and lemon sliced.

CALVES' AND PIGS' FEET FRIED IN BATTER.

Wash and cook the feet tender, the day before using. When wanted, wash and roll them in a little flour to dry. Set them by, and make a batter of flour, eggs, milk, and a little salt and pepper (one egg is sufficient to two feet); take out the largest bones and roll the feet in batter, or lay them in a pan with hot lard, and pour the batter over them. Fry a delicate brown and serve on toast.

CALF'S HEAD BOILED OR BAKED.

Have a head nicely cleaned, and soak it in salt and water to make it look white. Remove the eyes. Take out the tongue and salt it. Of the brains make a separate dish. To boil the head put it in a pot of lukewarm water and boil till very tender. Serve with sauce made of butter, flour and water, some lemon juice and tomatoes. If to bake, dredge flour over it, put on bits of butter, season with pepper, salt and sweet herbs, set in a hot oven and baste with the water in which it was boiled.

POTTED CALF'S HEAD.

Boil a calf's head or half a beef's head with a cow-heel
until very tender. When done, pick out all the bones and
chop the meat and tendons very fine; strain the liquor they
were boiled in, and set it away to cool; skim off the fat and
pour the jelly over the meat. Season with a teaspoonful of
black pepper, salt, and thyme, powdered; boil all together
for a few minutes, and pour into bowls or jelly moulds. Serve
with parsley. Add a little garlic if the flavor is liked.

COLLARED CALF'S HEAD WITH BRAINS. COLD DISH.

Boil half, or the whole of a calf's head, as you require.
Cover it with water and let it simmer for two hours; take it
up, remove the bones, and put them back into the broth;
let it continue to stew, adding to it sage leaves, and an onion.
Cut the meat of head and brains into a stew pan, adding to it
some slices of ham, pepper and salt, the chopped tongue and
an eschalot; let these cook two hours. The brains should be
beaten up with two eggs, before putting them in, which should
be the last thing. Then pour all in a mould and fill up with
the liquor from the head, which should be boiled to a jelly.

CURRY OF COLD ROAST FOWL.

Take two large onions, two apples, two ounces of butter, a
dessert spoonful of curry powder or paste, half pint of gravy
or soup-stock, one spoonful of lemon juice and two tomatoes.
Fry the fowl and the onions in butter to a light brown
color; stew the apples, or fry them also. Put all, onions,

apples, gravy and fowl, with the tomatoes and lemon juice into a stewing pan and let it stew thirty minutes; then serve with boiled rice. If curry paste is used instead of curry powder, no lemon is required.

WELSH RAREBIT.

Cut a pound of cheese in slices a quarter of an inch thick, fry them together five minutes in butter, then add two well-beaten eggs, a little mustard and pepper; stir it up and send it to table hot, on slices of buttered bread.

HAM TOAST FOR LUNCHEON.

Beat the yolk of an egg with a tablespoonful of sweet milk; set it on the fire to warm, and thicken it with grated or finely chopped ham; let it simmer a few moments and pour it on buttered toast. This is for one person.

WINTER DISH OF BAKED BEANS AND PORK.

This is a very heavy dish, but nourishing, and it is well to know how to cook it, as it is economical.

Pick the beans, wash them, and put them to soak over night in plenty of water. In the morning pour this water off and put the beans in a kettle of cold water; place them on the fire and let them simmer till quite tender. Take them up and drain them; when thoroughly drained, put them in a baking pan with a large piece of salt pork; score the pork and lay it deep in among the beans, not upon them. Pour boiling water over them, and bake till brown. If in a range, leave them in all night. This constant change of water improves the beans very much, and makes them less flatulent.

MUTTON, BEEF AND HAMS.

REMARKS ON BOILING MEATS.

Meat, whether fresh or salted, smoked or dried, should always be put on the fire in cold water. Dried meats should be soaked before boiling. The delicacy of meat and fowls is preserved by carefully skimming while they are boiling.

STUFFED HAM.

Smoked hams are much liked stuffed with spices and sweet herbs, which is the only kind of stuffing a salt ham will admit, as bread, crackers or oysters would sour before the ham could be used. If you wish to stuff a ham, look at the receipt for "Aromatic Spices for seasoning Meat, Pies, etc." Soak your ham all night, scrape it nicely, and boil it half an hour to make the skin tender; then take it from the pot, gash it all over, introduce as much of the pounded spices as the incisions will hold, and then close the skin over the gashes and boil in the same manner, with vegetables thrown in, as in receipt for boiled ham.

BAKED HAM.

Soak and clean your ham, boil it with onions, cloves, parsley and sweet herbs until it is nearly done, then let it cool in its own liquor; when cold, pull off the skin and place the ham in the oven gate, with a little sugar and bread

crumbs over it till it is brown.   If it is to be eaten hot, serve
with vegetables and some acid or piquant sauce; if cold, send
up savory jelly, No. 21.

TO BOIL A HAM.

Run a knife, or skewer, into the thickest part of the ham
next the bone; if the knife comes out clean the ham is good,
if it smells rank and smears the knife the ham is not good.
Select your ham, then, according to this rule, and when good
lay it in cold water; scrape and wash it carefully, and let it
remain in the water all night. In the morning, when the water
—enough to cover the ham—is nearly boiling lay the ham in,
and keep the water in a simmer.   When it has boiled about
an hour throw in two carrots, four onions, two heads of celery,
a sprig of parsley, two or three blades of mace and four cloves.
If the ham is very salt, it is well to change the water before
putting in the seasoning.   To obtain tenderness and mellow-
ness the ham must not be allowed to boil hard, only simmer.
Too much heat hardens all meat, especially salt meat.   When
the ham is done set it off in its own water, let it cool in it;
by this means it will retain its moisture.   When cool take it
out, skin it, and dredge sugar over it, set it in the oven till
it browns, or hold a hot shovel over it.

DAUBE GLACÉE OF BEEF, FOR COLD SUPPERS.

Take a thick round of beef—from four to six inches is the
best size—make holes in it and stuff them with salted pork
or bacon; roll each piece, before it is drawn through the beef,
in pepper, salt, sugar, and vinegar, with minced parsley, and

a very little minced garlic. If the weather is cold it will be better to keep the meat till the next day before cooking it. Boil two calf's feet or four pig's feet until they drop to pieces; pick out the bones and strain the liquor; set it away to jelly, or put it on ice to make it jelly. The next morning, put one half the jelly in a large stew pan, then add the beef, and cover it with the remainder of the jelly. Paste the pan over very tight or cover it extremely well, so that none of the flavor can escape. Cook this about four hours; when done, take out, cover with the liquor, and set it aside till it is jellied. This is delicious to eat cold, for suppers and collations.

BOILED BRISKET OF BEEF, STUFFED.

A piece weighing eight pounds requires five or six hours to boil. Before boiling the beef make a dressing of breadcrumbs, pepper, butter, salt, sweet herbs, mace, and an onion, all chopped fine and mixed with a beaten egg. Put the dressing between the fat and the lean of the beef; sew it up to keep the dressing in. Flour a cloth, tie the beef up tight in it, and let it boil five or six hours.

ROUND OF BEEF STEWED BROWN.

Make incisions in the beef and stuff with chopped onions, salt, pepper, and sweet basil, thyme and parsley. Dredge the meat with flour, lay some slices of bacon over it, and put it to brown in a close oven. Slice two turnips, four carrots, four salsifies, three stalks of celery and two onions; add a quarter of a cup of tomato catsup or two large tomatoes; season with salt and put all in the oven to cook with the meat. After it has been cooking in the oven two hours and is brown, add a cup of water with the vegetables. Cover again closely, and let this stew for one or two hours more, or until the meat nd vegetables are tender.

TO FRY A STEAK TO TASTE AS IF BROILED.

It sometimes happens that when the fire is low and the coals gone out, you are called on to cook a steak. Then get up a quick blaze in the stove with some kindlings. Put in a pan, over the blaze, a little butter; when it is hot lay in your steak; let it fry quickly; while frying cover the pan. Work some butter, salt and pepper together in a tin pan, and when the steak is done to taste, let it lie in this mixture a few minutes, and then serve. Do not salt a steak until it is cooked, as salt will toughen it and draw out its juices.

ROUND OF BEEF À LA BARONNE.

Boil a fat round of beef for half an hour, take it up and put in a deep dish; cut gashes in the sides of the meat, put pepper and salt into each gash; fill the dish the meat is in with claret wine; set it in to bake, adding as it goes in the stove three blades of mace, a cup of pickled capers, or nasturtiums, three white onions cut small, and a bunch of parsley cut fine. Stew or bake all together until the meat is tender. Toast some slices of bread very brown, lay them in the bottom of a dish, lay in the beef and pour the gravy around it, unless it is preferred in a sauce boat.

ROASTED BEEFSTEAKS.

Tenderloin or porterhouse steaks are the best for broiling. Have a clear fire of coals to broil on ; rub the gridiron with a little fat of the meat; lay on the steak without salting, let it broil gently until one side is done, then turn. Catch the blood as you turn it, to make the gravy rich. If the steak is a large firm one, take a quarter of a pound of butter and work into it pepper and salt. When the steak is done lay it on to this seasoned butter, keep it hot until the butter melts, turn the steak in it a few times, put the blood with the gravy, and serve hot, with tomato sauce or catsup.

TO ROAST BEEF IN A STOVE.

A fine roasting piece of beef may, if properly managed, be baked in a stove so as to resemble beef roasted before a large, open fire. Prepare the meat as if for roasting, season it well with salt, pepper, and a little onion if liked. Set the meat on muffin rings, or a trivet in a dripping pan, and pour into the pan a pint or so of hot water to baste the meat with. Keep the oven hot and well closed on the meat ; when it begins to bake, baste it freely, using a long-handled spoon ; it should be basted every fifteen minutes ; add hot water to the pan as it wastes, that the gravy may not burn; allow fifteen minutes to each pound of meat unless you wish it very rare. Half an hour before taking it up, dredge flour thickly over it, baste freely, and let it brown. Take the meat from the pan, dredge in some flour and seasoning if needed ; throw into the gravy a cup of water, let it boil up once, and strain into a sauce boat or gravy tureen.

LEGS OF MUTTON BOILED A L'ANGLAISE.

Select a fat, fine leg of mutton, put it on the fire in warm water; when it boils skim it, and let it simmer gently for two hours and a half; throw in a tablespoonful of salt. When the mutton is done garnish with turnips mashed in cream, butter, pepper and salt, and send it to table with a sauce boat of caper sauce No 11.

ROAST LEG OF MUTTON.

Select a fine fat leg, cut holes in it, and lard it with fat bacon; season with parsley, pepper, and salt and put it to bake in a slow oven. Roast it for two hours, and serve with tomato sauce.

MUTTON STUFFED WITH MUSHROOMS.

Chop up half a pint of mushrooms, put them in a stew pan with some chopped parsley, and onion, and a tablespoonful of grated lean, and same of fat ham; season with salt and pepper, add the yolks of four eggs, stir it all together, and introduce it in the leg by taking out the bone or by making incisions in the mutton. Bake very brown, froth it up by dusting flour over it, and serve with a good brown gravy, in which some currant jelly is melted. Sauce No. 28 is very nice for stuffed leg of mutton.

MUTTON HAUNCH.

Let it lie in vinegar and water a few hours before it is put to cook. When wanted, rub it all over with pepper and salt, and when going to put it in the oven, cover it with a paste made of flour and water, to keep in the juices while baking; allow fifteen minutes to each pound of mutton. When half done, take off the flour paste, baste the meat well and dredge flour over it. Half an hour before serving, stir into the pan a quarter of a pound of butter, baste the meat freely, dredge flour over it again, and brown. Serve with port wine and jelly in the gravy, or if preferred, use one of the sauces mentioned for roast mutton.

MUTTON THAT WILL TASTE LIKE VENISON.

Take a hind quarter of lamb or mutton ; rub it well all over with brown sugar, half a pint of wine, and same of vinegar. Let it stay in this pickle for a day or two, if the weather is cold. When it is wanted, wash it, dry it, and roast it, or it may be cut into steaks, or made into a pie like venison. Sugar is a great preservative, and gives a finer flavor than salt, which hardens delicate meats. Salt drains out the juices of mutton or lamb.

CURIOUS !

Item 1880

40. *Bouki fait gombo, lapin mangé li. (Le bouc fait le gombo, le lapin le mange.)

"He-goat makes the gombo; but Rabbit eats it."[1]—[*Louisiana.*]

333. Vié coq, zène poule. (Vieux coq, jeune poule.)

"An old cock, a young hen."—[*Mauritius.*]

43. *Ça qui bon pou zoie, bon pou canard. (Ce qui est bon pour l'oie, est bon pour le canard.).

"What is good for the goose is good for the duck."—*Martinique.*

Item 1880

80. C'est lhé vent ka venté, moun ka ouer lapeau poule. (C'est quand le vent vente qu'on peut voir la peau de la poule—lit.: que le monde peut voir.)
"It's when the wind is blowing that folks can see the skin of a fowl."—True character is revealed under adverse circumstances.—[*Trinidad.*]

272. Quand poul ou tini zé, pas mette li dans canari. (Quand votre poule pond des œufs, ne la mettez pas dans le pot.)
"When your hen is laying, don't put her in the pot."[2]—[*Martinique.*]

[1] This proverb is founded upon one of the many amusing Creole animal-fables, all bearing the title: *Compè Bouki épis Compè Lapin*) "Daddy Goat and Daddy Rabbit".) The rabbit always comes out victorious, as in the stories of Uncle Remus.
[2] Like our saying about killing the goose that laid the golden eggs.

Gombo Zhèbes 1885

FOWLS AND GAME.

BOILED CHICKENS.

After the chickens are cleaned and trussed fold them in a nice white cloth, put them in a large stew pan and cover them with boiling water; boil them gently, and skim carefully so long as any scum rises ; let them simmer slowly as that will make them plump and white, while fast boiling will make them dark and lose flavor. When done lay them on a hot dish, and pour celery, oyster, or egg sauce over them. Serve some also in a boat, as it keeps hot longer than when poured over the fowls. Boiled tongue or ham should be served with boiled chicken. If the chicken is not very tough, an hour or an hour and a quarter is sufficient to boil it.

COUNTRY FRIED CHICKENS.

Take a young fat chicken, cut it up, pepper and salt it, dredge it over with flour, and set it by while you mix a cup of lard, and some slices of fat bacon in a frying pan. Let the lard get very hot, then drop in a few pieces of the chicken, always allowing room in the pan for each piece to be turned without crowding. As fast as you fry the pieces, put them on a dish over hot water to keep the heat in them while you make the gravy. Pour off some of the grease the chicken was fried in, and then dredge into the fryingpan some flour; let this brown nicely and then pour into it a cup of sweet milk, little at a time ; let it froth up, and then place your chicken back into the gravy for three minutes. If you like the chicken brown and dry, pour the gravy under it on the dish for serving.

BOILED CHICKENS WITH STUFFING.

Truss and stuff the chicken as for roasting, dredge it all over with wheat flour, and put it in a pot of boiling water ; take the pot off the fire for five minutes after the chicken is put in, or the skin will crack; then let it boil gently according to its age and weight, an old fowl requiring twice as long to boil as a young one; allow fifteen minutes to the pound. Take off all the scum as it rises, and when done serve with hard-boiled egg sauce, or parsley, or oyster sauce. This is a nice way to cook a fat old chicken, as it is much more tender and nourishing than baked, for if the chicken is old baking toughens it.

STEW, OR FRICASSEE OF CHICKEN.

Clean and wash the chicken, cut it up as for frying, lay it in a stew pan with water to cover it; add a teaspoonful of salt and half as much pepper ; set it to boil very gently, take off all scum as it rises. When the chicken is tender, which will be in an hour, take a teacup of butter, a tablespoonful of flour worked in it, and a bunch of parsley, put them in the stew pan with the chicken ; let all stew twenty minutes, and serve on toasted bread. Egg-balls around the toast add much to the beauty of this dish.

CHICKEN FRICASSEE À LA MARENGO.

Cut the chicken up as for a fricassee, put it in a saucepan with a wineglassful of salad oil, and allow it to cook rather briskly for twenty minutes; then put in with it a quarter of a pound of truffles cut up, a bunch of parsley, six chives or small green eschalots, a bruised clove of garlic, and pepper and salt; let them stew for twenty minutes; then pour off the oil and take out the parsley. If only one chicken is used, throw in half a pint of button mushrooms, a ladleful of brown gravy sauce, and the juice of a lemon. Garnish this dish with pieces of fried bread and large crayfish.

ROAST CHICKENS.

Draw them and stuff with rich bread and butter stuffing; baste them with butter and a little fat bacon, seasoned with sweet herbs; brown nicely, and serve with their own gravy made by sifting in a tablespoonful of flour and a cup of hot water; add a little chopped parsley, and serve with hard-boiled eggs on the dish with the chickens.

CHICKEN SAUTÉ WITH OYSTER SAUCE.

Cut up the chicken as for frying, roll each piece in salt, pepper, and sifted flour, and fry a light brown. Pour off most of the grease the chicken was fried in, and in the same pan put three dozen oysters with a pint of their juice, and a spoonful of lemon juice. Let them simmer a few minutes, and serve with pieces of fried bread around the dish.

COLD CHICKEN ESCALOPED.

Mince cold chicken without the skin, wet it with gravy or hot water (gravy is best), and season with salt and pepper. To the minced meat of one chicken, put two ounces of sweet, fresh butter, cut small. Rub tin or silver scallop pans with butter, strew over the bottom powdered cracker, lay the minced chicken in, strew cracker over the top, and bake in a hot oven long enough to brown the top. Serve with celery or pickle.

TO BROIL A CHICKEN.

Clean it as usual and split it down the back, break the breast-bone with a stroke of the potato beetle, spread it out flat and lay it on the gridiron over clear coals; put the inside of the chicken to the fire first. Put a tin cover over it, let it broil quickly until nearly done, then turn it and finish without the cover. When nicely browned take it on a dish, season it with salt and pepper, and butter it freely; turn it once or twice in the butter and serve it hot.

CHICKEN CURRY.

Cut up the chicken and stew it as usual for the table. When done add a tablespoonful of curry powder. Serve rice with the dish.

CHICKEN PIE, À LA REINE.

Cut two chickens up as for frying, lay some veal cut in small pieces in the bottom of your pie dish, cut up over the veal a slice of fat ham; on this place your chickens; place hard boiled yolks of eggs in among the chicken. Take half a pint of white sauce, made with butter, flour, and milk or water;

pour this over the chickens, season with a cup of chopped mushrooms, some parsley, pepper and salt (a good pie can be made if you omit the mushrooms and ham, but not so rich as this recipe); now cover your pie with a good paste, and bake for an hour or two.

PLAIN CHICKEN PIE.

Take two nice chickens, or more if they are small, cut them up as for frying, and put them in a pot to stew with some slices of fat meat. Let them cook for half an hour, then add a few onions and four Irish potatoes sliced small, so that in cooking they may be thoroughly dissolved in the gravy. Season with pepper, salt, a little parsley, and a quarter of a pound of sweet butter. When it is cooked well there should be gravy enough to cover the chickens. If you want it very nice, beat up two eggs, and stir into the stew with half a pint of milk. Line a five-quart pan with a crust made like soda biscuit, only more shortening; put in the chickens and gravy; then cover with a top crust. Bake until the crust is done and you will have a good chicken pie.

CHICKEN POT PIE.

Cut up a chicken, parboil it, save the liquor it was boiled in. Wash out the kettle, or take another one, and in it fry three or four slices of fat salt pork, and put it in the bottom of the dish in which the pie is to be made; then put in the chicken and the liquor, also a piece of batter of the size of a teacup, and sprinkle in some pepper; cover with a light crust and bake an hour.

BONED TURKEY.

Chop up one pound of white veal, with a pound of fat bacon; season high with chopped mushrooms, parsley, pepper, salt, and a bunch of sweet herbs; when chopped fine, pound them in a mortar or pass them through a sausage grinder; add to this the yolks of three eggs, and place it by in a basin for use. Peel a pound of truffles, and cut up a boiled smoked tongue, a pound of fat bacon, or a pound of calf's udder or veal. Next bone a turkey, or two fine capons, or fowls, and draw the skin from the legs and pinions inside. Take the turkey on a napkin—it is now limp and boneless—cut slices from the thick breast and place it on the skin where it seems to be thin, distribute the flesh of the fowl as evenly as you can on the skin; season it slightly with pepper and salt. Spread a layer of the prepared force-meat in the basin, let it be an inch thick; then place the cut-up tongue, bacon and veal, lay a row of chopped truffles and a layer of the force-meat until the skin is covered, or as full as it will hold. It must be sewed up the back, the ends tied, like a cushion, or roly-poly; to do this you must butter a cloth and put it tightly over the turkey skin, as it will be quite too tender to stand the cooking, etc., unless supported by a napkin. Tie it up tightly and place it in a round stew-pan with the bones and any trimmings of veal or poultry at hand, add to it two boiled calf's feet, or an ounce of gelatine, two onions stuck with four cloves, a bunch of parsley, six green onions, a bunch of sweet basil, and a bunch of thyme, two blades of mace, and a dozen pepper corns, or whole peppers; moisten all with half a pint of wine or brandy. Warm this up and put in your tied-up gelatine, pour over it as much white veal stock as will cover it well, put it back on the stove to simmer gently for two hours and a half; let the gelatine get cold in its own seasoning, and then take it out and put it under a weight while you remove the stock or gravy; take off all the cold grease from the surface and clarify with eggs in the usual way. When the gelatine is quite cold, remove the weight, take it from its napkin, wipe it, and glaze it, and place it on a dish. Decorate it with the strained gravy, which should have been placed on ice as soon as clarified and strained. It will now be a firm jelly; if not, put it on ice again, and trim the boned turkey or fowls with it.

Gelatines of turkeys, geese, capons, pheasants, partridges &c., are made in the same way. This is from the finest source, and will repay any one who tries to make this magnificent dish. It has never to my knowledge, been given in any American cook-book, as it was obtained from one who was *Chef de Cuisine*, to a crowned head in Europe.

WILD TURKEY.

If the turkey is old, or tough, it must be boiled one hour before being stuffed for baking. Then stuff it with oysters, bread and butter, and season with pepper and salt; baste with butter, and the juice of the turkey. Make the gravy by putting in the pan a pint of oysters, or button mushrooms, throw in a cup of cream, or milk, salt and pepper, and send to table hot, with the turkey.

A PLAIN WAY TO COOK A TURKEY BY ROASTING.

Make a dressing to suit you; there are several to choose from in this book, made from bread, or forcemeat. Stuff the

turkey, season it with salt, pepper, and a little butter, dredge
it with flour and put it in the oven; let the fire be slow at
first, and hotter as it begins to cook. Baste frequently with
butter; when the turkey is well plumped up, and the steam
draws toward the fire, it is nearly done; then dredge again
with flour, and baste with more butter until it is a nice
brown. Serve with gravy and bread sauce; some like chestnuts stewed in the turkey gravy, and served with it. A very
large turkey will take three hours to roast, one of eight
pounds will take two hours.

ROAST TURKEY A LA PERIGORD.

For this purpose choose a fine young hen turkey; make an
incision at the back of the neck, and through this take out
the entrails, as the turkey looks so much nicer than when
otherwise cut. Cut away the vent, and sew up the place with
coarse thread; singe off the hairs and scald the legs to get off
the black skin, if the skin is black as it sometimes is. The
neck should be cut off close into the back, and the crop left
entire; some cooks can do this and some think it too much
trouble. Break the breast bone and take it out. Lay a little
salt on the turkey, and cover it up, while you prepare the
stuffing. Wash three pounds of truffles, if the hen turkey is a
large one; if it is small two pounds will do. Peel the truffles
and slice them; throw them into water, and scald them;
add two pounds of fat ham, or bacon, also, the turkey
liver, and a quarter of a pound of veal liver; season
this with pepper, salt, nutmeg, chopped thyme, and a
clove of garlic. Set the stew pan, containing all these

ingredients, on a slow fire, and let them cook for an hour, stirring them occasionally, with a wooden spoon. Mash them all up and let it get cool; when cool, stuff the turkey full of the truffle dressing, and fill the crop also; sew it up carefully, and tie it with a string, then truss the turkey, and if time allows, put it away for the next day. It should then be roasted, keeping it well basted with the liquor the truffles were boiled in, and butter added to it.

BOILED TURKEY AND CELERY SAUCE.

Draw a fine young turkey hen, and remove the angular part of the breast bone; take two pounds of fat veal dressing and stuff the turkey with it. Put over the fire to cook, the veal, bones, and turkey giblets, to make some white soup stock; season this and let it boil until you want to put the turkey on to cook. Now truss your turkey and put it in a boiling pot with a carrot, two onions, a head of celery, and a bunch of sweet herbs; now pour over the turkey the stock from the veal and giblets; cover with it, if enough; if not, put in water to cover it and set it to boil; when it has boiled one hour, put it on the back of the stove, and let it simmer and braise, until dinner. Take off any strings that may look badly; dish it up. Pour over it a well made *purée* of celery, or oyster sauce, and send to table. This is an elegant mode of serving turkey.

BOILED TURKEY WITH OYSTER SAUCE.

Clean and truss it the same as for baking. Stuff the turkey with oysters, bread crumbs, butter and mace, all mixed and seasoned. Put it on the fire in a kettle of water not hot, but slightly warm; do not drop it into boiling water or it will break the skin and spoil the appearance of the turkey. Cover it close, and when the scum rises take it off. Let the boiling continue for one hour, then put the pot containing the turkey on the coolest part of the stove, and let it simmer for half an hour. Serve with oyster sauce in a sauce boat.

DUCK ROASTED.

Pick, draw and singe the duck; wash it out carefully and stuff it with potatoes, mashed with butter, onions, and parsley. Put it down, to a good fire or in a hot oven, pour in a cup of water; let it roast for half an hour if it is fat and tender, longer if tough. As soon as the duck is cleaned, boil the giblets, and before serving, chop them up fine with some of the gravy from the duck, two tablespoonfuls of catsup, a lump of butter, and a little brown flour. Have lemons cut on side dishes, or serve with brown duck sauce No. 1. See sauces for meats, ducks &c.

DUCKS, TAME AND WILD.

Tame ducks are prepared for the table the same as young geese, that is, stuffed with bread, butter, pepper and onion, or with mashed and seasoned Irish potatoes. Wild ducks should be fat, the claws small and supple; the hen is the more delicate. Do not scald wild ducks, but pick them clean and singe over a blaze. Draw and wipe them well inside with a cloth; rub pepper and salt inside and out; stuff each duck well with bread and butter stuffing. If the ducks are at all fishy, use onion in the stuffing, and baste very freely. It is well to parboil them in onion and water before stuffing; throw away the water and then proceed to stuff and roast them. Put in the pan a teacup of butter, baste well with this, and when nearly done, dredge flour over the ducks, and brown them nicely. For the gravy you must boil the giblets; while the ducks are cooking mince these fine; add pepper, salt, and a teaspoonful of browned flour. Take a glass of wine and a large spoonful of currant jelly; heat them and serve with the ducks, mixed with the giblets, or serve it in a dish alone, as you like.

CANVAS-BACK DUCKS.

These are cooked the same as wild ducks, without onion however, in the basting, as they have no disagreeable taste. Serve wine and currant jelly with canvas-back ducks.

TO STEW DUCKS WITH GREEN PEAS.

Truss the ducks as for baking and boiling, and put them away in the pantry; then put two ounces of butter in a stew-pan on the fire, stir in two tablespoonfuls of flour, stir until it becomes brown or a fawn color; then pour in a pint of broth or gravy made from veal, or from water in which ducks or chickens have been boiled. Stir this while cooking, and when it boils, put in the ducks; let them cook for half an hour, or until done or nearly so, then add a quart of green peas, an onion chopped, and a sprig of parsley; allow these to stew gently until done; remove the parsley and the ducks, and if there is too much sauce, cook it down a little; dish up, pour the peas and gravy over the ducks and serve.

ROASTED DUCK.

Clean, draw and truss the duck, or ducks, wash them nicely, salt and pepper them, and get ready a sage and onion stuffing (see roast goose), or stuff with mashed potatoes, or bread, butter, onions, pepper and salt mixed, and bound together with an egg.

BROILED TEAL DUCK.

Split the duck like a partridge down the back, broil on clear coals, butter freely, and serve on buttered toast; pepper and salt when broiled, just before putting on the butter; if salted before it extracts the fine flavor.

WILD DUCKS.

There are several kinds of ducks South, and some are very fine. Truss wild ducks and lay them in a pan to bake with a small onion in the body; put butter over them, with a bunch of celery, a little pepper and salt; cook slowly and garnish with lemon. Wild ducks should be wiped dry after they are drawn, and rubbed on the inside with pepper and salt, except the canvas-back, which should be left to its own delicious flavor.

WILD GEESE.

Wild geese should be cooked rare, and stuffed with a dressing of bread, butter, and a small quantity of pungent seasoning, such as onion, cayenne, or mustard.

ROAST GOOSE, WITH SAGE AND ONION.

Draw a fine fat goose, stuff it with a seasoning of the following mixture: Take four onions, peel them and boil them ten minutes in plenty of water to take from them the strong taste. When the onions have boiled take them from the fire, chop fine, and add to them a large spoonful of sage leaves dried and powdered, then add a cupful of stale white bread crumbs, a teaspoon of black pepper, a little cayenne, and a teaspoon of salt. Mix all together with a cup of milk or beef water, and stuff the goose with it. Put it in the oven and brown it nicely; baste often with butter; when done dish it with its own rich brown gravy, and send to table with a boat of apple sauce.

GOOSE, WITH CHESTNUTS À LA CHIPOLITA.

Get the goose ready as usual. To prepare the stuffing take sixty large chestnuts, peel them by scalding, then put them in a stew pan with two ounces of butter, one onion chopped fine, and a sprig of parsley; chop and mix all together and stuff the goose with it; mix with the chestnuts one pint of good broth, and stew them down in it before stuffing the goose. Boil down the gravy very much, and when the goose is served, add the juice of two oranges, half a pound of currant jelly, and a lemon peel in the gravy. Pour this over the goose when it goes to the table.

GAME, VENISON ETC.

Venison is the finest game we have South. The haunch or saddle is always roasted; it requires constant attention, and should be turned and basted frequently while cooking. Cover the fat with thick white paper while cooking; when nearly done, take off the paper and baste well with claret wine, butter and flour. Currant jelly is the usual accompaniment of roasted venison, and is preferred by some to wine, in cooking it.

VENISON STEAK.

Venison steak is good fried or broiled. If to be broiled, season with pepper, salt, and butter, and cook quickly on a hot gridiron. If the meat is not fat, make a gravy for it of wine, flour, and butter. Serve hot.

VENISON PASTY.

This is a pie made from the bones, meat, &c., of venison, after the steak and haunch are taken off. Cut up and stew, or braise the parts of meat intended for the pie; season with pepper, salt, port wine, butter, and if liked, mushrooms; stew all until tender, then make a paste and finish like chicken pie. This is better to eat cold than hot, and should be rich enough to be a solid jelly when cold.

SQUIRREL, OR YOUNG RABBIT PIE.

Cut up two or three young squirrels or rabbits; put them in a saucepan to cook with two ounces of butter, a handful of chopped mushrooms, a bunch of parsley and two shallots chopped; season with pepper and salt, and a little thyme or sweet herbs; cook them a light brown. Throw in a glass of white wine, a half cup of brown gravy from veal or chicken, and the juice of half a lemon. Toss all up on the fire fifteen or twenty minutes, and it is ready to be put in the pie. If you have no gravy on hand, add to the rabbits a cup of sweet milk, and a piece of butter, as large as a hen's egg. Make a nice paste, line the sides of the pan, pour in the stewed rabbit, and cover with paste. Bake until a light brown, and eat cold or hot. It is almost as good as venison pie.

HARE OR RABBIT, ROASTED.

If the hares and rabbits are young, the ears will be tender. Clean the rabbits and wash them through several waters. If to be roasted, they must be stuffed with grated bread crumbs, suet or butter, a chopped onion, the liver of the rabbit chopped, and a lemon peel grated. Moisten with eggs and a little claret. Put this in the rabbit and sew it up; baste with butter, and cook for two hours. Make the gravy with the drippings in the pan, a little cream or milk, and flour. If the rabbits are old, they are good stewed slowly with sweet herbs, wine, water, and chopped onions, and thickened with flour and butter.

CEDAR, OR CAROLINA RICE BIRDS.

These are very small, but make a delicious pie by stewing them with butter and sweet herbs, and baking them in a light paste, with plenty of gravy.

PARTRIDGE OR QUAILS

Are nice roasted or broiled, and served on toast. If baked they require constant basting.

PIGEON PIE. VERY NICE.

Take six pigeons, truss them, and stuff them with their own livers, a little bacon, some butter, parsley, and rolled cracker or a small piece of bread; salt to taste; cover the bottom of the baking dish with slices of veal or beef; season with chopped parsley, mushrooms, pepper, salt, and butter. Place the pigeons on this, and cover with a nice pie crust. When the pigeons are placed in the pan, lay between each two pigeons the yolks of two hard-boiled eggs Be sure and have enough gravy to keep the pie very moist. This can be done by adding plain beef-stock or water as the pie bakes. Parboil the pigeons a little, also the beef, before putting them in the pan, and then keep the water they were boiled in to fill up the pie.

ROAST PIGEONS.

Truss them when plucked and drawn, lay thin slices of fat bacon on their breasts; bake them three-quarters of an hour, and then make a gravy with their giblets, which should have been boiling for the purpose. Chop up the livers etc., brown them and serve with the pigeons. Thin the gravy with the stock the liver was boiled in.

TO ROAST A SUCKING PIG.

In selecting a pig for the table, one four weeks old is to be preferred. Let the pig be prepared in the usual way by the butcher, that is scalded, drawn, etc. Stuff it with a mixture of two or three onions, say half a pint when sliced and chopped, and a dozen leaves of sage, pepper and salt; set this to simmer on the fire, then throw in half a pint of bread crumbs if the pig is small—if a large one, put a pint of crumbs—a quarter of a pound of butter, and the yolks of four eggs. Cook this and stuff the pig with it; sew the pig up and put it in the oven to roast; baste it often with a brush or swab dipped in olive oil, dust a little sugar over it, and brown it evenly. Take off the head before serving, take out the brains, put them in a stew pan; add to them some chopped parsley, pepper, and salt, a cup of the gravy from the pig, and the juice of a lemon. Stir this over the fire, and send it to the table hot in a separate boat.

ILLUSTRATED LETTERS FROM THE PEOPLE—NO. II.

Item 1880

271. *Quand patate tchuite, faut mangé li. (Quand la patate est cuite, il faut la manger.)

"When the sweet potato is cooked, it must be eaten."[1]—[*Louisiana*.]

[1] This differs a little from the spelling adopted by Gottschalk in his *Bamboula*— "*Quand patate-la couite ma va mangé li.*" The proverb is used in the sense of our saying: "Strike the iron while it's hot."

278. Quiquefois wou plante zharicots rouze; zharicots blancs qui poussé. (Quelquefois vous plantez des haricots rouges, et ce sont des haricots blancs qui poussent.)

"Sometimes you sow red beans, and white beans grow." "The best-laid plans of mice and men gang aft a-gley."—[*Mauritius.*]

76. *C'est couteau qui connaite ça qui dans cœur geomon. (C'est le couteau qui sait ce qu'il y a dans le cœur du giromon.)

"It's the knife that knows what's in the heart of the pumpkin."[2]—[*Martinique.*]

[2] This proverb exists in five Creole dialects. In the Guyana patois it is slightly different: *Couteau oûnso connain qu'or iniam* (le couteau seul connait le cœur de l'igname.) "It's only the knife knows what's in the heart of the yam."

Gombo Zhèbes 1885

VEGETABLES.

IRISH POTATOES, MASHED AND BROWNED.

Boil them without peeling; peel them while hot, mash them up with sweet butter, a little milk, pepper and salt. Many like them better when mashed and smoothed over with a knife blade, and slightly browned in the oven. They can be kept hot in this way if the meal is kept back for a guest, which is convenient on some occasions.

STEWED IRISH POTATOES. A NICE BREAKFAST DISH.

Wash, peel, and slice six potatoes; throw them for a few moments into cold, salted water, take them out in five minutes and place them in a stew pan on the fire; cover them with cold water; when tender, throw off all the water, pour over them half a cup of sweet milk, a little salt, pepper, and chopped parsley, and thicken them with a spoonful of butter, rolled in flour, or a teaspoonful of flour, beaten in carefully to prevent it from lumping; stew a few moments and serve in a covered dish.

PUFFS.

Very nice potato puffs may be made by mashing seven or eight potatoes smoothly, and mixing in with them two well-beaten eggs, two tablespoonfuls of melted butter, also well-beaten, and a cup of milk. Pour it into a pan and bake in a hot stove.

FRIED POTATOES.

Wash and pare a sufficient quantity for the meal. Slice them in the machine, taking care to bear down lightly, so as to have the slices very thin. Have ready a vessel of very hot lard, and drop the sliced potatoes into it, letting them remain till they begin to brown. Take them out with a wire ladle, scatter a little fine salt over them, and serve while hot. Success depends almost entirely upon having the lard sufficiently hot. If the potatoes do not brown, but absorb fat, and are limp and greasy, be sure the lard must be made hotter. Properly fried, they may be eaten with relish when cold, as they are crisp and palatable.

FRIED POTATOES.

Pare and cut the potatoes in thin slices; throw them as you cut them into salted water to cool, and make them crisp. Put them piece by piece on a dry towel and wipe dry, then drop them into boiling fat, enough to float them. As they brown, dip them out with a skimmer, and salt them a little.

POTATO CROQUETS.

Take six boiled potatoes (cold mashed potatoes will do), add three tablespoonfuls of grated ham, a little pepper, salt, and chopped parsley, also, the yolks of three eggs; form into balls, dip in egg and roll in bread crumbs; fry in hot lard; garnish with parsley.

SWEET POTATOES

Are good baked plain in their skins; or boiled, peeled and sliced, served with butter; or boiled, and then sliced in a pan, butter and sugar thrown over them, and baked in the stove. Some persons like them boiled and mashed with butter, and browned in the oven like Irish potatoes.

TURNIPS, TO COOK.

Boil or steam them after peeling; when they are quite tender, you must mash them like potatoes, and season with pepper, salt and butter.

ONIONS BOILED AND FRIED.

Trim and peel them, and boil them in water until quite tender, then dish them. Season with salt, pepper and butter. Many like them cut in slices and fried a light brown; they are good on a beefsteak when washed in two or three waters after being sliced, then put into hot lard and some of the beefsteak gravy, fried gently until a light color, and served around the steak.

GREEN CORN ON THE COB.

Get it as fresh from the field as possible, and if you desire it boiled on the cob you must (when it is well silked) throw it into boiling salted water. Corn requires only fifteen minutes boiling; too long boiling takes out the sweetness from the grain.

STEWED GREEN CORN.

Take a dozen fresh, tender, ears of corn; cut it off the cob, and put it in a stew pan with a quart of cold water. No salt at first. Let it cook half an hour and then stir in a lump of fresh butter, a spoonful of flour, and salt and pepper to taste. If too dry, add a cup of sweet milk, or water if the milk is not convenient.

GREEN CORN FRITTERS.

Beat three eggs with a cup of milk; to this add a pint of boiled green corn grated; throw in flour enough to make a batter thick enough to drop from a spoon; salt and pepper to taste, beat it very hard, and drop into boiling lard one spoonful at a time. This is a great luxury and a good substitute for oysters during the hot season.

SUCCOTASH, OR CORN AND BEANS MIXED.

Boil for half an hour two pints of green shelled beans, or the same amount of string beans; then pour off the water, cut the corn from two dozen ears, put it in the pot among the beans; add salt and pepper, and cover them with boiling water. Let it boil for half an hour, and add a lump of butter as big as a hen's egg, rolled in flour; let this boil up once and it is done.

CORN OYSTERS.

One pint of grated green corn, one cup of flour, one dessert spoonful of salt, one teaspoonful of pepper and an egg. Mix all together, and drop and fry in hot lard. This is a nice breakfast dish.

ROASTING EAR PUDDING.

Cut as much corn from the cob as you require; a dozen ears make a large pudding. To every three ears allow an egg, a spoonful of butter, a little pepper and salt, to suit your taste; fill and cover it with sweet milk. Let this bake an hour.

OKRA AND CORN FRICASSEE.

Put a pint of cut okra in a frying pan in which there is a cupful of hot lard, or the fat of side meat; let it fry a little, then cut into it a pint and a half of corn; fry it until it is thoroughly cooked, pour off some of the grease, and dredge in a little flour, and a half-cup of milk; pepper and salt, to taste, must be added just before dishing it up.

A NICE WAY TO COOK OKRA OR GOMBO.

Take a pint of young tender okra, chop it up fine, add to it half as much skinned, ripe, tomatoes, an onion cut up in slices, a tablespoonful of butter, a little salt and pepper, and a spoonful of water; stew all together till tender, and serve with meat or poultry.

SALSIFY FRIED IN BATTER.

Scrape the salsify, throw it for a few moments into cold water, then parboil it, drain it and cut it into lengths of three inches; allow it now to steep until cold, in a bowl with two tablespoonfuls of olive oil, one of French vinegar, pepper and salt; let it remain in this, occasionally turning it until ready to fry it. Then make a batter with eggs, milk, and flour; dip the salsify in this batter, and fry in hog's lard; fry parsley with it and serve.

TOMATOES STUFFED.

Take five large tomatoes, slice off that part which joins the stalk, cut out a little of their pulp, take out the seeds, and strain them; chop up the pulp with a handful of parsley, a slice of fat bacon, a slice of ham, and a cup of bread crumbs; fry all these, and season with butter, pepper, salt, thyme, and the yolks of two eggs; take it off the fire as soon as the eggs are beaten in, and stuff the tomatoes. Bake them for half an hour, pour some brown sauce or gravy over them and serve.

TOMATOES, TO BROIL.

Take ripe, red tomatoes, place them on the gridiron, broil, and turn until done through; then serve them whole, so that they can be seasoned at the table.

STEWED TOMATOES, WITH OR WITHOUT SUGAR.

Pour boiling water over six or eight large, ripe tomatoes, let them remain in it a few minutes to scald the skins, then take them out and skin them. Chop them up and put them to stew with a little salt, pepper, and a small piece of butter; then add a spoonful of rolled cracker or toasted bread, and a tablespoonful of sugar, if liked; if not, omit the sugar, and let them stew gently, for half an hour longer.

TO COOK SPINACH.

Wash in two or three waters, as the grit adheres very closely to spinach; when well-washed, boil it one half hour in clear water; add a little soda, if it does not look a nice green. When soft, drain it well and chop very fine— it cannot be too fine; add butter, salt if needed, and pepper to taste; garnish with hard-boiled eggs cut in fancy shapes; or, in early spring, it is nice to poach two or three eggs, and lay on the freshly cooked spinach.

ASPARAGUS ON TOAST.

The fresher this vegetable is the better, and in picking and mashing it, all stalks not crisp and tender should be thrown aside. Cut off nearly all the horny white parts, tie the rest in neat bunches, and boil in salted water for twenty minutes or half an hour; then take it out, let it drain a minute and lay on buttered toast, the heads all one way; cover with rich drawn butter sauce.

ASPARAGUS WITH CREAM.

When cream is plentiful, cut the asparagus in inch pieces, boil, and then throw it into rich hot cream, with seasoning of pepper and salt.

STEWED MUSHROOMS ON TOAST.

Pull out the stems of the mushrooms, and peel them; melt a tablespoonful of butter in a stew pan, throw into the butter a little salt, pepper, and powdered mace (if liked), lay the mushrooms in this, upper side down, and stew till they are tender, which will be in about twenty minutes. Fry a slice of bread until it is a light brown, and then arrange the mushrooms over it. Serve hot.

EGG PLANT.

Parboil egg plant, slice it and dip each piece in beaten egg and roll it in pounded cracker; then drop it in hot lard and fry brown. Season with salt and pepper. They are delicious cooked this way, and taste like soft-shell crabs. Another way is to parboil them, mash them up and season with eggs, onions, pepper, salt and butter; then place the mixture back in the shell, and bake. Serve in their shells.

ANOTHER WAY TO COOK EGG PLANT.

Parboil, slice them, and without rolling them in anything drop them into boiling lard; season with salt and pepper.

Some like them mashed and added to a batter of eggs, flour and milk, seasoned with pepper and salt, and then dropped like fritters into hot lard.

BURR ARTICHOKES.

Get them young or they are not tender, wash them in salted water, and put them to boil. Boil until you can pull off a leaf easily; salt them and serve with drawn-butter sauce, with vinegar in it, or mustard and oil, as preferred.

SNAP BEANS, STEWED AND BOILED.

Pick and snap them when green and tender, cut them small, and throw into boiling water; let them cook gently for two hours; then stir in a half cup of broth, and a cup of milk; let them stew in this for half an hour longer; season with salt and pepper to taste. Many like them cooked with a piece of lean side bacon. They require several hours boiling, if not very young. Put the beans in first, and when half done, put in a pound or so of bacon to an ordinary mess of beans.

GREEN ENGLISH PEAS, TO STEW.

Shell a quart of green peas for a small mess. Wash them in cold water, and put them on to cook in a stew pan with a pint of boiling water, or enough to cover them. Let them cook half an hour, and then stir in a large lump of butter rolled in flour; let this cook a few minutes, and add a teaspoonful of white sugar, same of salt and pepper, and serve while hot. Do not let them cook dry. Lamb and green peas is a favorite dish in the spring of the year.

MARROWFAT PEAS.

This is a late sort of green pea, and is much richer in taste than the earlier ones, but not so delicate. They must be dressed like the early peas, by boiling in water, and when soft, pour off the water. They are sometimes a little strong if the water is not changed. Fill up with milk, or milk and water, and boil a little longer, then season with butter, pepper and salt, and thicken with a teaspoon of flour stirred in among the peas.

LIMA, OR BUTTER BEANS.

Shell them, and lay them in cold water for an hour or so before cooking; this renders them more delicate and mealy. When ready to cook, put them in a stew pan in boiling water enough to cover them; let them boil fast and keep them covered while cooking; examine them in an hour, and if soft, pour off nearly all the water and stir in a lump of butter, some pepper and salt. Lima beans and sweet corn make the finest succotash, although string beans are generally used.

SQUASH, STEWED.

If not very young, you must peel the squashes, steam or boil them until tender, and season them with sweet milk or cream, and a little butter, pepper and salt; let them stew down in this until they are thick, and of the consistence of mashed potatoes. Another way is to take them from the steamer, mash them with a cut-up onion, and a slice or two of ham; then stew them down thick, adding pepper and salt to taste.

STEWED SUMMER SQUASH.

Gather them while young and tender. Peel, cut them up, take out the seeds, and put them on to boil; let them cook rapidly until very tender. Drain them well in a colander, and mash with a wooden spoon. Put this pulp in a stew pan with a small piece of butter, a gill of cream, and a little pepper and salt; cook this, and stir constantly until the squash is dry. Serve very hot.

PUMPKIN WITH SALT MEAT.

This is very good cooked with salt meat and brown sugar. Slice the pumpkin and put it in the oven with brown sugar, or good molasses; slice some smoked meat and lay it in among the pumpkin; cook it tender. It is better than many things with more reputation.

CAULIFLOWER, WITH WHITE SAUCE.

Remove the green stalks, and if the heads are large, divide them into quarters; wash and boil them with a little pepper, butter and salt; serve with drawn butter or white sauce, when they become soft and tender.

STEWED CABBAGE.

Cold cabbage left from dinner can be drained from the pot liquor in which it was boiled, and then simmered for half an hour in water, or milk and water: pour off all the water when it is tender, and stir in the pot a lump of butter or clarified drippings; let it cook gently, then throw in a cup of milk or cream; thicken it with flour, and season with pepper and salt. Serve with the cream gravy poured over the cabbage.

BEETS, BOILED.

Wash the beets clean, but do not trim the roots, or they will bleed and lose their sweetness. If the beets are young and tender, they are nice cooked whole, and then stewed in a little butter, with sugar, salt and vinegar added. Let them simmer in this batter for twenty minutes, and serve. If the beets are large, boil, and slice them when cooked, and season with vinegar, pepper and salt, or slice them, and serve with butter.

PARSNIP FRITTERS.

Boil the parsnips in salted water until they are done; make a batter of an egg, a spoonful of milk and flour, pepper and salt, and when the parsnips are cool enough to handle cut them in rounds, dip them in the batter and drop them into hot lard; fry a light brown, turn them and fry the other side. When brown on both sides, drain them from the grease. They are good, mashed like turnips.

MACARONI IN A MOULD.

Boil macaroni till it is tender, line a mould with it, fitting it in closely. Make a mince of any kind of meat, raw or cooked; season with sweet herbs, butter, pepper, chopped eschalot, and a couple of eggs; fill the mould with this and boil for twenty minutes. Serve with white sauce No. 10 put around the macaroni.

MACARONI AND GRATED CHEESE.

Take a quarter of a pound of macaroni, break into lengths, and throw it into cold water to soak, an hour or so after breakfast. Boil it an hour, take it out of the pot and put in the bottom of the pan a layer of the boiled macaroni and then a layer of grated cheese; strew over the top a teaspoonful of salt and some lumps of butter as big as a nutmeg. Then fill up the pan with new milk and bake until browned on top, but never let it get dry; it is better to put water in, if your milk has given out, than to let it get the least dry. This is a rich dish when well made, but a poor one if badly made, and served dry.

THE ORGAN GRINDER.

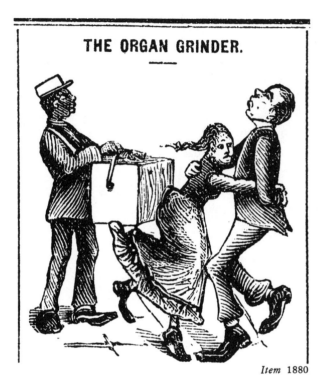

Item 1880

128. Dizéfs canard plì gros qui dizéfs poule. (Les œufs de cane sont plus gros que les œufs de poule.

   "Ducks' eggs are bigger than hen's eggs."—Quantity is no guarantee of quality.—[*Mauritius.*]

129. Dizéfs coq, poule qui fére. (Les œufs de coq, c'est la poule qui les fait.)

"It's the hen that makes the cock's eggs."—[*Mauritius.*]

150. Janmain nous ne pas douè ladans quiou poule compté zè. (Il ne faut jamais [nous ne devons jamais] computer les œufs dans la derrière de la poule.)

"We should never count the eggs in the body of the hen."—(The Creole proverb is, however, less delicate.)—[*Martinique.*]

49. Ça qui mangé zé pas save si bonda poule fait li mal. (Ceux qui mangent ne savent pas si le derrière de la poule lui fait mal.)

"Those who eat eggs don't know whether the chicken suffered." [5]—[*Martinique.*]

EGGS, OMELETS, ETC.

In choosing eggs hold each one up to the light: if fresh, the white will be clear and the yolk distinct; if they are not good, they will have a clouded appearance.

Eggs for boiling must be as fresh as possible; they may be kept fresh for several weeks by packing them in bran. Lay the small end of the egg downward in the box. You may also keep them for months by greasing them with melted lard, or beef fat, or in a weak brine of lime water and salt; strong lime water will eat the shell, and if *very* strong will cook the eggs. Add to a common bucket of water a pint of salt and a pint of lime; stir it well, and it is ready to receive the eggs.

Omelets require a thick-bottomed pan, as an ordinary pan is too thin and would scorch the eggs before they could be properly cooked. For turning omelets, eggs, fried parsley, etc., have a skimmer spoon with a flat, thin blade, with holes to let the fat from the fry.

TO BOIL EGGS IN THEIR SHELLS, SOFT OR HARD.

Wash the eggs clean, drop them as wanted in a stew-pan of boiling water; if you desire them soft, let them boil just three minutes by the watch; if only the yolk is to be soft five minutes will do it; but if wanted very hard for salad, sandwiches, etc., let them boil ten or fifteen minutes. Then put them in cold water, to make them peel easily. If soft-boiled eggs are kept in the shell before eating them, they will harden very much from the heat of the shell.

EGGS, AU GRATIN, FOR LENT.

Boil the eggs hard, peel and cut them in slices, and lay them in a deep dish in close circular rows. Make a sauce of a tablespoonful of butter, the yolks of four eggs, a little grated cheese and half a cup of sweet milk. Stir this over the fire until it thickens, pour it over the eggs, strew some bread crumbs on the top, and bake for about ten minutes; then send to table hot.

POACHED EGGS WITH TOAST AND ANCHOVY PASTE.

Toast six pieces of bread, shape them round, before browning; keep them where they will be hot until you poach the eggs. Take a tin dipper, half fill it with boiling water, and drop it gently into the pot again, holding it so that none of the water from the pot can get into the dipper; keep it firm by holding it yourself or getting it held for you, and break a nice fresh egg into the dipper; let it stand until the white is firm. Lay each egg on one of the slices of hot toast, use butter and salt on the toast for both egg and toast; break each egg in this way until your six eggs and six pieces of toast are used; butter very freely, and serve hot. Anchovy paste may be spread on the toast before the eggs are put on, but it is a nice dish without it and very suitable for a delicate breakfast.

POACHED EGGS AND HAM.

Poach your eggs in a tin dipper, as directed, and when done put them on round slices of broiled or fried ham. Many prefer this to fried ham and eggs.

EGGS WITH BROWNED BUTTER AND VINEGAR.

Put four ounces of butter into an omelet pan over the fire; as it begins to sputter, break the eggs into it without disturbing the yolks, season with pepper and salt; fry the eggs carefully and remove them on to the dish in which they are to be served. Put two ounces more butter in the pan, fry it of a brown color; put to the butter two tablespoonfuls of vinegar, pour it over the eggs and serve.

OMELETTE AU NATUREL.

Break eight eggs into a bowl; add a teaspoonful of salt, half as much pepper, beat up the whole very hard and throw in a tablespoonful of water. Have the omelet-pan on the fire with a cup of sweet butter heated to a gentle heat (fierce heat would scorch the eggs); pour the eggs into the heated butter; raise it as it cooks, with a skimmer-spoon, turn in the brown edges, or turn one half over the other, as it keeps in the lusciousness of the omelet. Keep gently rolling it, as it cooks, until, when done, it is round like a small roly-poly pudding. Omelette au naturel is the basis of all omelets, for, by substituting different seasonings, you have all the varieties of them. Parsley and onion chopped fine and mixed with the eggs is one variety; grated ham and parsley is another; sugar makes another class, and so on.

A NICE OMELET WITH GREEN ONION.

Beat the whites and yolks of six eggs separately, put in a tablespoonful of butter, a spoonful of chopped green onion and one of fine-cut parsley, and mix with the eggs; then put it into a thick-bottomed pan, in which you have placed a half cup of butter. Roll it up as it cooks, and tilt the pan on one side, that the omelet may cook on the other side; roll up again as it cooks. Do not let it get hard and brown but keep it soft. Keep on rolling as well as you can; a little practice will make you perfect. When the eggs cook, butter, pepper and salt them, and turn on a dish.

OMELET FOR ONE PERSON.

Beat two eggs—yolks and whites separately; in a bowl put a tablespoonful of water, a little parsley, a teaspoonful of butter, and a little green onion, if liked; beat the eggs into this, and whisk all very rapidly for a few minutes; then pour it into a pan, where there is a tablespoonful of butter just hot enough to color the eggs; cook them very slowly, and roll up the omelet as it cooks until it is like a rolled pancake; pepper and salt it at the last moment of cooking, as putting in salt too soon makes eggs tough.

OMELET WITH PARMESAN CHEESE.

Break six eggs into a bowl, add a gill of cream, four ounces of grated cheese, some pepper and a little salt; beat the whole together, pour into a pan, roll up and bake as directed. Butter it well before sending to table.

OMELET WITH SUGAR.

Beat six eggs, whites and yolks separately, with seven spoonfuls of powdered sugar. Flavor with lemon, and bake like a pudding for ten or fifteen minutes, or just long enough to set the eggs. Longer baking will spoil the jelly-like consistency of the omelet.

OMELETTE SOUFFLÉE.

Beat six eggs, the whites and yolks separately; put to the yolks four dessertspoonfuls of white sugar powdered, and the yellow rind of a lemon chopped very fine; mix them thoroughly, whip the whites to a high froth and add them to the yolks. Put quarter of a pound of butter into the pan, over a brisk fire, and as soon as it is completely melted pour in the mixture; stir it that the butter may be completely incorporated with the eggs. When it is so, put it in a buttered dish and set it over hot embers or ashes, strew powdered sugar over the top and color it with a hot shovel; this may be done in the oven. Serve as soon as possible, as it soon falls and so the appearance is spoiled.

OMELETTE SOUFFLÉE, IN A MOULD.

Break six fresh eggs, separate the whites from the yolks, put with the yolks three spoonfuls of rice flour and a tablespoonful of orange-flower water; stir these well together, whip the whites of the eggs to a high froth, and mix them with the yolks. Pour the mixture into a buttered mould, about half full; bake in a moderate oven for half an hour. When done turn it on to a dish and serve quickly. This omelette must be clear and shake like a jelly.

A DELICIOUS OMELET.

Beat separately, and lightly, six eggs; add to them a table-spoonful of chopped green onion, and the same of parsley, chopped fine; beat them into the eggs with two tablespoonfuls of water, and at the last moment a little salt. Have a thick-bottomed skillet, or pan on the fire, put in a teaspoonful of nice sweet butter, and when this is hot put in the eggs. Take a broad-bladed knife and keep rolling the omelet as it sets; do not let it get too brown, but roll it in an oblong shape; never turn an omelet over, but push and roll it, as described, then slide it on a hot dish, pour a spoonful of melted butter over it, and send it to table hot. A wood fire is the best, over which to cook an omelet, as you want only a blaze; a great heat in the stove makes it impossible to have the eggs of the light delicate brown required.

SPANISH OMELET.

Beat up six eggs until quite light, add to them a cup of chopped ham and two small onions minced very fine. The onions should be cooked a little before being put into the eggs, or they will not be cooked enough. When mixed together put it into a thick-bottomed pan and commence rolling. When it is a light brown, give it the last roll, let it lie a moment in the pan, then dish it. Put fresh butter as it goes to table, for the butter the omelet is fried in is never good to send to table.

OMELET, WITH OYSTERS.

Break eight or ten eggs in a basin, whip them up well, add a gill of cream, a tablespoonful of sweet butter, a spoonful of chopped parsley, pepper and salt to taste; beat it again very light, then stir in a pint of chopped oysters, and when the butter is hot put in the omelet. When the eggs have partly set roll the omelet in form of a cushion, which you can do by using the tin slice. Brown delicately, and serve with a little melted butter or some sauce you prefer.

Grated Parmesan cheese is very fine in place of the chopped oysters; also, ham, in the above omelet, is an acceptable addition.

THE AMATEUR MUSICIAN.

"Madam Caba,
   Tiyon vous tombe;
Madame Caba,
    Tiyon vous tombe;
Ah, la reine,
   Piye la su' moi;
Madame Caba
   Piye la su' moi;
Madame Caba
   Chandelle 'te teigne," etc.

Item, 1880

SALADS AND RELISHES.

GARNISHES.

Parsley is most universally used to garnish all kinds of cold meats, boiled poultry, broiled steak and fish of many kinds. Horse-radish is much liked on roast beef; slices of lemon are liked by many on broiled fish or boiled calf's head, etc. Mint is liked by many on roast lamb, and currant jelly is generally liked on game, ducks, etc.

MUSHROOM CATSUP.

Lay fresh mushrooms in a deep dish, strew a little salt over them, then a fresh layer of mushrooms and salt, till you get in all the mushrooms. Let them stay in this brine three days; then mash them fine, add to each quart a spoonful of vinegar, half a spoonful of pepper and a teaspoonful of cloves; pour all this in a stone jar, and place the jar in a pot of boiling water; let it boil two hours, then strain it without squeezing the mushrooms. Boil the juice fifteen minutes, and skim it well; let it stand a few hours to settle; bottle it and cork it well. Keep it cool, or it will ferment.

A DELICIOUS FLAVOR FROM THYME, ETC.

A delicious flavor from thyme, mint, sweet marjoram and rosemary may be obtained when gathered in full perfection. They should be picked from the stalks and put into a large jar, then pour strong vinegar or brandy over them; let them stay in this twenty-four hours, then take the herbs out, and throw in fresh bunches; do this three times, then strain the liquor or vinegar. Cork and seal the bottles tight. Do not let the herbs stay more than twenty or twenty-four hours in the liquid before straining, for fear of imparting an unsavory taste. This is very useful in soups.

CELERY AND SWEET HERBS VINEGAR.

Take two gills of celery seed, pound them and put them in a bottle; fill the bottle with sharp vinegar, shake it every day for two weeks, then strain and bottle it for use.

GREEN TOMATO SOY, OR SAUCE.

Slice a peck of green tomatoes thin, salt them thoroughly, using a pint of salt. Let them stay in this all night, and in the morning drain them from the salt, wash them in cold water, and put them in a kettle with a dozen cut-up raw onions, two tablespoonfuls of black pepper, same of allspice, a quarter of a spoonful of ground mustard, half a pound of white mustard seed, and a tablespoonful of red pepper. Cover all with strong vinegar, and boil it until it becomes like jam. Stir it frequently while it is boiling or it will scorch.

SUPERIOR TOMATO CATSUP.

Get a bushel of ripe tomatoes, scald them until they are soft enough to squeeze through a sieve. When strained, add to the pulp a pint and a half of salt, four tablespoonfuls of ground cloves, same of cayenne pepper, a quarter of a pound of allspice and a tablespoonful of black pepper, a head of garlic skinned and separated, and a half gallon of vinegar. Boil until it is reduced one-half, then bottle.

TOMATO CATSUP.

Take enough ripe tomatoes to fill a jar, put them in a moderate oven, and bake them until they are thoroughly soft; then strain them through a coarse cloth or sieve, and to every pint of juice put a pint of vinegar, half an ounce of garlic sliced, quarter of an ounce of salt, and the same of white pepper finely ground. Boil it for one hour, then rub it through a sieve, boil it again to the consistency of cream; when cold, bottle it, put a teaspoonful of sweet oil in each bottle; cork them tight, and keep in a dry place.

TOMATO CATSUP. RECIPE FOR MAKING A SMALL QUANTITY.

Take a gallon of ripe tomatoes, skin them by pouring boiling water over them; let them get cold, and put them in a stewpan with four tablespoonfuls of salt, and the same of ground black pepper, half a spoonful of ground allspice, and three spoonfuls of ground mustard. Throw in eight pods of red pepper, and let all stew slowly until the tomatoes are soft and tender. Thin the mixture with enough vinegar to allow the catsup to be strained through a sieve; cook it fifteen minutes, and bottle up when cold. This will last in any climate, if well boiled and made according to these directions. Keep always in a cool, dark closet or cellar. Light ruins all catsups, pickles, or preserves, when they are exposed to it. This is a fine recipe.

FRENCH CHICKEN SALAD.

Roast one or two nice chickens, season them well, and when cooked, put them by to cool. Just before serving the dish, carve the fowls in small pieces, taking out all the large bones. Make a dressing of the yolks of six hard-boiled eggs to each fowl, mash the yolks very smooth with a wooden spoon and pour gently on them in a little stream a cup of olive oil; beat the eggs all one way till they are creamed. Add now a cup of vinegar to two fowls, a half a cup to one, pepper, salt, and drop a little vinegar on the fowl, then pour on the dressing. Arrange on the dish, cool, fresh lettuce heads quartered, and slice six more hard-boiled eggs over all as a garnish. A few red beets are a handsome addition, mixed with the green lettuce and yellow eggs.

CHICKEN SALAD FOR A SMALL COMPANY.

Boil four eggs hard, throw them in cold water; when cool, take the yolks of two in a bowl, pour over them a spoonful of mixed mustard, an ounce of sweet oil, a saltspoonful of salt, and a little black pepper; mix this carefully, pouring in the oil a little at a time; when it is smooth, pour in four table-spoonfuls of good vinegar, and one-half a teaspoonful of sugar. This is the dressing for your salad.

The chicken is supposed to be already boiled or baked. When cold, pick all the flesh from the bones and pile it in the centre of a glass bowl, or dish; mix with it three heads of celery, cut up fine, and season it with pepper and salt. About the time you wish it served, take six or seven heads of white-heart lettuce, split them, and place them closely around the cut-up chicken, and pour over it all the dressing. This is a plain and economical way, but if wanted richer, it is easy to add more eggs, and trim the salad with sliced hard-boiled eggs, over the top.

A NICE CHICKEN SALAD.

Cut up the white parts of four or five heads of celery, reserving the green leaves. Pick all the meat from a fine baked chicken, chop this up, and mix it with the cut-up celery; lay it in a glass or china dish, where it will be cool.

To make the dressing, rub the yolks of six hard-boiled eggs to a paste with two spoonfuls of mixed mustard, a teaspoonful of white sugar, and enough oil to make it perfectly smooth; put this in slowly, a little at a time, and finish the dressing by pouring in half a cup of vinegar. Pour this over the celery and chicken, and garnish with white heads of split lettuce, also the reserved celery leaves, and four sliced hardboiled eggs.

POTATO SALAD.

Slice a pint of cold potatoes, put them in a dish, chop over them six eschalots, pepper and salt them, and pour over them a dressing of two tablespoonfuls of oil, one of made mustard, and half a cup of vinegar; it is better without eggs.

POTATO SALAD.

Slice cold potatoes, add to them chopped eschalots, and season with pepper, salt, mustard, oil, tomato catsup and vinegar. Garnish with sprigs of parsley.

TOMATO SALAD, WITH OR WITHOUT SHRIMP.

Slice a dozen large tomatoes, slice with them three or four sweet peppers, then pepper and salt the tomatoes; lay slices of tomato and a little sweet pepper until the dish is full. Pour over all a dressing of oil, mustard and vinegar. A pint of shelled shrimp is a great improvement to this salad, but it is good without.

JAMBALAYA OF FOWLS AND RICE.

Cut up and stew a fowl; when half done, add a cup of raw rice, a slice of ham minced, and pepper and salt; let all cook together until the rice swells and absorbs all the gravy of the stewed chicken, but it must not be allowed to get hard or dry. Serve in a deep dish. Southern children are very fond of this; it is said to be an Indian dish, and very wholesome as well as palatable; it can be made of many things.

COLD SLAW, WITH HOT SAUCE.

Chop fine a firm white head of cabbage, or better than that, slice it with a patent slicer; lay it in very cold water for an hour, then take it out, drain it, and when drained thoroughly, place it in the dish it is to be served in and pour over it the following sauce. Take two cups of strong vinegar to a quart of cut cabbage, stir in it one teaspoonful of mustard and salt, a tablespoonful of butter, and three teaspoons of white sugar. Make this all hot, and at the last moment stir in the yolks of two or three eggs; stir rapidly and pour on to the chopped cabbage in the dish. It should be served instantly or the sauce will harden.

PLAIN COLD SLAW, WITH VINEGAR.

This is made by chopping or slicing the cabbage as in the above receipt. When it is soaked, and is cool and firm, dust pepper on it, throw in a little salt and pour over it a cup of cold, sharp vinegar. Sliced hard-boiled eggs are a great improvement if put over the cabbage when sent to table. Sliced onions also make a good salad when seasoned with salt, pepper and vinegar. Mix a little sweet, sliced vegetable pepper with the onions.

PICKLES.

Pickles should always have vinegar enough to cover them; those intended for immediate use, should be kept in wide-top stone-ware jars. Keep a cloth folded upon the pickles, and the jar covered with a plate or wooden vessel; they should occasionally be looked over, and the softest and least likely to keep, used first. Pickles intended for use the following summer, should be assorted from the remainder when first made; choose those most firm, and of equal size; put them into stone, or glass-ware, with fresh vinegar to cover them; cover the vessel close, with several thicknesses of paper, or a tin cover, or if wide-mouthed bottles are used, cork them tightly.

Cucumbers may be put down in a strong salt and water brine, to be greened and pickled as they are wanted. Keep them under the brine. When wanted, freshen them in two or three changes of water, for two or three days, until by cutting one open, you find it but little salt; then pour scalding vinegar over them three times, and keep them covered; add spices and seasoning to the vinegar, to suit the taste.

The vessels in which pickles have been, whether of glass, wood, or stone, will never be fit for preserved fruit; they will surely spoil if put in them. After the pickles are used, throw

out the vinegar, wash the vessels first in cold water, then pour
hot water into them, cover and let it remain until cold, then
wash, wipe, and dry them near the fire or in the sun, and set
them away for future use. Wooden ware will require to be
wet occasionally, or to be kept in a damp place, that it may
not become leaky. Should catsups seem frothy or foamy,
put them in a bright brass, or porcelain kettle, over the fire;
boil slowly, and skim until no more scum rises, then turn
into an earthen vessel to cool, after which, put in bottles
and stop them tight.

TO PICKLE CUCUMBERS PLAIN WITHOUT SPICES.

Take one hundred small cucumbers, or more, if you wish,
salt them freely, and let them remain eight or ten hours; then
drain them, put them into boiling vinegar enough to cover
them, and place vine leaves among and over them to green
them; let them scald a few minutes in the vinegar, and take
them from the fire, but place them near it to keep warm and
become green; if the leaves turn yellow, put fresh ones among
them. When green you can pack them away in jars; season
them at any time you may desire, as they will keep well if
scalded thoroughly with the boiling vinegar.

CUCUMBER PICKLES IN WHISKEY.

Prepare your cucumbers as usual by letting them stay a
few days in brine, or if time is an object scald them in brine,
and then proceed to pickle them. The same brine may be
used many times, pouring it boiling hot on each mess of cucumbers. If you have no vinegar convenient drop your
scalded sucumbers into a mixture of one part whiskey and

three parts water. Secure them carefully from the air, and by Christmas they will be fine, firm, green pickles, and the whiskey and water will be excellent vinegar. Add spices after they are pickled. If you do not wish all your pickles spiced, keep a stone-pot of well-spiced vinegar by itself, and put in a few at a time as you want them.

CUCUMBER AND ONION PICKLE.

Take a dozen fine crisp cucumbers and four large onions. Cut both in thick slices, sprinkle salt and pepper on them, and let them stand. Next day drain them well and scald them in boiling vinegar; cover close after scalding. Next day scald again with a bag of mace, nutmeg and ginger, in the vinegar; then place them in jars and cork close. If the vinegar seems to have lost its strength, replace with fresh, and put the bag of spices in again to keep the flavor.

OLD-TIME SWEET PICKLED CUCUMBERS.

Put your cucumbers in brine for eight days; slice them without soaking; let the slices be an inch thick. When cut, soak them until the salt is nearly out, changing the water very often. Then put them in a kettle, with vine leaves laid between the layers; cover them well with leaves, and sprinkle pulverized alum all through them, to harden and green them, then cover with vinegar, and set them on the back of the stove until they become green. Take the cucumbers out and boil them a little in ginger tea (half an hour will be enough). Make a syrup of one quart of strong vinegar, and one pint of water, three pounds of sugar to four pounds of cucumbers, with one ounce of cinnamon, cloves, mace and white ginger to every ten pounds of fruit. Make this syrup hot, and put in the cucumbers and boil them until clear. When they are clear take them out and boil the syrup until it is thick enough to keep. Pour it over the cucumbers, which should have been placed in jars ready for the syrup. They are now ready to use, or seal up, as may be desired. If not convenient to pickle after eight days' salt brining, it does not hurt to let them remain a few days longer.

PICKLED EGGS.

When eggs are abundant and cheap, it is well to pickle some for a time of scarcity. Boil three or four dozen eggs for half an hour, let them cool, and then take off the shells, and place them in wide-mouthed jars, and pour over them scalding vinegar. Season the vinegar with whole pepper, cloves, or allspice, ginger, and a few cloves of garlic. When cold, they must be bunged down very close. Let them be well covered with the vinegar, and in a month they will be fit for use. The above pickle is by no means expensive, and as an accompaniment to cold meat is not to be surpassed for piquancy and goût.

SWEET PICKLE OF FIGS.

Put the figs in brine at night; in the morning, or after being in brine about twelve hours, take them out, wash off the salt, and put them in alum water for three hours. Then take them out and scald them in hot water until heated through. Make a syrup of a quart of vinegar, a pint of sugar with a tablespoonful of cinnamon, mace, and cloves each; boil half an hour, and pour on the figs boiling hot. Repeat the boiling next day, and bottle up and seal for future use.

SWEET PLUM PICKLE.

Take eight pounds of fruit, four pounds of sugar, two quarts of vinegar, one ounce of cinnamon and one of cloves. Boil the vinegar, sugar and spices together; skim it carefully and pour it boiling on the fruit; pour it off, and skim and scald each day for three days; it will then be fit for use. If for putting away, scald it the fourth time and cork up tightly. Plums prepared in this way are superior to the old way, with sugar alone.

GREEN TOMATO SWEET PICKLE.

Slice tomatoes until you have seven pounds, sprinkle them with salt, and let them stand twenty-four hours. Then soak them for the same length of time in fresh water to get the brine from them. When drained off and ready, allow four and a half pounds of sugar, one ounce of cinnamon, one ounce of cloves, and enough vinegar to cover them. Boil the compound together and pour it over the tomatoes; let them stand twenty-four hours, then bring all to a boil, and tie away in jars, and keep in a cool place away from the light.

CANTALOUPE SWEET PICKLE.

Take a ripe cantaloupe, quarter it, remove the seeds and cut it into pieces an inch square. Put the cut pieces in a stone crock, and pour on scalding vinegar; when it cools heat it again, and return it to the cantaloupe. Repeat this next day.

On the fourth day take out the fruit and add fresh vinegar to cover it. To every quart of this vinegar add three pounds of loaf sugar, and five pounds of cantaloupe. Put to them nutmeg, cinnamon and mace, to taste. Put all in a porcelain-lined kettle and simmer until the fruit can be pierced with a straw. Pack it in small jars and keep in a cool place.

CHOPPED CABBAGE PICKLE.

Put together one pint of chopped onions, three gills (or three wineglassfuls) of white mustard seed, three table-spoonfuls of ground mustard and the same of celery seed; add a pound of brown sugar and three quarts of good vinegar. Cook this compound slowly until it begins to thicken, then pour it hot upon two gallons of chopped cabbage, which should be shaved or chopped very thin. This pickle is ready to bottle for use when it has boiled fifteen minutes.

TO PICKLE CABBAGE. A VERY NICE, YELLOW PICKLE.

Cut four cabbage heads into eighths, if large, or quarters, if small; they must be white and tender. Soak it in strong brine for three days and scald it in clear water until you can pierce it with a straw. Take it out and dry it on large dishes for twenty-four hours. Then put it into strong vinegar, with powdered turmeric, sufficient to color the cabbage yellow. Let it remain in this vinegar ten days; then take it out and drain on a sieve for several hours. Have the following spices prepared, then pack in a jar alternately one layer of cabbage and one of spices. For each gallon of vinegar allow five pounds of sugar, three ounces of turmeric, two of ginger, four of horse radish, two of white mustard seed, one-half ounce of celery seed, quarter of an ounce of mace, two ounces of whole pepper, white if you can get it, and four ounces of garlic. Scald the vinegar and sugar together, and pour hot on the cabbage and the spices. Cover tight, and you will have an admirable pickle.

TO PICKLE RED CABBAGE.

Slice the cabbage and sprinkle with salt. Let it remain three days; drain, and pour over it boiling vinegar in which you have put mace, bruised ginger, whole pepper and cloves; let it remain in this until next day. Then give one more scald, and it is ready to put up for use. The purple red cabbage is the best.

CHOW-CHOW PICKLE.

Take a quarter of a peck, each, of green tomatoes, pickling-beans, and white onions (scald the onions separately), add one dozen cucumbers, green peppers, and a head of cabbage chopped. Season with ground mustard, celery seed, and salt to taste. Pour over these the best cider vinegar to cover them, and let all boil two hours, and while hot add two tablespoonfuls of sweet oil and the same of white sugar. Bottle and seal up carefully in wide-mouthed glass jars.

PICKLED CAULIFLOWER.

Take large, ripe, full-blown cauliflowers; divide the pieces equally and throw them into a kettle of boiling water; boil them until a little soft, but not as much as if for the table. Take the pieces out and let them cool, then scald an ounce of mace, to each quart of good cider vinegar, and pour it hot on the cauliflower. Spices such as are usually used in pickling, improve this receipt, and should be tied in a bag and thrown in with the pickle at the last, remembering not to use dark spices, as they discolor the cauliflower. White pepper, white mustard seed and ginger are the spices suitable for this pickle.

PICKLED LEMONS.

They should be small and have a thick rind. Rub them hard with a piece of flannel, then slit them through the rind in four quarters, but not through the pulp; fill the slits with salt hard pressed in, set them upright in a crock four or five days, until the salt melts. Turn them each day in their own liquid until they get tender. Make the pickle to cover them of vinegar, some of the brine of the lemons, pepper and ginger; boil this pickle and skim it well, and when cold put it over the lemons with two ounces of mustard seed and two cloves of garlic, to six lemons. This is fine for fish when the lemons are all used.

TO PICKLE ONIONS.

Peel the onions, boil some strong salt and water and put it over them, cover, and let them stand twenty-four hours, then take them up with a skimmer; make some vinegar boiling hot, put to it whole pepper and mustard seed, and pour it over the onions to cover them ; when cold cover close.

PREMIUM MUSTARD PICKLE.

Soak three quarts of small cucumbers, gherkins, or green tomatoes, in strong salt water for three days ; then put them into fresh cold water for a day or two, then scald them in

plain vinegar and set them by in a place to cool. Take a
gallon of vinegar, add to it one ounce of white mustard seed,
two ounces of turmeric, three of sliced ginger, two of shred-
ded horse-radish, one-half pound of mustard, three pounds of
brown sugar, one-half pint of sweet oil, one ounce each of
celery seed, black pepper, cloves, mace, and one teaspoonful
of cayenne pepper. Boil all these ingredients for fifteen minutes and pour it on the cucumbers, gherkins, or other scalded
vegetable you may wish to pickle.

WALNUT PICKLE.

Pick the walnuts about the fourth of July. They should
be so soft that a pin can be run through them. Lay them in
salt and water ten days, change the water two or three times
during the ten days. Rub off the outside with a coarse cloth
and proceed to finish the pickle. For one hundred nuts, make
a pickle of two quarts of vinegar, one ounce of ground pepper,
same of ginger, half an ounce of mace, cloves, nutmegs and
mustard seed. Put these spices in a bag, lay it in the vinegar
and boil all together a few minutes; then set the pickle away
for use. If the vinegar is not very strong, add fresh vinegar
to the last scalding of the pickles.

PICKLED OYSTERS.

Take fine large oysters, put them over a gentle fire in their
own liquor, and a small lump of butter to each hundred
oysters. Let them boil ten minutes, when they are plump
and white; take them from their liquor with a skimmer and
spread them on a thickly folded cloth. When they are firm
and cold take half as much of their own liquor and half of

good vinegar, make this hot, and take a stone crock, put in a layer of oysters, a spoonful of ground mace, a dozen cloves, allspice, and whole pepper alternately. If to be kept, put them in glass jars with a little sweet oil on top. Stop them and seal tight, and they will, if kept in a cool place, be good for months.

COUNTRY GREEN PICKLE.

One peck of tomatoes, eight green peppers to be chopped fine. They must be the vegetable or sweet pepper. Soak the tomatoes and pepper twenty-four hours in weak brine; drain off the brine, and add to the green tomatoes a head of finely chopped cabbage; scald all in boiling vinegar twenty minutes. Skim it out from the vinegar, and place in a large jar, and add three pints of grated horse-radish and such other spices as you please. Fill the jars with strong cold vinegar and tie up for use.

TOMATO SAUCE PICKLE.

One gallon of tomatoes and one gallon of vinegar. Slice the tomatoes (green ones are firmest), and sprinkle salt between each layer. Let them remain thus twelve hours, then rinse them, and put them to drain on a sieve. Put your vinegar to boil with a dozen onions cut up in it, season high with cloves, pepper and ginger, and when this boils throw in your tomatoes and let them boil five minutes. Finish by stirring in one-quarter of a pound of mustard and a pound of sugar; then add a quart of vinegar and bottle it.

PLAIN PEACH PICKLE.

Take eight or ten fine, nearly ripe peaches; free-stone are preferred by some, but experience teaches that clings make the firmest pickle. Wipe off the down with a flannel rag, and put them into brine strong enough to bear up an egg. In two days drain them from this brine, and scald them in boiling vinegar, and let them stay in all night. Next day boil in a quart of vinegar, one ounce of whole pepper, one of broken-up ginger, eight blades of mace, and two ounces of mustard seed; pour this boiling on the peaches, and when cool, put them in jars, and pack away carefully in a cool place.

PEACH PICKLES.

Take ripe, sound, cling-stone peaches; remove the down with a brush like a clothes brush; make a gallon of good vinegar hot; add to it four pounds of brown sugar; boil and skim it clear. Stick five or six cloves into each of the peaches, then pour the hot vinegar over them, cover the vessel and set it in a cold place for eight or ten days, then drain off the vinegar, make it hot, skim it, and again turn it over the peaches; let them become cold, then put them into glass jars and secure as directed for preserves. Free-stone peaches may be used.

PEACHES AND APRICOT PICKLE.

Take peaches fully grown but not mellow; cover them in strong salt and water for one week. Take them from the brine and wipe them carefully, rubbing each peach to see if it is firm. Put to a gallon of vinegar half an ounce each of cloves, pepper corns, sliced ginger root, white mustard seed, and a little salt. Scald the peaches with this boiling vinegar, repeat this three times; add half as much fresh vinegar, and cork them up in jars. Keep them dark and cool. Light will spoil pickles or preserves as much as heat does. Apricots may be pickled in the same way.

GREEN PEACHES PICKLED.

Brush the down from green peaches (cling-stones); put them in salt and water, with grape leaves and a bit of saleratus; set them over a moderate fire to simmer slowly until they are a fine green, then take them out, wipe them dry, and smooth the skins; take enough vinegar to cover them, put to it whole pepper, allspice, and mustard seed, make it boiling hot, and turn it over the peaches. Repeat the scalding three successive days.

PEACH MANGOES.

Steep some large free-stone peaches in brine for two days, then wipe each peach carefully, and cut a hole in it just sufficient to allow the seed to come out; then throw them into cold vinegar until you make the stuffing, which is to fill up the cavity occupied by the seed. Take fresh white mustard seed which has been wet with vinegar, and allowed to swell a few hours, scraped horse radish, powdered ginger, a few pods of red pepper, a few small onions, or, better still, a clove of garlic. Mix all with vinegar, and add half as much chopped peach. Stuff the peaches hard with this mixture, replace the piece cut out, and tie it up tight with pack-thread. Boil a quart of vinegar for each dozen peaches; season it with the same spices as the stuffing. Boil the spices in a small bag, and then put in the peaches and let them scald ten or fifteen minutes, just long enough to be thoroughly hot all through. Place the peaches in jars, and pour scalding vinegar well spiced over them—the vinegar must cover them; add at the top a tablespoonful of salad oil. Cover the jar tight by tying leather over it.

MELON MANGOES.

Get the late, small, smooth, green melons, they should not be larger than a teacup; cut out a piece from the stem end large enough to allow you to take the seeds from the inside; scrape out all the soft part, and when done, cover with the piece cut out and lay them in rows in a stone or wooden vessel as you do them. Make a strong brine of salt and water, pour it over the melons and let them remain in it twenty-four hours. Prepare the following stuffing: sliced horse-radish, very small cucumbers, nasturtiums, small white onions, mustard seed, whole pepper, cloves and allspice ; scald the pickles and cool them. Rinse the melons in cold water, then wipe each one dry and fill it. Put a cucumber, one or two small onions, with sliced horse-radish and mustard seed, into each melon : put on the piece belonging to it and sew it with a coarse needle and thread; lay them in a stone pot or wooden vessel, the cut side up; when all are in, strew over them cloves and pepper, make the vinegar (enough to cover them) boiling hot, and put it over them, then cover with a folded towel; let them stand one night, then drain off the vinegar, make it hot again and pour it on, covering as before. Repeat this scalding four or five times, until the mangoes are a fine green; three times is generally enough. Be sure the melons are green and freshly gathered. The proper sort are the last on the vines, green and firm. If you wish to keep them till the next summer, choose the most firm, put in a jar and cover with cold fresh vinegar; tie thick paper over them.

My Office in My Hat.

An' what are ye drivin' at?
I deals in corn, in hay an' oats,
    An' all that, an' all that.
Nor care I how the people votes,
As I ride upon my tandem floats
    With me office in me hat.

Item 1880

215. Napas éna fromaze qui napas trouve so macathia. (Il n'y a pas de fromage qui ne trouve son pain bis.)

"There's no cheese but what can find brown bread."[1]—[*Mauritius.*]

Item, 1880

42. Ça ou pédi nen fè ou va trouvé nen sann. (Ce que vous perdez dans le feu, vous le retrouverez dans la cendre.)

"What you lose in the fire, you will find in the ashes."—Meaning that a good deed is never lost. "Cast your bread upon the waters," etc.—[*Martinique.*]

[1] That is to say, whoever has a bit of cheese can always find a bit of brown bread to eat with it. There never was a girl so ugly that she could not find a husband.

Gombo Zhèbes 1885

BREAD AND YEAST.

REMARKS ON YEAST.

Without good yeast to start with, it is impossible to make good bread, therefore I devote a few moments to this important consideration. There are several kinds of yeast used for raising bread and rolls. Brewers' yeast is given to start with, though too strong for a family bread. Bakers' is better, but not always to be had. A housekeeper should get a little of any good yeast to commence with, and when she finds it is good, and is well risen and sweet, instead of pour-ing it into flour, and baking it, it is better to thicken it with corn-meal, cut the cakes out, dry in a cool place, and keep the cakes always on hand for any purpose to which they are suited, *i. e.*, in the making of bread, rolls, pocketbooks, loaf-cake, sally lunn, or any kind of light biscuit.

TO MAKE RISING WITH YEAST CAKE.

Take a heaping spoonful of good yeast cake pounded, one-half a cup of warm water, a lump of sugar, and enough sifted flour to make a thick batter. Set this to rise in a cool place in summer, and a warm place in winter. It will be light and ready to use in about three hours, unless it is kept very cool. A heaping spoonful is the proper quantity for one quart of flour ; half a cup of lard will make the bread better and richer. It is well to grease the bread on top before baking.

LA CUISINE CREOLE.

TURNPIKE CAKES, COMMONLY CALLED HARD YEAST.

Put a cup of hops into a pint of water; when boiling hot, strain it over a pint of corn-meal; add a teacup of bakers' yeast, and when cool roll the dough in flour, and cut it out into cakes, and dry them for use.

LIQUID YEAST OF PARCHED CORN AND HOPS, WHICH DOES NOT TURN SOUR.

Take two teacupfuls of corn, parch it thoroughly, being careful not to burn it; add a good handful of hops; boil in water enough to cover well, for an hour and a half. Pare six good-sized potatoes, and boil them for half an hour with the corn and hops. Sift the potatoes (when done) through a colander, and strain the liquor through a cloth on to the potatoes; add a tablespoonful of ginger, one cup of sugar, and a half cup of salt; put in cold water enough to make up a gallon. Put the whole in a jug, having added a teacupful of good yeast to raise it. Set the jug, without corking, in a warm place till it begins to "work," then cork it and put it in the cellar, and the longer it stands the better it becomes. When wanted for bread, you should (at noon) take five or six boiled potatoes, mash them very fine, stir in a teacupful of flour, and pour on a quart of boiling water; then put in a cup nearly full of yeast, and set the ferment in a warm place till night; then set a soft sponge, with warm water and flour, adding the ferment; it will be ready to mould up hard the first thing in the morning. Let it rise till quite light, then mould it out in loaves, rise again, and bake in the usual way. The sponge should not be set near the stove. The superior qualities of this yeast are shown by the fact that you never use saleratus in the bread, and it never sours. If the directions are followed, with good flour, you may be sure of sweet light bread every time.

MISS BEECHER'S POTATO YEAST.

Mash six boiled potatoes, mix in half a coffeecup of flour, two teaspoonfuls of salt, and add hot water until it is a batter; beat all well together. When it is blood-warm add to it one-half cup of brewers' yeast, or a whole cup of home-brewed yeast. When this is light, put it in a bottle, and cork it tight for use. Keep it as cool as possible.

ANOTHER POTATO YEAST WITHOUT HOPS.

Boil and mash sufficient potatoes to fill a pint cup; add to them a pint of water, boil them together, stir in flour enough to form a thick batter, and when cool, add a yeast cake, or a cup of good yeast. Bottle and put away in a cool place.

YEAST WITH HOPS.

Peel and boil eight large Irish potatoes. Boil a handful of hops in a little water, or in the water the potatoes were boiled in; mash the potatoes fine, and strain the water from the hops over them. Put in a cup of flour to the potatoes before the water is poured on, as it mixes better when dry; mix all together and beat it, then put in half a cup of good yeast, or a yeast cake. This will keep good for a week if kept cool.

HOME-MADE YEAST.

Boil one pound of good flour, one-quarter of a pound of good sugar, and a tablespoonful of salt in two gallons of water. Boil for two hours, and bottle it for use. This will do if you are where you cannot get bakers' yeast, or turnpike cakes to start your yeast, but is not always reliable.

SALT RISING YEAST.

Take a pint of new milk, warm from the cow if possible. Put in a teaspoonful of salt, and thicken it with flour to the consistency of batter cakes. Set this in a warm place to rise, and make your biscuit or bread up with it, and some new milk, or milk and water warmed together.

SALT, OR MILK, RISING FOR BREAD, AND HOW TO BAKE IT.

Take a pint of new milk, stir in nearly a pint of boiling water, then salt it with a teaspoonful of fine salt; thicken this with flour enough to make a thick batter. Set it in a warm place to rise, and it is ready to mix into bread. Mix the yeast in a soft dough with fine flour, a little lard, and a cup of water; mould it, and set it to rise. When well risen, bake it a nice brown. Wrap it in a damp cloth for a few minutes, and let it cool slowly before it is cut. This is a good bread for a delicate stomach, which is sometimes painfully affected by hop-yeast bread.

HARD FIG-LEAF YEAST MADE WITHOUT HOPS.

During the war we could get no hops, and found that fig-leaves were a good substitute. *To Make Fig-Leaf Yeast.*— Take a pint cup of the leaves, put them to a quart of cold water, and boil them until a strong tea or decoction is made—this is to be put away to cool; then pour off the tea carefully, leaving the dregs and leaves. Now boil and wash Irish potatoes enough to fill a pintcup, put them to the tea of fig-leaves, beat them up with a tablespoonful of brown sugar and flour, to make a stiff batter, and put it in a covered vessel to rise. When this yeast is light and frothing, thicken it immediately (as keeping too long injures it) with cornmeal, until it is thick enough to be rolled out like biscuit. Roll it out, cut and dry the cakes, turning them very often until dry. This will be a supply of yeast for several months. When you wish to make bread, take one of the cakes in the morning, put it in a covered mug or pitcher; put on it a cup of cold water, and when it is dissolved, put to it a spoonful of brown sugar, and make a batter of the water and yeast cake. Make this batter as stiff as pound-cake batter, and when it rises well, mix with two quarts of flour, and the bread will be most excellent, if carefully made according to these directions. Use lard as usual in making the bread up for baking.

TO MAKE A LOAF OF GOOD BREAD.

One large spoonful of hop yeast, or a yeast cake; put this to a pint of water, mash to this two Irish potatoes, and stir all together. Sift in flour until you have a stiff batter, and set it to rise. When it is very light, stir in a spoonful of lard, and enough flour to enable you to mould it into a loaf. When moulded, grease the top, and set it to rise again. If really light, you can now bake it; but if *not*, work it down again, and mould it over and let it rise again.

This is made plain and definite, for nothing is more discouraging for a young housekeeper than to feel that she really *tried,* and yet could *not* make good bread. This is in such small quantities that a young person could try it, without feeling that she was wasting much, if she does not succeed the first time. Any one who tries this simple recipe will have the pleasure of presenting a nice loaf of bread to her family.

TO MAKE GOOD BREAD.

Make a pint of meal into mush, then pour it on to two quarts of flour; when cool, add a little salt and warm water, or milk, and a cup of yeast; work it with a spoon, and set it by to rise until morning. Knead it well; yes, *very* well, and make it into loaves; place in the pan, and when light, bake it. Add a little lard, if liked.

A VERY NICE POTATO BREAD.

To two pounds or pints of flour, add one pound or pint of warm, mashed mealy Irish potatoes. Add to this milk and water, a cup of yeast and a little salt. Make it after kneading it very well, into loaves, and place them in a pan to rise. If you desire a rich, short bread you may add a little lard or butter, but it is nice without.

RAISED WHEAT BREAD WITH POTATOES.

Take one half a cup of hop yeast, or yeast made from turnpike cake will do, also two boiled hot Irish potatoes, mash them, and add to the yeast and potatoes one pint of water. Make a sponge of this by beating in sifted flour until it is a soft dough. Set it to rise by the stove; when it is light, pour the sponge in the bread tray and mould it rather stiff with sifted flour, knead it well and set it to rise *again.* When it is light, work in a little more flour, shape it in loaves in the baking-pans; and when light the second time bake it; this allows the yeast to lighten or rise *once,* and the dough or bread to rise twice, making three fermentations the dough undergoes before it is baked into bread.

LIGHT BREAD, INVARIABLY GOOD.

Take *nine* pintcups of flour, one pintcup of good yeast made from hops, two pintcups of warm water and a pint-cupful of warm milk. Make into a sponge, let this rise; when risen, knead it with all your strength, work more flour into it, and let it rise again. When it is light, you must bake it in loaves.

EXCELLENT FAMILY BREAD.

Take a peck of sifted flour, half a pint of family yeast, or a gill of brewers' yeast; wet all up soft with new milk, or milk and water warm. Add a cup of shortening, and a teaspoonful of salt. Knead it faithfully, and set it in a warm place to rise. It is better to take the dough when risen, and work it down again; but some dislike the trouble, and bake it as soon as it rises. You must keep your dough for wheat bread, very soft; but for rye, you may have it stiff.

SPONGE BREAD.

Take three quarts of wheat flour, and three quarts of boiling water, mix them thoroughly; let them remain until luke-warm, then add twelve spoonfuls of family yeast, or six of brewers'. Place it where it will be warm; keep the air from it, and leave it to rise. When it is light, work in flour to mould it, and a little salt. Let it stand for a second rising, then shape into loaves and bake.

RYE AND INDIAN BREAD FOR DYSPEPTICS.

Take a pint of rye flour and a pint of Indian meal, scald the meal with a cup of boiling water, and when lukewarm, mix in the flour and a cup of yeast; add a little salt, and knead it as for other bread. Bake for two hours.

GRAHAM BREAD.

Get good, fresh, ground unbolted flour, and sift it through a common hair sieve. Take three quarts of this wheat meal, one half a cup of good yeast, and three spoonfuls of molasses. Mix to a sponge with water, work in flour enough to mould it, and proceed as you do with common wheat bread. You must put a little soda in the batter before moulding, as it is more disposed to ferment than fine or bolted flour.

MISS SHATTUCK'S BROWN BREAD.

One quart of rye meal, two quarts of Indian meal, two tablespoonfuls of molasses; mix thoroughly with sweet milk. Let it stand two hours, and bake in a slow oven.

BOSTON BROWN BREAD.

One and a half pints of Indian meal, half a pint of wheat flour, one cup of sweet milk, one cup of sour milk, with a teaspoonful of soda in it; three tablespoonfuls of molasses, one tablespoonful of yeast, and a pinch of salt. Put it in a warm place to rise, then let it bake steadily for four hours; warm by steaming it when wanted to use.

CORN BATTER BREAD.

Take six spoonfuls of flour, and six of corn meal; add a little salt, sift them together; make a batter with four eggs, and a cup of milk; stir in the flour and meal, make it a soft batter, and bake in small tins for breakfast. Some use yeast powder or soda with this batter, but that is a matter of taste. If yeast powder is used, sift it in the flour; if soda is used put it in the milk.

MISSISSIPPI CORN BREAD.

One quart of buttermilk, two eggs, three spoonfuls of butter, and a teaspoonful of saleratus; stir in meal, to the milk, until it is as thick as buckwheat batter. Bake in squares about one inch thick. It will require half an hour in a hot oven. If it is not nice, it will be because you have put in too much meal, and made the batter too thick. But try again, and you will succeed.

SODA OR MILK BISCUIT.

To a pound of sifted flour, put the yolk of an egg; dissolve a teaspoonful of carbonate of soda in a little milk; put it and a teaspoonful of salt to the flour, with as much milk as will make a stiff paste; work it well together, beat it for some minutes with a rolling-pin, then roll it very thin. Cut it in round or square biscuits, and bake in a moderate oven until they are crisp.

RICH SODA BISCUIT WITH CREAM OF TARTAR.

To each quart of flour add two teaspoonfuls of cream of tartar sifted through it. Put in a tablespoonful of lard or butter; dissolve a tablespoonful of soda in a cup of water, pour it on the flour; mix with milk, or milk and water, to a soft dough, roll out on the floured biscuit board, cut with the biscuit cutter, and bake quickly. Add a little salt.

A NICE WAY TO MAKE YEAST POWDER BISCUIT.

Take a quart of flour—which is about the quantity required by an ordinary family of six persons; sift one pint of the flour in a tin basin, and sift into it two heaping spoonfuls of yeast or baking powder. Add to the flour a tablespoonful of lard; put this also in the basin and make, with a little salt, a nice batter; beat the flour, lard and water very briskly until it is light. Take down your biscuit board and sift on it the other pint of flour, make a hole in the flour, and pour in your batter, gently stirring it until it is a soft dough; keep it as soft as possible, roll it out, cut it with the biscuit cutter, and bake quickly. These biscuits never have that screwed or drawn-up look that most biscuits made with yeast powder have.

SPONGE BISCUIT WITH YEAST.

Stir half a teacup of melted butter, a teaspoonful of salt and a cup of good yeast, into a pint of lukewarm water; then add flour to make a stiff batter. Set this to rise; when light drop this mixture on to flat buttered tins; drop them several inches apart so as to leave room for them to rise. Let them stay in a warm place fifteen minutes, before being put in the oven to bake. Bake them quickly to a light brown color; they will take about six or eight hours to lighten, though the time depends always on the yeast, and the coldness or warmth of the weather.

SPONGE BISCUIT WITHOUT YEAST, MADE WITH CREAM.

Mix half a pint of thick cream, four eggs, a little salt, soda, and flour enough to make a stiff batter; if too stiff to drop nicely, thin it with a cup of sweet milk. Drop on tins like the above recipe. Bake in a quick oven.

CREAM OF TARTAR BISCUIT FOR BREAKFAST.

One quart of sifted flour, three teaspoonfuls of cream of tartar and one of soda mixed in the flour, and a little salt, two large spoonfuls of shortening; mix soft with warm water or milk, and bake.

MILK BISCUIT OR ROLLS.

Warm a pint of milk and half a pound of butter; pour this into nearly two quarts of flour (you must take out a handful for finishing the biscuit); add two eggs and a cup of yeast, knead it very well and make into round balls, flatten each one on the palm of your hand and prick it with a fork; bake.

NICE ROLLS OR LIGHT BISCUIT.

Beat together one egg, one spoonful of sugar, a small lump of butter and a gill of yeast, or a yeast cake; add to this a quart of flour, and enough warm milk, or milk and water, to form a dough; work it and set it to rise. When it has risen, take down your bread-board, flour it *well*, roll your dough out on the board, and spread over it a tablespoonful of lard or butter. Sprinkle a dust of flour over the butter, roll it up into rolls and bake quickly. Rolls are often made dark by allowing them to get too light.

VIRGINIA ROLLS.

One tablespoonful of good yeast, one egg, one large spoonful of butter, one pound or pint of flour, a little salt and enough milk to form into a stiff batter. Set it to rise in a warmed pan until it is light; sift a cup of flour into the bread-tray, and pour the light batter in; work it well and keep the dough very soft, which is the most certain way to have light rolls or bread. Now, that it is well worked, moist and soft, set the dough to rise; when light, make into rolls, and lay them on a warmed and buttered pan; set them by the fire to rise again, baste the top over with butter, and bake in a quick oven as soon as they are light. Do not keep them too long rising or they might become sharp or sour.

LIGHT FLOUR PUFFS FOR BREAKFAST.

Take a tumbler of sifted flour, a tumbler of milk and two eggs. Put a teaspoonful of yeast powder in the flour before sifting; beat the eggs separately. Mix all together, and add a teaspoonful of melted butter or lard just before baking in little fancy pans. Put salt in the flour with the yeast powder, and then bake as quickly as you can.

ROLLS FOR BREAKFAST.

Sift at night a quart of flour; add half a pint of milk, a spoonful of salt, two well-beaten eggs, and a half cup of yeast. Work it well, cover it, and set it in a warm place to rise. Next morning work in two tablespoonfuls of butter, and mould the dough into rolls. Rub over each roll a little butter, and bake.

FINE ROLLS.

Warm half a cup of butter in a half pint of milk; add two spoonfuls of small beer yeast, or a cup of home-made yeast, and a little salt; pour this on to two pounds of flour. Let it rise an hour, knead it, and make into loaves or rolls.

RICE CAKES.

Take a pint of rice that has been boiled soft; add to it a teacup of flour, two eggs well beaten, a pinch of salt, and enough milk to make a nice thick batter; throw into the batter a tablespoonful of melted butter or lard, and bake on a hot griddle.

SALLY LUNN.

One cup of warmed sweet milk in a cup of yeast, one cup of sugar, one quart of sifted flour, and four eggs, with a cup of lard and butter melted together. Pour this mixture, after it has been well beaten, into a cake mould; let the mould be warmed and well greased. Set it now to rise in a warm place, let it rise until very light, and bake like a cake. With a sharp knife divide the cake, severing the top from the bottom crust; butter both, set the top crust down on the under half, and bring it to table hot.

SALLY LUNN.

Pour a cup of risen yeast into a bowl, add a cup of warm sweet milk, one-half a cup of white sugar, and a large spoonful each of lard and butter mixed and warmed; also add four eggs well beaten, three and one-half cups of sifted flour, and a little salt. Beat all this well, and pour into a warm and well greased cake pan and set it to rise in a warm place in winter, and a cool one in summer. If you wish it for tea, make it up five hours beforehand, having set the yeast to rise after breakfast. If wanted for breakfast make it up at nine o'clock the night before. Remember if made up at night, you add a little more flour, or make the dough a little stiffer, and do not put it in a pan at night, but allow it to rise in a tureen or crock, and pour it in the pan and let it rise a little before baking. It must be baked like a cake. This is a never failing recipe and has been much liked.

MUFFINS AND CRUMPETS WITH YEAST.

Take two pints of milk, four eggs, and a small teacupful of yeast, or a yeast cake; melt a piece of butter (the size of an egg) in a little of the milk, add a teaspoonful of salt, and thicken with sifted flour until it is like buckwheat batter. Set it to rise for eight or ten hours, and then bake in muffin rings, or pour it like batter cakes, on a hot griddle. Butter them, when cooked this way, just as they come from the griddle. Some like sugar and ground cinnamon, sifted over each crumpet as it is baked.

NICE MUFFINS.

To a quart of milk, one quarter of a pound of butter, four eggs, and enough flour to form a very stiff batter, add a cup of yeast; set it to rise three hours, then bake in greased muffin rings. Split, butter, and serve them hot.

GRAHAM MUFFINS FOR DYSPEPTICS.

Take a quart of Graham flour, one half cup of brown sugar, one teaspoon of salt, two tablespoonfuls of yeast, warm water or milk enough to soften it sufficiently to stir readily with a spoon. When it is light, stir up again and drop in rings and bake. If made over night, add a little soda in the morning. Bake soft.

POCKET BOOKS, FOR TEA. VERY MUCH LIKED.

Take a cup of light and warm yeast, a cup of warm, sweet milk, two eggs beaten, a cup of sugar, a spoonful of grated orange peel and nutmeg; add to this, flour enough to make a thin batter, and set it in a warm place to rise. If you wish it for tea, you must make this batter up about nine o'clock in the morning, and in two hours it ought to be full of bubbles, and light. Then pour this batter into sifted flour, enough to form into a rather stiff dough; add salt and a lump of butter as big as an egg. Work it thoroughly, and set it in a tureen to rise again. When it is risen it is ready to form into shapes, called pocket-books. To do this you must flour the board and roll out the dough half an inch thick, smear the surface with butter, cut into strips about six inches long, and two inches wide, fold them over and over, and lay them within an inch of each other on a warm and greased baking tin, or pan; swab the tops over with warmed butter and a beaten egg; set them now to rise, which will require an hour. Just before you put them in the oven, you must sift some sugar over them.

"PAIN PERDU" OR, LOST BREAD.

Take a pint of fresh milk, and sweeten it with a cup of sugar; stir two beaten eggs in it, and season with any flavoring you like. Cut six slices from a loaf of bread, soak each piece of bread a few minutes in the custard of milk and sugar already prepared, take the pieces out one by one, and fry them in butter made hot in a frying pan, pile them up and serve hot.

INDIAN BREAKFAST CAKES.

Take a quart of milk or milk and water, make it scalding hot, pour half of it hot, on as much fine corn meal as it will wet; let it cool, then beat up in it two eggs—beat the eggs light; add a little salt and a teaspoonful of saleratus; thin the batter a little with the rest of the milk; butter pans and pour in the mixture. Bake in a quick oven.

INDIAN-MEAL GRIDDLE CAKES, WITHOUT EGGS.

One quart of milk or milk and water, one pint of corn meal, four tablespoonfuls of flour, one tablespoonful of salt, and a teaspoon of butter; beat up and bake on a griddle or in shallow pans.

HALY'S BUCKWHEAT CAKES.

One quart of fresh buckwheat flour, half a cup of yeast, one tablespoonful of salt, one and a half quarts (or a little less) of milk and water warmed. Beat all well with a large spoon, and pour the mixture in a tall jar, as in that it rises better than in a flaring or open crock. In the morning add a teaspoonful of soda or saleratus, just before frying the cakes. Then grease the griddle and fry them brown; eat with syrup or honey.

BUCKWHEAT GRIDDLE CAKES.

Put three pints of warm water into a stone jar, add half a gill of baker's yeast, or an inch square of turnpike cake dissolved in a little warm water; add a heaping teaspoonful of salt, and half a small teaspoonful of saleratus. Have a pudding-stick, and gradually stir in enough buckwheat flour to make a nice batter; beat it perfectly smooth, then cover it and set it in a moderately warm place until morning. A large handful of cornmeal may be put with the flour, and it is by many persons considered an improvement. If the meal is added it will require an egg and a cup of milk.

NOODLES.

There are few things nicer than " noodles " when they are properly made. Make a stiff dough with two eggs, a little salt, and sufficient flour. Roll this out very thin, shake on a little flour and rub it in; fold the dough over, and roll it up, after which cut it fine with a knife. Have ready a pot almost full of boiling water into which you have put a little salt. Drop the noodles in, and boil them for five or six hours. Pour the water off, and fry the noodles in plenty of butter, and they will be splendid.

RUSKS, DOUGHNUTS AND WAFFLES.

MISS LESTER'S TEA RUSK.

One quart of flour, one half pint of milk, one quarter of a pound of butter, two eggs; add mace, nutmeg and a cup of yeast. Set it to rise, and then make up into rusks; bake on buttered tins when light, and serve hot.

DOUGHNUTS WITHOUT YEAST.

Half a pound of butter, a pint of sour milk or buttermilk, three quarters of a pound of sugar, a small teaspoonful or saleratus dissolved in a little hot water, two well-beaten eggs, and as much flour as will make a smooth dough; flavor with half a teaspoonful of lemon extract and half a nutmeg grated; rub a little flour over a breadboard or table, roll the dough to a quarter of an inch in thickness, cut it in squares, or diamonds, or round cakes, and fry in boiling lard as directed. These cakes may be made in rings and fried.

SOUR-MILK DOUGHNUTS WITHOUT YEAST.

Take a quart of flour, three eggs, three-fourths of a pound of sugar, and half a cup of shortening; add a teaspoonful of soda, and mix to a soft dough with buttermilk. Roll out, cut them, and fry in boiling lard.

DOUGHNUTS WITH HOP YEAST.

Take two quarts of light hop or potato yeast sponge, mix in it a pint of new warm milk, three beaten eggs, a cup of butter or lard, one large cup of sugar, a large spoonful of cinnamon, and a little salt; beat this well, and sift in flour to make a soft dough. Set this in a warm place to rise, and when it is light roll it out on the board a little thicker than pie crust, and cut with a knife in squares of about three inches. Let them stand a little and fry them in plenty of boiling lard. If fried in a little lard they will soak the fat, which will spoil them. Throw them, or any other kind of cakes you wish to fry, into a pot half full of boiling lard, and it insures their being light and nicely browned.

PLAIN DOUGHNUTS.

Take two pounds, or pint cups, full of light risen dough; add to it half a pound of butter, one half pound of sugar, one half pint of milk, three eggs, a little cinnamon and nutmeg. Cover it and set it to rise; when light, cut it into shapes and fry in boiling lard. Add a little flour to stiffen the dough.

CREAM DOUGHNUTS WITHOUT YEAST.

A quart of cream, sweet or sour, five eggs, and a cup of sugar. If the cream be sour, add soda to sweeten it; if sweet, put in two tablespoonfuls of yeast powder, or any good baking powder, and flour to mix, then roll out and fry in boiling lard.

WAFFLES. ECONOMICAL WAY.

Take two eggs, a cup of sweet milk, one cup of water and three cups of flour, with two tablespoonfuls of yeast powder mixed in it before sifting; add a tablespoonful of melted lard or butter, and a teaspoonful of sugar. Mix all well, and bake in waffle irons. This is a nice cheap waffle.

CRULLERS.

Two cups of sugar, one cup of butter, three eggs, one cup of sour milk, one teaspoonful of soda. Flavor to taste, and fry in boiling lard, or bake lightly in the stove.

CRULLERS.

One cup of butter, two cups of sugar, three eggs, half a pint of sour milk, one teaspoonful of soda, half a nutmeg, flour to roll thin. Cut in fancy shapes. Sprinkle sugar over them when done. Put two pounds of lard in a deep skillet, and when it is very hot, begin to fry the crullers. You will have to replenish once or twice with lard, as it will become brown and scorched if you do not. The crullers should be a light-brown, of uniform color. One-half this quantity makes a large dishful of crullers.

ILLUSTRATED LETTERS FROM THE PEOPLE—NO. 5.

Item 1880

35. Bon-temps pas bosco. (Le bon temps n'est pas bossu.)
   "Good fortune is never hunch-backed." (Same proverb in Martinique
   dialect, and in that of Louisiana.) *—[*Trinidad*.]

Gombo Zhèbes 1885

CAKE AND CONFECTIONS.

ICING.

Take one pound of powdered or flour sugar (not the common pulverized) and the whites of four eggs. Put the sugar to the eggs before you beat it at all; then beat till it is stiff. Spread it on the cake with a wet knife, wetting it in cold water each time you use it. Set it in front of the stove to dry, or in an oven with the least particle of heat. The cake must be nearly cold. You can flavor the icing with rose, orange, or lemon; if the latter, add a very small portion of grated rind. It is much nicer to add sugar to eggs before beating than afterward.

CHOCOLATE ICING.

To one pound of fine loaf sugar add half a pint of cold water; boil over a brisk fire until the sugar, when pressed with the fingers, presents the appearance of strong glue; add six ounces of grated chocolate; flavor with vanilla.

TO MAKE ICING FOR CAKES.

Beat the whites of two eggs to a froth, then add to them a quarter of a pound of white sugar, ground fine like flour; flavor with extract of lemon or vanilla; beat it until it is light and very white, the longer it is beaten the firmer it will become. No more sugar must be added to make it so. Beat the frosting until it may be spread smoothly on the cake. This quantity will ice quite a large cake over the top and the sides.

FROSTING FOR CAKE.

To each egg used take ten teaspoonfuls of finest powdered sugar, and a teaspoonful of lemon extract. Beat quickly, and allow at least five minutes for each spoonful of sugar. The excellence of icing depends on the purity of the powdered sugar and the rapidity of beating given the eggs; it is much to be regretted that the most of powdered sugar is adulterated with foreign materials, especially with the white earth called "Terra Alba," which causes the sugar to harden like stone, and prevents the cake and frosting from being, as it should be, light and good.

POILED ICING. VERY NICE.

Boil, until very thick, a pound of white sugar in a cup of water. It should be as thick as for candy ; when boiled, pour it gently on the beaten whites of three eggs. Beat this rapidly until well mixed with the eggs, then flour the cake with flour or corn starch, and ice it with a knife in the usual way. You must use flavoring to suit your taste. Much of the perfection of icing depends on the quality of the sugar, which should be pure and ground, not pulverized, as that sugar is now often adulterated.

HOT BOILED ICING FOR CAKE.

Dissolve one pint of powdered sugar in two large table-spoonfuls of water (or three if the spoon is small) ; set it on the fire to boil. While this syrup is heating on the stove, beat the whites of four eggs to a strong froth, take off the boiling syrup, and beat it to the white of eggs, holding it high over the pans, and pouring it in a stream on the eggs; then flavor with lemon, or vanilla, and spread it on the cake, while the icing is warm; set the cake for a few moments in the oven to harden the icing, it is then ready for the table.

CHARLOTTE RUSSE.

Boil one ounce of isinglass or gelatine, in one and a half pints of milk, sweeten it with half a pound of white sugar, and beat in the yolks of six eggs; flavor it with vanilla. When this mixture begins to stiffen as it grows cold, stir into it one pint of cream whipped to a froth. Ornament the glass dish it is to be served in, with strips of sponge cake, and pour the Charlotte Russe in. Set it in a cool place until wanted.

SPLENDID FRUIT CAKE.

One pound of butter washed and creamed, one and one-fourth pounds of white sifted sugar, creamed with the butter; add the yolks, beaten lightly, alternately, with the whites beaten to a stiff froth, of twelve eggs; stir in carefully a pound of sifted flour. The day before, wash and dry two pounds of currants, pick and seed two pounds of large raisins, and slice one pound of citron. Pour all this fruit into a large pan, and dredge it well with a quarter of a pound of sifted flour; stir all well into the butter, add a grated nutmeg, a glass of wine, and the same of brandy. Bake in a large cake mould very carefully, four hours. It is safer to have it baked by a confectioner, if it is convenient to do so.

NICE FAMILY CAKE WITH FRUIT.

Three cups of fine sugar, two cups of butter, five cups of sifted flour, half a pound of chopped raisins, and half a pound of dried currants; flavor with brandy, and nutmeg, or extract of nutmeg, or lemon. Put the same flavor in the frosting, if the cake is to be used for special occasions.

CHEAP FRUIT CAKE.

To one quart of sifted flour, add a teacupful of sugar, half a cup of butter, one cupful of raisins, two teaspoonfuls of cream of tartar, and one of soda, two tablespoonfuls of mixed spices; rub thoroughly together the flour, cream of tartar, soda and butter, stir in sufficient cold water to make a stiff batter, then add the spices and raisins; pour it into a small tin pan, bake one hour.

WISCONSIN FRUIT CAKE.

Take three quarters of a pound of raw salt, fat pork, chopped very fine ; then pour on a pint of boiling water, one cup of sugar, two cups of molasses, two teaspoonfuls of cloves, one of cinnamon, one nutmeg, two teaspoonfuls of saleratus, one pound and a half of raisins, also a pound of citron and currants if liked, and flour as stiff as can be stirred; bake very slowly an hour, or longer if necessary, as it will burn without great care. This will make three loaves, and will keep well. This is convenient in the winter when eggs are scarce.

NOUGAT FRUIT CAKE.

Make the batter the same as for fruit cake, but instead of the same quantity of fruit, add two pounds of seedless raisins, one pound of citron, one of blanched and cut almonds, and one pound of grated cocoanut. Pour over the cocoanut a cup of sweet milk. Add the wine, brandy and nutmeg. This is much admired. It is an experiment of my own, and has been very much in request.

RICH WEDDING CAKE, OR BLACK CAKE.

One pound of flour, nine eggs, the whites and yolks beaten separately, one pound of butter beaten to a cream, one pound of brown sugar, one teacupful of molasses, one ounce of grated nutmeg or ground mace, one teaspoonful of ground allspice, one teaspoonful of cinnamon, and a gill of brandy; beat this mixture well. Having picked, washed, and dried three pounds of currants, stone and cut three pounds of raisins, strew half a pound of flour over them, mix it well through, and stir them with a pound of citron, cut in slips, into the cake. Line tin pans with buttered paper, put the mixture in, an inch and a half or two inches deep, and bake in a moderate oven an hour and a half or two hours. Ice according to directions.

BRIDE'S CAKE. A SPLENDID RECIPE.

Take three-fourths of a pound of butter, wash and cream it, add one pound of white sugar; beat them well together, then add the beaten whites of seventeen eggs, alternately with a pound of sifted flour. Flavor with lemon or rose, and bake. This is a most delicious and delicate cake.

RICH BRIDE'S CAKE.

Take four pounds of sifted flour, four pounds of sweet fresh butter, beaten to a cream, and two pounds of white powdered sugar; take six eggs for every pound of flour, an ounce of ground mace or nutmeg, and a tablespoonful of lemon extract or orange-flower water. Wash through several waters, and pick clean from grit, four pounds of currants, and spread them on a folded cloth to dry; stone and cut in two, four pounds of raisins, cut two pounds of citron in slips, and chop or slice one pound of blanched almonds.

Beat the yolks of the eggs with the sugar to a smooth paste; beat the butter and flour together, and add them to the yolks and sugar; then add the spice and half a pint of brandy, and the whites of the eggs beaten to a froth; stir all together for some time; strew half a pound of flour over the fruit, mix it through, then, by degrees stir it into the cake.

Butter large tin basins, line them with white paper, and put in the mixture two inches deep, and bake in a moderate oven two hours. The fruit should be prepared the day before making the cake.

CHEAP JELLY CAKE.

One cup of fine white sugar, one cup of milk or water, two tablespoonfuls of butter, one egg, two cups of flour, one teaspoonful of cream of tartar and one half teaspoonful of carbonate of soda· flavor with nutmeg or lemon. It is best with plum or currant jelly.

DELICIOUS POUND CAKE.

Cream three quarters of a pound of butter, sift a pound of flour gradually into it, and cream them together. Beat the yolks of nine eggs light in another pan; stir into the eggs a pound of sifted sugar, mix well; beat the whites of twelve eggs to a froth, add them to the yolks and sugar, then pour this into the pan containing the butter and flour; beat all well together; add a little brandy or wine, and nutmeg. Bake carefully in a large pan. Do not have the oven hotter on the top than at the bottom, for the cake must be allowed to rise. Then bake from the bottom. This is a superior way of making cake, and if properly baked is delicious.

MAIZENA CAKE.

Half a pound of butter rubbed to a cream with one pound of powdered sugar, six eggs beaten lightly and one pound of corn starch. Flavor and bake in small patty pans.

A GENERAL RULE FOR MAKING SPONGE CAKE.

Take of sugar the weight of the eggs used, and half the weight of flour; beat the yolks and sugar together, then add the flour, and, lastly, the whites, having first beaten them to a high froth; then stir them thoroughly together, put into a paper-lined basin, or pan, and bake in a quick oven. The cake may be flavored with lemon, rose, or vanilla extracts, and a little nutmeg, or with a little brandy. Pounded almonds or grated cocoanut, may be added to sponge cake mixture.

BOILED SPONGE CAKE.

Put three quarters of a pound of loaf sugar in a stew pan with nearly half a pint of water, and the peel of a lemon cut very thin; let it simmer twenty minutes. Beat the yolks of eight eggs, and the whites of four, for ten minutes; then pour in the boiling syrup, and beat it well for half an hour. Have your cake pan well greased and a paper in the bottom. Stir gently into the mixture 5-8 of a pound (which is ten ounces) of sifted

flour ; pour the batter immediately into the pan, and bake in
a rather quick oven about half an hour. Have the oven in
baking order before you put the flour in, as sponge cake will
be tough if it is not baked immediately the flour is added,
and it should not be beaten after the flour is stirred in. This
is one secret of having fine light sponge cake.

JENNY'S SPONGE CAKE.

Beat ten eggs separately, put the yellow with a pound of
sifted fine sugar in a bowl ; beat it again very light, and then
put in the whites ; last of all stir in half a pound of flour,
but do not beat the batter after the flour is stirred in. Flavor
with lemon or orange-flower water. Pour the mixture into
pans lined with buttered paper, and do not place more than
one and a half inches of batter in each pan. Bake twenty
minutes. If the oven is too hot, be sure and cover the top of
the pans with a paper or pasteboard, to prevent scorching.

WHITE SPONGE CAKE.

The whites of ten eggs, beaten to a froth ; one tumbler of
sifted flour, one and a half tumblers of sifted white sugar,
half a teaspoonful of cream of tartar, and a pinch of salt ;
stir the cream of tartar and salt well into the flour.
Add the sugar to the whites first, then last of all stir in
the flour very lightly, and flavor with any . delicate extract,
and bake immediately. No soda required.

SPONGE GINGER BREAD.

One cup of sour milk, one cup of molasses, one-half cup of
butter, two eggs, one and a half teaspoons of saleratus, one

tablespoonful of ginger. Flour to make as thick as pound cake. Warm the butter, molasses and ginger, then add the milk, flour and saleratus, and bake as quickly as you can.

GINGER SNAPS.

One cup of butter and lard mixed, one cup of sugar, one cup of molasses, half a cup of water. one tablespoonful of ginger, one teaspoonful of soda in hot water, flour enough to roll the dough soft.

GINGER-NUTS.

Take three pounds of flour, one pound of butter, one quart of molasses, four tablespoonfuls of allspice, the same quantity of cinnamon, and eight tablespoonfuls of ground ginger. Roll thin, cut out in the shape of the small ginger-nuts sold at the confectioners', and bake in a rather quick oven.

ANOTHER RECIPE.

Take two cupfuls of butter, the same quantity of molasses, one cupful of sugar, two tablespoonfuls of ginger, four of cream, one teaspoonful of soda, one-half an ounce of cinnamon, and about one and a half pounds of flour—or enough to make a stiff dough. Roll, cut, and bake in a moderate oven.

TEA CAKES. CHEAP AND NICE. NO EGGS.

One cup of butter or a large spoonful of lard, two cups of sugar, one cup of sour milk, one teaspoonful of soda, some grated orange peel or nutmeg; flour enough to roll out. Roll very thin; cut with fancy cutters, and bake in a quick oven. If you use lard, add a pinch of salt.

PORTUGAL CAKE.

Make a batter with half a pound of butter, one pound of sugar, one pound of flour, and six eggs, two tablespoonfuls of lemon juice or white wine. Add one pound of seeded raisins, or citron, dredged with a little of the flour; one and a half pounds of blanched almonds cut fine, and one grated nutmeg.

CHEAP WHITE CAKES. FOR TEA.

Take half a pound of sifted flour, rub into it one ounce of butter, and a quarter of a pound of fine sugar; add one egg, half a teaspoonful of caraway seeds, and as much milk as will make it a paste; roll it out to quarter-of-an-inch in thickness, or thinner; cut it in small round cakes, and bake on tin plates, in a quick oven, ten or twelve minutes.

LADY CAKE.

One pound of flour; 1 pound of sugar; $\frac{5}{8}$ of a pound of butter; whites of 17 eggs; 2 or 3 drops of oil of bitter almonds. Cream the well-washed butter; add the sugar and cream again; alternate the whites with flour; flavor last of all. The confectioners nearly always bake in a square or long pan.

YELLOW LADY CAKE.

Take a pound of fine white sugar, with half a pound of butter beaten to a cream ; the yolks of eight eggs beaten smooth and thick; one cup of sweet milk, a small teaspoonful of powdered volatile salts or saleratus, dissolved in a little hot water ; half a nutmeg grated ; a teaspoonful of lemon extract, or orange-flower water, and as much sifted flour as will make it as thick as pound-cake batter. Beat it until it is light and creamy; then having taken off the skins, and beaten to a paste, a quarter of a pound of shelled almonds, stir them into the cake, and beat well. Line buttered tin pans, with white paper; put in the mixture an inch deep, and bake half an hour in a quick oven, or forty minutes in a moderate oven. This is a delicious cake.

WHITE LADY CAKE.

Beat the whites of eight eggs to a high froth, add gradually a pound of white sugar finely ground; beat a quarter of a pound of butter to a cream; add a teacupful of sweet milk with a small teaspoonful of powdered volatile salts or saleratus dissolved in it; put the eggs to the butter and milk, add as much sifted flour as will make it as thick as pound-cake mixture; add a teaspoonful of orange-flower water or lemon extract, then add a quarter of a pound of shelled almonds, blanched and beaten to a paste with a little white of egg; beat the whole together until light and white; line a square tin pan with buttered paper, put in the mixture an inch deep, and bake half an hour in a quick oven. When done take it from the pan, when cold take the paper off, turn it upside down on the bottom of the pan and ice the side which was down; when the icing is nearly hard, mark it in slices the width of a finger, and two inches and a half long.

ISABELLA CAKE.

Two cups of butter, four cups of sugar, sixteen eggs, six cups of sifted flour, two teaspoonfuls of yeast powder. Cream the butter and sugar together; add the beaten yolks, then alternately the flour and the beaten whites. Put the yeast powder in the flour. Flavor with vanilla or lemon. Bake carefully in a four-quart cake mould, the bottom and sides of which you have well oiled. Always lay paper in the bottom before oiling, as it prevents the cake from burning and sticking to the pan. This cake is delicious, finished with a chocolate icing.

A NICE CUP-CAKE RICH ENOUGH FOR ANY COMPANY.

Take one cup of butter and three of sugar ; work this to a cream. Beat five eggs separately ; then stir in five cups of sifted flour ; add a cup of sour cream and a teaspoonful of soda; flavor with a glass of wine and a little nutmeg. Bake in a quick oven in round tins, and ice while it is warm.

CUP CAKES.

One cup of butter, three cups of sugar, five cups of flour, one cup of milk, three eggs, one teaspoonful of soda, a little brandy.

TEACUP CAKE WITHOUT EGGS.

One cup of butter, two cups of sugar, one cup of sour cream or thick milk, a teaspoonful of saleratus dissolved in hot water, a gill of brandy, half a grated nutmeg, a teaspoonful of essence of lemon, or the yellow rind of a grated lemon; stir in flour until the batter is as thick as pound cake, and bake an inch deep in a buttered basin.

LITTLE JESSIE'S CAKE.

Two cups of fine sugar, one cup of butter, one cup of sweet milk, four cups of flour, six eggs. Flavor with a glass of wine or brandy, with a nutmeg grated into it. Add a cup of currants.

NICE AND CHEAP JUMBLES. NO EGGS.

One cup of butter, two cups of sugar, one cup of clabber, a teaspoonful of soda stirred into the clabber, a little grated orange or lemon peel, and a good quart of sifted flour. Roll it, and cut in rounds with a hole in the middle, and bake in a quick oven. If you wish, sprinkle sugar over them, and stick strips of citron in each cake when you place them in the baking pan. They are quite nice. Instead of clabber, you can use sweet milk and yeast powder in the flour.

MARBLE CAKE—WHITE PART.

Whites of four eggs, one cup of white sugar, half a cup of butter, half a cup of sweet milk, one teaspoonful of cream tartar, half a teaspoonful of soda.

MARBLE CAKE—BLACK PART.

Yolks of four eggs, one cup of brown sugar, half a cup of molasses, half a cup butter, half a cup of sour milk, one teaspoonful of soda, and plenty of all kinds of spices to suit the taste. Put first black, then white, dough, until all is in; then bake. It is very nice.

FRENCH LOAF CAKE.

Five cups of sugar, three of butter, two of milk, ten of sifted flour, six eggs, three small nutmegs, one teaspoonful of saleratus, one pound of raisins, and one-third of a pound of citron. Stir the butter and sugar to a cream, then add part of the flour, the milk and the beaten yolks of the eggs, then add the rest of the flour and the whites of the eggs; add the fruit as you get the cake ready for the oven; season to taste. This will make four loaves. Bake one hour.

LOAF CAKE. PLAIN.

Three cups of sweet milk, two of sugar, and one of yeast; stir in flour to make it quite thick, and let it rise over night. In the morning add two eggs well beaten, fruit and spice to taste; let it rise till light. Bake in a slow oven.

EGG KISSES.

Four whites of eggs, one-half pound powdered sugar; beat well and bake quickly. Flavor with extract of rose or lemon.

GENOESE CAKES.

Half a pound of butter, half a pound of sugar, four eggs, half a pound of flour, a small glass of brandy or wine. Bake in a square sheet; ice it and cut into diamonds; ornament with dots or stripes of any kind of bright jelly or preserves.

FRANCATELLI'S SPANISH CAKE.

Put half a pint of milk or water into a stew-pan over the fire, with four ounces of butter and two ounces of sugar. As soon as these begin to boil, withdraw the stew-pan from the fire, and stir in five ounces of flour. Stir well for a few minutes, add essence to taste, and, one by one, three eggs and a small pinch of soda. Drop this paste on a baking-sheet in small round balls (the size of a hickory nut), and bake a light brown in a quick oven. Garnish with preserves.

CHOCOLATE CAKE.

Half a pound of butter, one pound of sugar, one pound of flour, four eggs, one half pint of milk, one teaspoonful of soda, and two of cream of tartar sifted into the flour. Mix all these ingredients well together, and bake in two cakes.

Beat three whites of eggs with three cups of sifted sugar, and add chocolate to taste. Spread a layer of this icing between the cakes and on the top and sides.

CHOCOLATE CAKE.

Take one cup of butter, two cups of sugar, one cup of milk or water, three and a half cups of flour, half a teaspoonful of soda, one teaspoonful cream of tartar, the yolks of five eggs and the whites of two. Bake on jelly cake tins.

CHOCOLATE MIXTURE FOR FILLING THE ABOVE CAKE.

One and a half cups of sugar, the whites of three eggs, three tablespoonfuls of grated chocolate. Flavor with vanilla.

RING JUMBLES.

One pound of butter, one pound of sugar, four eggs, one and a quarter pounds of flour, or enough to make a soft dough. Line a pan with buttered paper, form the dough into rings. Bake quickly and sift sugar over them.

The dough must be kept very soft, or if not wanted in rings put in more flour, and cut the cakes out with a cutter.

GERMAN LADIES' FINGERS.

Beat the yolks of five eggs with half a pound of sugar. Add half a pound of blanched almonds, cut fine or pounded. Grate the rind of a lemon, mix well, and add gradually enough sifted flour to make into a dough. Roll out and cut in strips the length and size of the forefinger ; wet them with the beaten white of two eggs, and bake.

LADY FINGERS.

Four eggs, half a pound of sugar, half a pound of flour. Flavor to taste. Drop by teaspoonfuls, and bake quickly.

CITRON CAKE.

One pound of butter, one pound of sugar, one pound of flour, and eight eggs. Add to this batter one pound of blanched almonds, cut small, and half a pound of sliced citron dredged with flour; beat all up well. Beat in a half teaspoonful of soda, moistened with sweet milk, or if preferred, a tablespoonful of yeast powder, rubbed in the flour before mixing. Beat this mixture well, and bake it in a cake-pan ; put buttered paper in the bottom of the pan, and cover the top of the cake with something to protect it from the heat of the stove, until the bottom is nearly done. This is the best way to cook all delicate cakes.

LOUISIANA HARD-TIMES CAKE.

Cream half a pound of butter, with one pound of sifted sugar. Add to this the beaten yolks of six eggs. Beat this again, and set it by until you beat the whites of the eggs to a stiff froth. Sift a pound of flour, and put into it two teaspoonfuls of yeast powder. Then pour in alternately a little flour and beaten eggs until all is used. Then mix in a cup of cold water and two teaspoonfuls of brandy, wine or extract of lemon. Butter a four-quart cake-pan or mould, have the oven ready, and pour in the mixture, and bake immediately. Cover the top of the cake while baking. When done you will have a nice cake, and one that is very inexpensive.

INDIAN BREAKFAST CAKES.

Take a quart of milk scalding hot; stir into it as much corn-meal as will make a thick batter, add of salt and saleratus in fine powder, each a teaspoonful, and when a little cooled, two well-beaten eggs; bake in buttered pans, in a quick oven. This is a nice breakfast cake.

DELICATE CAKE OF CORN STARCH.

Take half a pound of sugar, one-fourth of a pound of butter, the whites of eight eggs, and a quarter of a pound of corn starch mixed with quarter of a pound of common flour. Beat all very light, add to the flour a teaspoonful of cream of tartar, and a half-spoon of fine soda (not saleratus). Flavor with lemon or rose.

SODA TEACAKES WITHOUT EGGS.

Take half a pound of sugar, and half a pound of butter; beat it to a cream. Dissolve a teaspoonful of fine soda in a cup of milk, and pour it into the batter, half a nutmeg and flour to make a stiff batter. Bake in tin squares or a shallow pan, cook twenty minutes.

A VERY GOOD CHEAP CAKE.

One cup of butter, one and a half cups of brown sugar, one cup of milk, sweet or sour, yeast powder or soda—if yeast powder is used, put two teaspoonfuls; if soda, put one heaping teaspoonful—one cup of molasses, four eggs, one nutmeg, one pound of raisins, five cups of flour.

TRIFLES.

Beat two or three fresh eggs a few minutes, add a salt-spoonful of salt, and enough of sifted flour to make into a stiff paste; roll very thin; cut into small round cakes; fry in boiling lard, and sprinkle sugar over them. They are a delicious dish for tea.

A NICE MOLASSES CAKE.

One cup of molasses, one and a half cups of sugar, one cup of butter, four eggs, a cup of sour milk and a heaping spoonful of soda. If desirable, you may add one pound of seeded and chopped raisins, or the same of currants; grease the pan carefully as molasses cake is liable to stick, and is always more difficult to get out of the pan than sugar cakes. You may add flour to roll it out like biscuit if you wish, or it is *better* made only as thick as pound-cake batter, and baked in a pan like that cake. Make the batter stiff with flour, as it turns out better than when soft.

SILVER CAKE.

Cream two coffee-cups of butter with two pints of fine white sugar; add the beaten whites of eighteen eggs, and four pints of flour—one of these pints must be maizena or corn starch flour, as that gives a delicacy which common wheat flour cannot. You must thin this mixture gradually as you beat in the flour and eggs, by pouring in two coffee-cups of water. Flavor with almond, and bake in a large pan. When you sift the flour you must add to it two teaspoonfuls of yeast powder.

SILVER CAKE.

Two pints of sugar and two cups of butter; cream the butter and sugar together. Add two cups of cold water; beat to a froth the whites of eighteen eggs, mix them with the butter and sugar, four pints of flour, and two teaspoonfuls of yeast powder; mix flour and yeast powder together, and stir gently into the batter. Flavor with almond. For a small cake take half the quantity of ingredients. It makes a nicer cake to allow one of the pints of flour to be corn starch, instead of common flour.

SUPERIOR GOLD CAKE.

Take half a pound of butter, one pound of sugar, one pound of flour, the yolks of ten eggs, one teaspoonful of soda mixed with a little hot water. Cream the butter and sugar together; beat the eggs light, and add them to the butter and sugar. Then stir in the flour and soda.

CHEAP AND RELIABLE GOLD AND SILVER CAKE.

Two cups of butter and four of sugar creamed together, two cups of sweet milk, or water, if you have no milk; eight cups of sifted flour well mixed with four teaspoonfuls of cream of tartar, and two of soda; beat separately the yolks and whites of eight eggs. Take half the batter; use the yolks for the gold cake, and the whites for the silver cake. Flavor differently, as with rose and lemon.

SUPERIOR SILVER CAKE.

Take half a pound of butter, one pound of sugar, three-quarters of a pound of flour, the whites of ten eggs beaten to a froth. Cream the butter and sugar together, then add the eggs, and lastly, stir in the flour.

COCOANUT SILVER CAKE.

Cream one cup of butter and two cups of sugar, add a cup of milk, the whites of six eggs, and three cups of sifted flour with one teaspoonful of cream of tartar, and half a teaspoonful of soda mixed in the flour. Grate a small cocoanut, dry it in a skillet over the fire by stirring it about ten minutes. Stir the cocoanut into the batter. Bake in a moderate oven about three-quarters of an hour.

COCOANUT CAKES.

Grate a cocoanut, place it in a skillet over the fire, and stir until it is as dry as flour. Beat one cup of sugar and the white of an egg to a froth. Mix well, and make into small cakes; put them on buttered paper and bake. The oven should not be very hot.

COCOANUT CAKES.

Take a cocoanut, pare it and grate half a pound; allow the same quantity of loaf sugar. Dissolve the sugar in two tablespoonfuls of water, place it on the fire; when the syrup is boiling hot, stir in the cocoanut. Continue to stir it until it is thick like candy, then pour it out on a buttered pan, and cut it across in shapes, or use a round cake cutter.

COCOANUT POUND CAKE.

Take three coffee-cupfuls of flour, one of butter, and two of white sugar; one cupful of milk; the whites of six eggs;

one teaspoonful of cream of tartar; one-half teaspoonful of carbonate of soda; grated cocoanut—a small one. The cocoanut should be laid in water as soon as the shell is broken; take out a piece at a time to pare it; lay it in a dry cloth as soon as pared, and cover it up, that the air may be kept out and the moisture absorbed. If the cocoanut goes in wet it will make the cake heavy. Cream the butter; add the sugar, and beat well; then put in the milk, slowly; the whites of the eggs, well beaten, alternately with flour; the cocoanut last of all. One-half of this quantity makes a good-sized cake. Bake in a moderate oven; increase the heat at the last. It takes about one-half or three-quarters of an hour to bake.

COCOANUT CAKE.

Make a batter of one cup of butter, two cups of sugar, three cups of flour and four eggs. Bake in jelly cake pans. Spread a layer of icing between each cake with grated cocoanut on top of the icing; finally, ornament the top with a thick layer of cocoanut.

COCOANUT DROPS.

Take a grated cocoanut, the beaten whites of four eggs, and half a pound of white sugar; flavor, mix, and bake on paper in drops.

PECAN CAKE.

Half a cup of butter, one and one half cups of sugar, two eggs, three quarters of a cup of sweet milk, two cups of sifted flour, one and one half teaspoonfuls of soda, and one teaspoonful of cream of tartar in the flour, one cup of pecans picked out and cut fine. Bake in a small cake pan.

WINE CAKES.

One quarter pound of butter, one half pound of sugar, one egg, a few drops of essence of lemon, and a good half pound of flour. Mix, roll thin, and cut out in round cakes. They are very nice with wine.

NAPLES BISCUIT.

Beat four eggs light; add half a pound of fine white sugar, and half a pound of sifted flour. Flavor with essence of lemon.

SHREWSBURY CAKE.

Beat to a cream half a pound of butter, and three-quarters of a pound of sugar ; add five well-beaten eggs, a nutmeg, some essence, and about a quart of flour. Sift the flour, mix it well, and drop the mixture with a spoon on buttered tins. Add currants if you wish.

COFFEE CAKE.

One cup of butter, two cups of sugar, one cup of molasses, one cup of strong coffee, two eggs, five cups of flour, one teaspoonful of soda, one cup of currants, one cup of raisins. Spice to taste.

NICE DROP CAKES.

One half pound sugar, one quarter pound of butter creamed together, four well-beaten eggs, one half pound of currants, a spoonful of brandy, grated nutmeg or lemon peel, and flour sufficient for a stiff batter. Beat well. Drop by spoonfuls on buttered tins and bake in a quick oven. They are light and tender.

DIAMOND BACHELORS.

Biscuit dough rolled thin, cut into diamonds and boiled in lard.   Ladies are very fond of them.

VELVET CAKE.

One cup of yeast, three eggs well beaten, one quart of warm milk, one quart of sifted flour, salt, a large spoonful of butter well beaten ; let it rise.   Pour into greased muffin rings and bake.

DELICATE CAKE.

Two eggs, two cups of sugar, half a cup of butter, one cup of sweet milk, three cups of flour, one teaspoonful of cream of tartar, half a teaspoonful of soda.   Bake in squares.

LITTLE DROP CAKES.

Half a pound of sugar, four eggs, half a pound of flour, quarter of a pound of butter.

CREAM CAKES.

Boil a cup of butter with half a pint of water; while it is boiling, stir in two cups of sifted flour; let it cool, and when cool, add five eggs well beaten, and a quarter of a spoonful of soda dry.   Drop this mixture with a teaspoon on tins and bake in a quick oven.

FOR THE INSIDE OF THE CAKES.

Take a pint of milk, one half a cup of flour, one cup of sugar and two eggs.   Boil the milk and flour together, add the eggs and sugar; flavor the custard with lemon.   Now, you must take the first or outside cakes, and split each one gently, so as to place in it the cream or custard which must be cold before you introduce it. Put into each cake about a teaspoonful of the cream. These are delicious. One half this quantity makes a large dishful of cakes.

ANOTHER CREAM CAKE WITH CRUST AND CREAM.

CRUST.—Three-quarter pint of water, half a pint of butter, three-quarters of a pound of flour, eight eggs; boil the water and butter together, and while boiling stir in the flour, take it off and let it cool, then add your eggs (beaten separately), and a teaspoonful of dry soda. Use about a spoonful of the crust for each puff; bake on tins for about twenty minutes. When done cut the crust open and put in the cream.

CREAM.—Two pints of milk, one cup of flour, two cups of sugar, four eggs; while the milk is boiling add your flour, sugar and eggs (previously well beaten together), let it cook until it begins to thicken, take it off, and flavor with rose water.

TIPSY CAKE.

Place a sponge cake weighing about a pound in a glass bowl, pour over it half a pint of sherry and Madeira (mixed). Make a rich custard of six eggs and a quart of milk, sweeten to taste, flavor and let it cool. Blanch half a pound of almonds, stick them in the top of the sponge cake and pour over it the custard.

PLAIN TEA CAKES.

Half a cup of butter, or a large spoonful of lard, one and a half cups of sugar, one teacupful of milk, one teaspoonful of soda, seven cupfuls of sifted flour. Roll thin.

EASY CAKE FOR YOUNG COOKS.

Take two cups of flour, sift it, and to each cup put a teaspoonful of yeast powder. Beat the yolks of three eggs and one cup of fine white sugar, together with half a cup of water mixed with extract or wine; beat this well in the yolks and sugar (only half a cup); froth up the whites of the eggs, add them, and last of all, beat in the flour with the powder in it. Bake quickly in square or jelly cake pans.

YOUNG COOKS' JELLY ROLL.

Make the sponge for your jelly roll by taking a cup of white sugar, one cup of flour, and three eggs. Mix, etc.; add baking powder with the flour. Bake in a stewpan with a quick fire; turn the cake out on a towel when done; spread the jelly while it is still warm and soft, and roll it carefully. Cut it in slices when cold; a spoonful of water beaten with the eggs makes the cake lighter, as it breaks the tissue of the eggs if it is added to them when beaten up.

ALMOND DROPS.

Blanch and pound five ounces of sweet, and three ounces of bitter almonds (or peach kernels), with a little white of egg. Put half a pound of sifted flour on your dough board, make a hole in the middle of the flour, in which put the almonds, with half a pound of sugar, four yolks of eggs, and a little salt. Make into a paste. Cut in pieces the size of a nut, lay them half an inch apart, on sheets of paper, in a baking-pan, and bake in a moderate oven for fifteen or twenty minutes.

ALMOND MACCAROONS.

Blanch and pound with a little rose-water half a pound of almonds; add half a pound of sifted sugar, the whites of two eggs (not beaten), form into a paste. Dip your hand in water, and roll the preparation into balls the size of a nutmeg; lay them an inch apart, on buttered paper, in a baking tin. Bake in a slow oven until a light brown.

ALMOND MACCAROONS.

To a pound of the best white sugar, sifted, add a pound of blanched almonds; put in a few drops of rose-water as you beat them together in a mortar. Add to them the well-beaten whites of six eggs, and form the paste into shapes in the palm of the hand by using a little flour; butter some sheets of white paper, and drop the maccaroons on it, leaving a space between them. Strew a little white sugar on them, and put in the oven to bake a light brown. Almonds are blanched by pouring hot water on them, and slipping off the brown coating.

FRENCH OPERA.

Item 1880

DESSERTS.

CHARLOTTE RUSSE IN VARIOUS WAYS.

There are many varieties of this Charlotte. They are always similarly made, that is with sponge cake or lady fingers, and whipped cream, custard or blanc-mange. One way is to beat the whites of three eggs to a high froth, with a quarter of a pound of sugar, and half a pint of cream, until it is quite thick and light; flavor this to your taste with lemon or vanilla, and pour it into a cake-lined mould; place some of the sliced cake or lady fingers on top of the mould and over the cream; set it on ice, and when wanted turn it on a dish and serve.

Or, having lined a basin or mould, or small tin cups with any convenient cake, such as lady fingers, sliced savoy cake, or yellow lady cake, fill them with mock cream, blanc-mange or custard, made from the yolks of eggs; let them become cold, then turn them out and serve.

ANOTHER WAY.

Break an ounce of isinglass small, and pour on it a teacup of hot milk or water; let it dissolve, then strain it through muslin, on half a pound of fine white sugar. When nearly cold add to it a quart of rich cream, already beaten to a froth; continue to beat it for a few minutes, holding the pan on ice.

Line your mould with sponges and pour your cream in. Cover with sponge cake or lady fingers. Turn it out and serve. The isinglass will make this very firm if held on ice long enough to solidify before serving.

PLAIN CHARLOTTE RUSSE.

Boil one ounce of isinglass in a pint of water until reduced one half. While it is boiling, make a custard of one half-pint of milk, yolks of four eggs, and one-fourth of a pound of sugar; flavor this with vanilla or lemon. Take a quart of cream, whip it up to a fine froth, and when the isinglass is nearly cold, so that it will not curdle the cream, stir it and the cream into the custard. Beat all thoroughly and set it on ice. This is a nice, easy way to make this dish, and may be made very ornamental, if wanted so, by lining a glass dish with lady-fingers, and then pouring in the cream and laying fine fancy sugar-drops on top. If you have no lady-finger sponges, you can slice any light sponge cake, and lay it on the bottom and sides of the glass bowl.

SICILIAN BISCUIT DROPPED ON TINS.

Take four eggs, twelve ounces of powdered and sifted sugar, and ten ounces of flour. Beat the eggs and sugar together in a stewpan on the fire, until the batter feels warm to the touch; remove it from the fire, and stir it thoroughly until it becomes cold; now add the flour, and flavor with vanilla. Butter some paper and place it on the baking tins, or pans. Drop the cake mixture in rounds or ovals on the buttered paper, and bake in a slow oven. When put in the oven sift white sugar over the biscuit.

QUEEN'S DROPS.

Beat up a quarter of a pound of butter, and a quarter of a pound of sifted sugar, two eggs, and six ounces of flour. Flavor with almonds, or vanilla, or lemon. Butter some paper, place it on baking-sheets or pans, and drop the mixture in drops about the size of a nutmeg. Bake in a hot oven.

ALMOND MERINGUE.

Beat the whites of two eggs with a quarter of a pound of powdered sugar and a quarter of a pound of blanched and cut almonds. Form them into rings on letter paper, put the paper on tin, and place them in the stove oven, to harden and brown lightly.

APPLE COMPOTE.

Make a syrup of three-quarters of a pound of sugar and a cup of water; let it boil while you are paring and taking out the cores of six nice sour apples. Throw them into the syrup and let them boil for half an hour, or until transparent. Pour into a glass or china dish, and serve for a lunch or tea. They are nice when served warm.

MAIZENA BLANC MANGE.

This can be made with maizena, corn starch, or potato flour, but maizena is preferable. Take a quarter of a pound of maizena and three pints of milk. Put two and a half pints of the milk on to boil, and wet the corn starch or maizena with the remaining half pint. When the milk boils add to it (or better before it boils), a quarter of a pound of white sugar and some lemon rind, sliced or grated. Let this boil a little, and then stir in the mixed maizena or corn starch. When cooked five minutes, pour it into moulds or bowls; wet the bowls first with cold water to prevent the jelly sticking to the sides. When firm and cold, eat it with cream or any kind of stewed fruit you may have.

GELATINE BLANC MANGE.

To one quart of milk add an ounce of Nelson's or Coxe's gelatine, which has been soaked an hour in a cup of cold water. Add to this half a pound of fine white sugar; let it simmer very gently on the fire in a stewpan until all the gelatine is dissolved. Strain it, and pour it in a mould; when it begins to thicken, put it on ice and serve it with cream.

GELATINE BLANC MANGE.

Take a quart of new milk, set it on to boil; stir into the boiling milk, half a box of gelatine, which should have been soaked in cold water ten or fifteen minutes. When the gelatine is dissolved, stir into the milk a cup of sugar; take the jelly from the fire, and last of all while the mixture is very hot, stir in four eggs; season with vanilla or lemon extract, and pour into moulds. Eat with cream. This is very nourishing for invalids.

CHOCOLATE *MANGE.*

Made the same as gelatine blanc-mange above described, except seasoning the jelly with six ounces of grated chocolate in the boiling milk. Eat with cream or wine sauce.

ISINGLASS JELLY.

Boil in one pint of water, one ounce of isinglass, and when well dissolved, add to it one pound of sugar, and a cup of pale wine. When the water is boiling, add to it the rind of a lemon, and when taken off the fire, add the juice and grated rind of another lemon. Strain this mixture and whisk it till it begins to thicken, then pour it into the vessel you wish to mould it in, and set in a cool place, or on ice to harden.

LEMON CUSTARD.

Boil a cup of water, and stir into it a tablespoonful of flour, or corn-starch. Beat the yolks of three eggs with a cup of brown sugar. Add the juice of a lemon strained ; beat it up with the yolks and sugar. Pour this in a paste, and bake it. While the custard is baking, take the whites of the three eggs and beat them up with a cup of pulverized sugar. Spread this icing on the baked custard, and brown it slightly.

NICE BOILED CUSTARD.

To every quart of milk, allow six eggs and a cup of white sugar. Set the milk to boil; beat the whites of the eggs with a half cup of sugar, and drop into the boiling milk for two minutes; then with a skimmer remove the boiled whites, and put on a dish to cool. When the whites are taken off, stir into the milk the yolks and sugar, previously well beaten up together. Add rose, lemon. or peach-leaf flavoring. Run this through a sieve into the bowl you expect to serve it in; then pile up the whites on the custard. The whites can be boiled without beating them with sugar.

APPLE CUSTARD. A NICE DISH.

Take a dozen apples, a large cupful of brown sugar, a tea-cupful of water, the grated rind of a lemon, one pint of milk, four eggs, and two ounces of loaf sugar. Peel, cut and core the apples ; put them in a saucepan with the water; as they heat, add the brown sugar and lemon-peel. When mashed and well cooked, take it off ; put the fruit in the bottom of a deep dish, and pour a custard of the milk, sugar and eggs, over it, and bake in a moderate oven. Grate over it before baking, a little nutmeg.

ALL THE YEAR ROUND PUDDING.

Line a pie dish with paste, spread on this three ounces of any kind of jam—strawberry or raspberry is best. Then beat well in a basin three ounces of bread crumbs, three ounces butter, the same of sugar, and the rind and juice of a large lemon; add this to the pastry and jam, and bake half an hour. If the lemon is not very juicy, add a tablespoonful of water to it.

TO GLAZE PASTRY.

Break an egg, separate the yolk from the white, and beat it well ; when the pastry is nearly baked take it out of the oven and brush it over with this beaten yolk of egg, then put it back in the oven to set the glaze.

TRANSPARENT PUDDING.

Beat eight eggs very light ; add them to half a pound of butter, and the same of sugar, which have been beaten to a cream together ; grate in half a nutmeg, set it on the fire in a stewpan, and stir it constantly until it is hot. Do not leave it more than five minutes on the fire, as you only wish to slightly cook the whites of the eggs to prevent their running when put on the paste. Line two pie pans with delicate paste, and pour in the mixture. Bake in a moderate oven,

and do not allow the top to burn, as it will, if not covered
when first put in the oven.   Cover with a pan until the bottom is cooked, and then a few moments colors the top.   This
pie has no meringue on top.   Serve it with a tart pie, as it
is a very sweet dessert.

APPLE TRIFLE—A SUPPER DISH.

Make a marmalade by stewing tart apples in sugar, seasoned
with lemon.˙ Lay it when cold in a deep glass dish, pour over
it a boiled custard made of two eggs, half a pint of milk,
sweetened with half a cup of sugar.   Finish it by whipping
a pint of rich cream to a froth, and pile it high on the custard.
Ornament with strips of citron and apple jelly laid on the
whipped cream.   This is a charming dish for the country
where cream is abundant.

TRIFLES.   DELICIOUS.

Cover the bottom of a glass bowl, or dish, with ladyfingers;
break up, and put also a half dozen maccaroons; pour over
them a cup of wine, or diluted extract to moisten them; then
put in three tablespoonfuls of jelly or jam.   Pour over this a
boiled custard, made with a pint of milk, three eggs and a
cup of white sugar.   Whip up the whites of two eggs with
a cup of white sugar and lemon juice to taste, and when it
will stand alone, put it on the custard, and serve.

GELATINE SNOW PUDDING.

Take two tablespoonfuls of good gelatine, throw over it
two spoonfuls of water, let it soak ten minutes, then pour
over it half a pint of boiling water, three quarters of a pound

of white sugar, and the juice of two lemons with the rind
thrown in. Let it come to a boil, take it off immediately,
strain it, let it cool a little, and when it begins to thicken add
the beaten whites of two eggs. Beat all thoroughly, and
pour it in a mould on ice to get firm. When cold and firm
send it to table in the middle of a glass basin or dish, and
pour around it a custard made from the yolks of the eggs,
and a pint of milk sweetened and flavored to taste. Sponge
cake should be served with this pudding.

A PRETTY DISH OF ORANGES CROQUANTÉ.

Take ten or a dozen oranges, remove the peel, all the
white part and the seeds. Do this carefully by quartering
them, retaining the transparent pulp and juice. Do not break
the skins of the sections. Boil a pound of loaf sugar in half
a glass of water until the syrup strings when lifted on a fork,
then take it from the fire and dip each section of orange in
this candy while it is hot; you can do this by placing each
one on a little stick cut for the purpose. As the pieces are
dipped, arrange them in some pretty form on a dish or bowl,
and fill up the hollow with whipped cream, sweetened and
seasoned with a glass of maraschino.

FRANCATELLI'S LEMON PUDDING.

The juice and grated rind of six lemons, a pint of milk or
cream, six ounces of sponge cake or maccaroons, eight yolks,
and the whites of four eggs (whipped to a froth), one pound
of sugar, and a little salt. Mix in a basin, and work all these
materials together for at least ten minutes. Put a border of

puff paste around a pie-dish, then pour in the batter; strew cut-up almonds over it, and bake. Sift powdered sugar over it, and serve.

WHIPPED CREAM WITH WINE.

To the whites of three eggs, beaten to a froth, add a pint of cream, four tablespoonfuls of sweet wine, and four spoonfuls of sugar. Put bright jelly, or light-colored marmalade in spots among the cream, and serve sponge cake with it.

BATTER PUDDING.

One quart of milk, six eggs beaten separately, and seven tablespoonfuls of flour. Boil the milk, stir in the eggs and flour, while the milk is nearly hot enough to boil; do not let it boil when you stir in the flour, but take it off the fire, or you will curdle the eggs. Bake this batter half an hour, and eat it with wine or lemon sauce. You should salt the milk slightly before boiling. When well and quickly made, this is a delightful pudding, but it should be eaten hot.

A SUPERIOR LEMON TART.

Squeeze the juice from six lemons, wash the rinds and boil them; if too strong of the lemon oil, it is better to change the water. You must grate or pound the rinds, and when tender and cold, add to them one pound of sugar, one-fourth of a pound of butter, and the yolks and whites of five eggs. Stir in the juice of the lemons, and cook the batter gently until it is thick as honey; then bake it in puff paste without tops. Ornament with fancy strips of paste.

SUET PUDDING.

Take a cupful of chopped suet, half a cup of molasses, one cup of raisins chopped, a teaspoonful of powdered cloves and cinnamon, one-half cup of sugar, two eggs well beaten, half a cup of sweet milk, a little salt, and two teaspoonfuls of yeast powder. Stir in flour until it is a thick batter; flour a cloth, and pour in the mixture, leaving room to swell. Boil two hours.

ROLL PUDDING OF ANY KIND OF FRUIT.

Make a light paste, roll out lengthwise, spread any kind of fruit over the paste, and roll it up in the dough; wrap it up in a cloth, tie it carefully, and boil it one hour. You will find this delicious if made of either blackberries, strawberries, peaches, or any kind of dried fruit stewed and sugared; if fresh fruit is used, it needs no stewing.

A DESSERT FOR A DELICATE PERSON.

Boil one cup of rice until perfectly soft, then add a teacup of rich sweet cream, and half a teacup of any acid jelly— currant is the best, but plum, strawberry or lemon will do. Put it over the fire a few minutes, turn it into a mould. Eat with sweetened cream.

MACCAROON PUDDING ICED.

Line a mould with maccaroons, as described for Iced Cabinet Pudding. Fill the mould with dried cherries seedless raisins and maccaroons, in layers; then pour a little Madeira or sherry wine over them, and finish by pouring over all a custard of a pint of milk, two eggs and flavoring to suit; sweeten it with half a pound of white sugar, and in summer cover the mould up in ice and salt until wanted. In winter steam it and serve with butter and sugar sauce.

STEAMED CABINET PUDDING, VERY FINE.

Butter a pudding mould, and line it with brioche, or any kind of cold sweet roll, or Sally Lunn, that has been left over. Fill the mould with layers of sponge cake, or maccaroons, alternately with currants, or seedless raisins, chopped citron, or other dried fruit; then make a boiled custard of six yolks of eggs (for a moderate size mould), a pint of milk or cream, six ounces of sugar, a glass of brandy, and the grated rind of a lemon. Moisten the maccaroons with extract of lemon, and then pour over the custard, which need not be previously boiled, as the pudding is to be *steamed*, and boiling the custard is unnecessary, except when it is to be iced. Serve with wine or hard butter sauce beaten up with a little wine.

MERINGUE PUDDING. VERY NICE.

Take a pint of bread crumbs, a quart of milk and four eggs. Make one pint of the milk boiling hot, pour it over the bread crumbs, and beat it smooth; when cool, add a cup of sugar, and the yolks of the four eggs, also a lump of butter (the size of an egg). Beat all well together, thin it by adding the rest of the milk, flavor it with peach or nutmeg, and set it in the oven to bake. You must only bake it long enough to cook the eggs, for, if you leave it to stew and simmer in the stove, it loses its jelly-like consistence, and the milk turns to whey. When slightly brown on top, take the pudding out of the stove, and set it to cool. When cool, spread over it a layer of acid preserve or jelly, such as plums, apples, grapes, or currants. Then finish it by making an icing or meringue of the whites of the eggs, beaten up with a full cup of white sugar; flavor this with lemon extract, and then put the pudding again in the stove and brown. If for a small family, use a pint of milk and half of all the materials mentioned. This is considered an elegant dish for any occasion.

A DELICIOUS PUDDING, VERY EASILY MADE.

Butter some thin cut slices of rolls; lay them in a pudding-dish with currants and citron cut up fine, and strewed between the slices. Then pour over the rolls, a custard made of a quart of milk, four eggs and half a pound of sugar; flavor this and bake lightly.

PRINCE ALBERT'S PUDDING.

Take one half pound of butter, one half pound of grated bread crumbs, one half pound of sugar, the juice of two lemons with the rinds grated in; add six eggs well beaten a glass of brandy and four tablespoonfuls of marmalade. Steam this pudding in a mould and serve with wine sauce.

COCOANUT PUDDING OR PIES.

Break a cocoanut and save the milk; peel off the brown skin, then throw each piece into cold water, and let it stay a few minutes to cool; take the pieces out, wipe dry and grate; add their own weight of white sugar and half the weight of butter; rub the butter and sugar to a cream, add five well-beaten eggs, and a cup of milk; last of all, throw into the mixture the milk of the cocoanut and the grated rind of a lemon. Bake in a pudding-dish, or make it into pies with a bottom crust. Ornament the top of the pies with fancy twists of paste.

CUSTARD COCOANUT PUDDING.

Grate one cocoanut; take a quart of milk, four eggs, and a cup of sugar. Beat sugar and eggs light, then stir in the milk, and last the cocoanut and such flavoring as you may prefer. Pour this into a deep pan lined with paste; put fancy strips of paste across it, and bake lightly.

A NICE ICE CREAM.

Put on the fire a stew-pan containing a quart of nice fresh milk, and while it is coming to the boil beat the yolks of eight eggs and a pound of fine white sugar; when these are well beaten, take off the boiling milk, let it stand to cool five minutes, and pour it very hot over the eggs and sugar; strain this mixture, and add for flavoring any favorite extract, either of lemon, orange, peach or vanilla. Let it stand to get cool, and pour it into the freezer and surround it with layers of ice, pounded fine, and coarse dairy salt, well beaten down, and fill up till within a few inches of the top of the freezer. Now, if you have it you may pour in one quart of pure cream, and beat it with a wooden spoon into the mixture in the freezer. Turn the crank of your freezer briskly if you have a five-minute freezer; if not, turn the can with your hand for fifteen minutes, and then pack round again with ice and salt. Draw off the melted ice and salt water, and fill up again and set away to harden before serving. Two tablespoonfuls of the extract are enough.

LEMON SHERBET.

If a gallon is wanted, take ten fine lemons, or more, if small ones. Place to them three quarts of cold water sweetened, with two and one-half pounds of loaf sugar. Just before placing it in the freezer, beat up the whites of three eggs with a little sugar and stir in. Then place the mixture of lemons, sugar, water and eggs in the freezer, and pack ice and salt around it. It freezes easily, with less trouble than ice cream. Pineapple or orange sherbet is also very nice made the same way.

BISCUIT CREAM IN MOULDS.

One quart of firm clabber and one quart of sweet cream, make it very sweet with white sugar; flavor with vanilla bean boiled in half a cup of sweet milk. Churn all together ten minutes, then freeze in moulds, or in an ordinary freezer.

ORANGE CREAM.

Squeeze the juice of four oranges, and put it with the peel of one into a sauce-pan; add to this a pint of water, half a pound of sugar, and the beaten whites of five eggs. Mix carefully, place it over a gentle fire, or it will curdle, stir it in one direction until it looks thick; strain it through a gauze sieve, and add to it, when cold, the yolks of the five eggs, and a cup of cream or sweet milk. Set it on the fire until hot enough to cook the eggs, or nearly ready to boil them, take it off, stir until cold, and set it on ice, or freeze it as you choose. This is a delicious cream, with or without freezing, and one much used by families in Louisiana.

STRAWBERRY, RASPBERRY, OR BLACKBERRY CREAM FROZEN.

Make a quart of rich custard, with eggs, and sugar and milk; when cold, pour it on a quart of ripe fruit, mash and pass it through a sieve. Add more sugar if required by the fruit, and freeze it.

PEACHES AND CREAM FROZEN.

Peel and stone a quart of nice mellow peaches; put them in a bowl, sweeten them well, and chop very fine. If you have sweet cream, put to the fruit a quart of it; if you have not, take a quart of milk, sweeten it with half a pound of sugar, let it boil, and when boiling, pour it on the beaten yolks of four eggs. When this custard cools, you may add the chopped peaches, which should be well sweetened. Pour all in the freezer and set it where it can be frozen.

BARLEY OR SAGE CREAM FOR INVALIDS.

Wash the sage or barley clean; take a cup of either; put it on the fire with water to cover it; boil it gently until it is soft. While boiling, put in a stick of cinnamon, or any seasoning that is agreeable. When the barley has boiled soft and thick, take it off and strain it; then add to it a rich boiled custard, sweeten it to taste; add a glass of wine, if liked, and serve it frozen, or not, as is liked best by the sick.

FROZEN PEACHES AND CREAM.

Peel and stone nice soft, ripe peaches, sprinkle enough sugar on them to make them very sweet; chop them up fine until they are a pulp, and add to them as much cream as you have peaches ; put them into the freezer and turn it briskly until the cream is well frozen. Figs and other fruits are good served in the same way.

ANOTHER ICE CREAM WITHOUT CREAM.

When cream cannot be procured, a custard made as directed, is a good substitute. To a quart of milk, add sugar until it is *very sweet,* for in freezing it loses some of its sweetness ; let this boil on the fire, when it boils gently, take it off and pour it scalding hot to the beaten yolks of eight eggs ; stir it constantly, but never boil it as the scalding milk will cook the eggs sufficiently ; it should also be stirred while cooling. Flavor with vanilla, or lemon or almond. If with a vanilla bean it is better to boil it in the milk before putting in the sugar. When the custard is cold, put it in the form or freezer. If you have no freezer you can make one, by using a tin kettle with a tight cover. Set this in the centre of a tub that is large enough to leave a space of four or five inches around it; fill the space with layers of cracked ice and coarse salt, a layer of ice last, and cover the whole with a woolen cover for half an hour. Then shake the kettle constantly, after that, until frozen. Cover up till wanted.

ICED CHOCOLATE CREAM.

Grate half a pound of vanilla chocolate, put it in a stew pan with half a pound of sugar, the yolks of eight eggs, and one pint of rich, sweet milk. Stir over the fire until it begins to thicken, strain through a sieve into a basin, add half a pint of whipped cream, and one and a half ounces of isinglass. Mix well and pour into a mould. Set it on ice if the weather is warm.

COFFEE CUSTARD.

Boil one quart of milk with five spoonfuls of white sugar. Beat four eggs separately, throw the whites into the boiling milk for two minutes and dip them out with a skimmer as soon as they are cooked. Beat the four yolks of the eggs with half a cup of corn starch wet with a little cold milk; set it aside until you can put into the hot milk a cup of hot strong coffee; then pour in the mixed corn starch and eggs, give it a little boil and take it off. Last of all, place the pure white boiled eggs on the rich brown of the custard, and you have a beautiful and appetizing dessert. Serve with sponge cake. Some boil the coarsely ground coffee in the milk first and strain it, proceeding after that as in other custards.

LEMON CHEESE-CAKES.

Boil the peel of two lemons until tender, and pound them. Take half a pound of sugar, the yolks of six eggs, and one-half pound of butter. Stir all well together, and add the juice of the lemons last. Lay puff paste in your pans, fill them half full of the mixture, and bake lightly.

ORANGE CHEESE-CAKES.

Boil the peel of four oranges in two waters, to take out the bitter taste. When tender, pound up with half a pound of sugar, one quarter of a pound of butter, and the yolks of six eggs. I make these confections to use up the yolks when I have been using the whites of eggs for icing or white cake. Beat the mixture well and add the juice of the oranges; if

the oranges are large the juice of two will be sufficient to
make two pies. Put puff paste in your pans, fill them half
full of the confection, and bake lightly.

WINE JELLY FROM SPARKLING GELATINE.

Take a package of an ounce, or an ounce and a half of
gelatine, pour upon it a pint of cold water, and let it remain
to soften for an hour or so. When ready to make the jelly,
pour on to the gelatine three quarters of a pint of boiling
water, and stir until the gelatine is dissolved; then add to it
one and a half pounds of white sugar, the juice and grated
rind of one lemon, and a spoonful of any essence. Then beat
the whites of two eggs well, and stir briskly into the
mixture; put it on a gentle fire, let it simmer slowly, take it
off as soon as it boils up, then add a pint of wine and two tablespoonfuls of extract of lemon or vanilla; then strain it through a
jelly bag until it runs clear. Some boil the extract and wine
in the gelatine before straining, but it injures the fine flavor to
do so. Boil the gelatine, the water, the sugar and eggs, and
strain it; after it is clear and still warm, pour in a pint of
wine and set the jelly on ice in summer, or to cool in the
winter. This should give great satisfaction.

YELLOW CUSTARD JELLY FROM GELATINE.

To one ounce of gelatine, soaked in one pint of water, add
a quart of milk; if the weather is warm take a little less milk.
Set the milk and gelatine (or double the quantity of isinglass)
on to get hot, let it give one boil up, then sweeten it, and when
a little cooled stir in the beaten yolks of eight eggs; do not

let the eggs boil up or you might curdle them. Flavor with vanilla or lemon, pour into moulds, and set in a cool place, or on ice to harden.

CALVES' FEET JELLY.

Take two calf's feet, add to them a gallon of water, which you must reduce by boiling to a quart; strain it while hot, and set away to get cold. When cold, take off the fat, and remove any settlings which may be in the bottom. Melt the jelly in a stewpan, and add to it the whites of six eggs, well beaten, half a pint of wine, half a pound of white sugar, the juice of four lemons, and rind of one grated. Boil this a few minutes, and pass it through a flannel strainer. This is a most delicate and nourishing article of diet for the sick and convalescent. If the jelly is dropped upon the sliced peel of a lemon instead of the grated peel, it will look prettier.

CALVES' FEET JELLY MADE WITH GELATINE.

Take three quarts of water, one pint of white wine, six teaspoonfuls of brandy, six lemons, juice and peel, six eggs, the whites slightly beaten, the shells crushed—the yolks not used—three pounds of white sugar, and four ounces of gelatine. First, soak the gelatine in one quart of the measured water; let it remain for one-half an hour. Mix the ingredients named with the other two quarts, and let all boil twenty minutes; strain it through a flannel bag without squeezing. Wet the jelly mould in cold water. Pour the jelly in, and leave it to cool, or put it on ice until wanted.

AMBROSIA OF ORANGE OR PINEAPPLE.

This is a pretty dessert or supper dish. You require a cocoanut and six oranges or a pineapple. Grate the cocoanut, and slice the oranges or pineapple; then in a glass dish lay a layer of fruit, and a layer of the grated cocoanut, until your bowl is full. Strew powdered sugar over each layer of fruit, and on the top, and it is ready.

FLOATING ISLAND, WITHOUT WINE.

Beat the whites of five eggs with a little currant jelly until they are quite thick. Sweeten a pint of cream, add a teaspoon of extract, pour it in the bowl, and then drop your whites of eggs and jelly by spoonfuls on the cream. If you cannot procure cream, you may make a substitute of a custard, made of a pint of sweet milk, yolks of two eggs, and half a cup of white sugar.

EGG-NOG.

Take the yolks of ten eggs; add to them ten tablespoonfuls of pulverized sugar, three pints of new milk, and one pint of the best brandy (whiskey will do). Beat up the whites the last thing, and stir in, after the liquor is poured in.

THE HAND-MAIDEN.

Item 1880

THE MILKMAN.

THIS IS A COW

MILK

Item 1880

44. Ça qui boudé manze boudin. (Celui qui boude mange du boudin.)
"He who sulks eats his own belly." That is to say, spites himself.
The pun is untranslatable."[1]—[*Mauritius*.]

45. Ça qui dourmi napas pensé manzé. (Qui dort ne pense pas à manger.)
"When one sleeps, one doesn't think about eating." [*Mauritius*.]

[1] *Boudin* in French signifies a pudding, in Creole it also signifies the belly. Thus there is a double pun in the patois.

Gombo Zhèbes 1885

PUDDINGS, PIES AND MINCE MEAT.

DIRECTIONS FOR MAKING AND BAKING PIES, TARTS, ETC.

The delicacy of pastry depends as much upon the baking as the making, therefore strict attention should be paid to the following directions:

Puff paste requires a quick, even heat; a hot oven will curl the paste and scorch it.

Tart paste or short paste requires a degree less of heat.

For raised or light crust, the oven may be heated as for puff paste.

When baking with coal, if the fire is not brisk enough do not put on more coal but add a stick or two of hard wood; or if nearly done, put in a stick of pine wood.

FAMILY PIE CRUST, SHORT.

Put a pound of sifted flour into a bowl, work into it half a pound of sweet lard or beef drippings, with a dessertspoonful of salt. When it is thoroughly mixed put to it enough cold water to bind it together. Flour the paste slab, or table, and rolling pin. Take a part of the paste and roll it to less than a quarter of an inch in thickness. This will be quite rich enough for health or taste. A bit of volatile salts, the size of a small nutmeg, dissolved in a little hot water and put to the paste, will make it more light and delicate.

FINEST PUFF PASTE, FOR PUFFS.

Heap one pound of flour in the centre of the breadboard, or slab; make a hollow in the centre; break one egg into it, then add a teaspoonful of salt and a piece of butter the size of an egg. Mix these lightly together with a little cold water, adding the water a little at a time, until the flour is made a nice paste; work it together, and roll it out to half an inch in thickness. Then divide a pound of butter in six parts, spread one part over the paste, then fold it and roll it out again, until you can perceive the butter through; then spread over another part, fold it up, and roll out again, and so continue until all the butter is used, and the paste has been worked over six times. It is now ready for making into pies, puffs, or any other purpose. Flour the slab and rolling-pin, and roll it out to a quarter of an inch in thickness. A marble slab and rolling-pin are best for pastry, and much more durable than wood. After using them, scrape them clean, wash them first with cold water, then pour scalding water over them, and wipe them dry. Have ·a sieve ready to sift any flour you may wish to use; this is but little trouble or delay and it is always best to sift flour. To gild pastry, wet it over when nearly done, with the yolk of an egg beaten with a little milk.

PIE-CRUST.

Three and a half cups of flour, one cup of sweet lard, one teaspoonful of salt, one teaspoonful of baking powder, and a cupful of very cold water. Mix with a knife, using the hands as little as possible. Roll and cut after the crust is on the pie plate.

BUTTERMILK PIE-CRUST—VERY WHOLESOME.

Take a pint of buttermilk, add one large teacupful of lard, one teaspoon of salt, and a teaspoonful of soda, and flour enough to form a soft dough. Mix the lard and flour by rubbing them together; then add the other ingredients. This is a tender and good pie-crust.

BOILED DUMPLING CRUST WITHOUT LARD OR BUTTER—FOR DYSPEPTICS.

Sift a pint of flour in a basin, salt it as usual, then pour on it a fine stream of boiling water from the spout of a kettle, pour it slowly, or you will overflow the flour; mix the flour and hot water with a spoon until it is a nice soft dough that you can handle; then pour it on the biscuit board, which should be well floured; give it two or three turns, and it is ready for the fruit. This is fine for dyspeptics, and altogether lighter and nicer than the old way of mixing with grease.

TO MAKE MINCE PIE MIXTURE.

Weigh two pounds of the chopped meat; put to it two pounds of suet free from strings or skin, and chopped fine; add two pounds of currants, picked, washed, and dried; four pounds of peeled and chopped rich tart apples, with the juice of two lemons, and the chopped peel of one; a pint of sweet wine, and one large nutmeg grated, or teaspoonful of ground mace; three pounds and half of sugar, quarter of an ounce of ground cloves, or allspice, and the same of cinnamon, and a large tablespoonful of salt. Mix the whole well together, put it in a stone pot, or jar, cover it close, and set it in a cool place for use. Mix it well together again before using.

TO FINISH THE PIE MIXTURE.

Pare, core, and chop, not very fine, some tart juicy apples; put to them one-third as much of the prepared meat; stone one pound of raisins, and cut a quarter of a citron in small bits; add a gill of brandy, and enough sweet cider to make the whole quite wet. A peck of apples, pared and chopped, with a quart bowl of the prepared meat, and the raisins, citron, and cider, as above-mentioned, with a large teacupful of brown sugar, is enough to make six or seven pies the size of a dinner plate. A teacupful of fine chopped suet may be added, if liked, or a tablespoonful of butter to each pie, as it is to be baked.

MINCE PIE MEAT.

Take a nice tender piece of beef which is free from gristle, skin or strings. The tongue is used for mince-meat, also the sirloin, the heart, head and skirts; the tongue and sirloin are best. Put the meat in hot water, enough to cover it; boil it gently until turning a fork in it will break it; set it to become cold, then take out all the bone and gristle parts. If the tongue is used peel off the skin, chop it very fine. To this meat, apples, raisins and spices are added, for which see recipe mince pie mixture.

MINCE PIE. HOW TO FILL AND BAKE.

Line a pie dish with a nice puff paste, rolled to twice the thickness of a dollar piece. Put in the *pie mixture* half an inch deep, and spread it to within a finger width of the edge; roll out a puff paste crust, turn a plate the size of the one on which the pie is made on to it, and with a knife cut the paste around the edge of the plate; then take the plate off, make three small incisions with the end of the knife on each side of the middle, take it carefully up and cover the pie with it, press it lightly with the finger against the bottom crust, put it in a quick oven for three-quarters of an hour. The top may be brushed over with the yolk of an egg beaten with a little milk. Pies made in this way should be served warm.

MINCE MEAT, FOR PIES.

Two pounds of beef chopped fine, one peck of apples, two pounds of raisins, two pounds of currants, one pound of citron, one half pound of suet, three pounds of sugar; powdered cinnamon, cloves and nutmeg, a spoonful each. Moisten with a bottle of champagne cider. When you bake the pies, place a spoonful of butter in each pie; but do not put butter in the jar with the meat.

MINCE MEAT, FOR CHRISTMAS PIES.

Boil a fresh beef tongue tender, let it get cold, then chop it fine, and add one pound of suet, one half peck of apples, two pounds of currants picked and washed carefully, one pound of citron sliced, half an ounce each of powdered cloves, allspice, cinnamon and ginger, three pints of cider, with half a pint of brandy; sweeten to taste, then pack away in a crock. Keep it cool, or it will ferment. Add apples when you bake the pie.

MINCE PIE WITHOUT MEAT.

Take one pound of currants, one pound of peeled and chopped apples, one pound of suet chopped fine, one pound of moist brown sugar, quarter of a pound of chopped and stoned raisins, the juice of four oranges and two lemons, with the peel of one lemon chopped. Add of ground mace and cinnamon each, a tablespoonful, and a wine-glass of brandy. Mix all carefully and put in a cool place. Eat this pie hot, and when it is baked, put in a tablespoonful of butter, but put none in the mixture.

MOCK MINCE PIES. VERY GOOD.

Take six crackers, soak them in one and a half cups of warm water, add to them one cup of good brown sugar, one cup of raisins, one cup of molasses, and one-half cup of cider or strong vinegar. Beat in half a cup of butter, season with a lemon and its rind, a nutmeg, one teaspoonful of cloves, and ground cinnamon.

ORANGE PIE.

To the juice and sliced pulp of two large fresh oranges, add the grated yellow rind of one orange. Beat the yolks of three eggs, with a cupful of sugar, and beat the whites to a high froth and add to them a cup of milk. Mix all the above together. Have ready a nice puff paste, and bake the mixture in it.

LEMON PIE.

Grate the rind and express the juice of three lemons; rub together a cup and a half of powdered sugar and three table-spoonfuls of butter; beat up the yolks of four eggs, and add to the butter and sugar, lastly the lemon; bake on a rich puff paste without an upper crust. While the pie is baking beat up the whites of the four eggs with powdered loaf sugar, spread it over the top of the pie when done; then set back in the oven a few moments to brown lightly.

LEMON PIE, WITHOUT CORN STARCH.

The juice and grated rind of a lemon, one cup sugar, two tablespoonfuls water, yolks of three eggs. Bake in a nice crust. Make an icing of the whites and a cup of sugar, pour it over the pie, put it back in the oven, and brown lightly.

LEMON PIE. RICH.

Five eggs, two lemons, one cup and a half of sugar. Beat all together except the whites of three eggs, which you must beat stiff with sugar, and when the pies are cold spread this icing on top and brown lightly. The crust of the pie is made of puff paste, or in any way that is liked; some ladies prefer plain family crust to puff paste.

CRANBERRY PIE OR TARTS.

Pick a quart of cranberries free from imperfections, put a pint of water to them, and put them in a stew pan over a moderate fire; add a pound of clean brown sugar, and stew them gently until they are soft; then mash them with a silver spoon and turn them into a dish to become cold, then make them in pies or tarts. Many persons put flour in cranberry pies; it is a great mistake, as it completely spoils the color of the fruit; but if they are strained and are too thin to jelly, it is well to add a spoonful of corn starch to thicken.

CRANBERRY TART WITH APPLES.

Mix half a pint of cranberries with half a pound of sugar and a spoonful of water; let them simmer a little until soft. Peel and cut thin a half dozen apples; put a rim of paste around a pie plate, strew in the apples, pour the cranberries over the apples and cover with a nice crust. Bake for an hour to cook the apples.

PORK AND APPLE PIE.

Make the crust in the usual manner (for many ways, see directions in this book), spread it over a deep plate; cut nice fat salt pork very thin, and slice some apples; place a layer of apples, then a layer of pork; sprinkle with allspice, pepper, and sugar, between each layer; have three or four layers, and let the last one be apples; sprinkle in sugar and spice; cover with a top crust, and bake an hour. This is a plain and wholesome dish; when the family is large and apples plentiful, it will be an economical way of giving the boys " apple pie."

MOLASSES PIE.

Take one pint of molasses, beat into it three eggs and a large spoonful of butter; pour the mixture into a rich crust, and bake.

A RICHER MOLASSES PIE.

One cup of molasses, one cup of sugar, four eggs, and four tablespoonfuls of butter. Mix together the sugar, butter and eggs, then stir in the molasses. Bake in a rich crust.

HUCKLE OR WHORTLEBERRY PIE.

Put a quart of picked huckleberries into a basin of water, take off whatever floats; take up the berries by the handful; pick out all the stems and unripe berries, and put the rest into a dish; line a buttered pie dish with a pie paste; put in the berries half an inch deep, and to a quart of berries put a teacupful of brown sugar, and half a teacupful of water; dredge a teaspoonful of flour over; throw in a saltspoonful of salt, and half a nutmeg grated; cover the pie, cut a slit in the centre, or make several small incisions on either side of it; press the two crusts together around the edge, trim it off neatly with a sharp knife, and bake in a quick oven for three-quarters of an hour.

BLACKBERRY PIE.

Pick the berries clean; rinse them in cold water, and finish as directed for huckleberries.

BOILED PLUM PUDDING. VERY FINE.

Prepare all the ingredients except the beating of the eggs, the day before making the pudding. Take one pound of grated bread crumbs, pour over them a pint of boiling milk; add a pound of chopped suet, half a pound of butter, one pound of sugar, half a pound of sifted flour, one dozen eggs, one pound of raisins, one pound of currants, half a pound of citron, one tablespoonful of ground cinnamon, one of cloves and allspice, also one grated nutmeg, a glass of brandy, the rind and juice of two lemons. Tie it in a piece of thick unbleached cotton, allowing room for the pudding to swell. Boil five hours. Serve with butter and sugar sauce. This can be steamed over, and be as nice as it was at first.

SIX-OUNCE PLUM PUDDING.

Six ounces of stoned raisins, six ounces washed and dried currants, six ounces of bread crumbs, six ounces of suet and six eggs. Flavor with half a nutmeg, half a lemon, and half a glass of brandy. Mix all these ingredients together, and put the pudding into a mould, or floured cloth, and boil three hours.

CHRISTMAS PLUM PUDDING.

One pound and a half of raisins, half a pound of currants, three-quarters of a pound of bread-crumbs, half a pound of flour, three-quarters of a pound of beef-suet, nine eggs, one wineglassful of brandy, half a pound of citron and orange-peel, half a nutmeg, and a little ground ginger. Chop the suet as fine as possible, and mix it with the bread-crumbs and flour, add the currants washed and dried, the citron and orange-peel cut into thin slices, and the raisins stoned and divided. Mix it all well together with the grated nutmeg and ginger, then stir in nine eggs well beaten, and the brandy, and again mix it thoroughly together, that every ingredient may be moistened; put it into a buttered mould, tie it over tightly, and boil it for six hours. This pudding may be made a week before using, boiled in a cloth, and hung up in a dry place, and when required put into a saucepan of boiling water and boiled for two hours or two hours and a half, then turned out, and served with sauce as above.

ANOTHER CHRISTMAS PUDDING.

One pound of raisins, one pound of currants, one pound of suet, three-quarters of a pound of bread-crumbs, one pint of milk, ten eggs, three-quarters of a pound of citron and orange-peel mixed, one small nutmeg, one glass of brandy. Stone the raisins and divide them, wash and dry the currants, and cut the peel into slices. Mix all these with the bread-crumbs, flour, and suet chopped very fine, add the grated nutmeg, and then stir in the eggs well-beaten, the brandy, and the milk. When the ingredients are well blended, put it into a mould, tie a floured cloth over it, and boil it six hours. When done turn it out, and serve with brandy and arrowroot sauce.

RICH PLUM PUDDING WITHOUT FLOUR.

One pound and a half of grated bread, one pound and a half of raisins, one pound and a half of currants, one pound of beef-suet, peel of one large lemon, three ounces of almonds, a little nutmeg or mixed spice, sugar to taste, three quarters of a pound of candied orange, lemon and citron, eight or nine eggs, half a pint of milk, two wineglassfuls of brandy. Stone the raisins, wash and pick the currants, chop the suet very fine, and mix with them a pound and a half of grated bread; add the candied peel cut into shreds, the almonds blanched and minced, and the mixed spice and sugar to taste. When all are thoroughly blended, stir it well together with eight or nine   ell-beaten eggs, two glassfuls of brandy, and half a pint of milk, tie it in a cloth, and boil it for five hours or five hours and a half, or divide it into equal parts, and boil it in moulds or basins for half the time.

COTTAGE PLUM PUDDING

One pound and a half of flour, four or five eggs, a pinch of salt, a little nutmeg, one pound of raisins, half a pound of currants, sugar to taste, and a little milk. Make a thick batter with five well-beaten eggs, one pound and a half of flour, and a sufficient quantity of milk. Then add the currants washed and picked, the raisins stoned, a little nut-

meg and sugar to taste. Mix all well together, and boil it
in a basin or floured cloth for quite five hours. The peel of
a lemon grated, and a few pieces of citron cut thin may be
added.

CHEAP PLUM PUDDING.

Take a cup of chopped suet, a cup of raisins, a cup of currants and citron mixed, a cup of sweet milk, two eggs, a cup
of molasses, and a teaspoonful of soda ; add to this three and a
half cups of sifted flour or bread crumbs, and a little salt.
Boil three or four hours. Serve with hard sauce of beaten
butter, sugar and nutmeg; or with butter, sugar and wine
sauce. This is inexpensive, but is modeled after the most
excellent recipes. The quantity suits a small company.

PLAIN PUDDING WITHOUT EGGS OR WINE.

One pound of chopped and stoned raisins, half a pound
of suet, one pound of flour, a cup of bread crumbs, two tablespoonfuls of molasses, a pint of milk or nutmeg grated, and a
lemon peel chopped. Cut the suet very fine and mix it with
the flour; add the bread crumbs, lemon and nutmeg, with
the stoned raisins, to a pint of milk ; mix all together and put
in the molasses ; keep it closely covered in a cool place. When
it is wanted, pour it in a floured cloth and boil it five hours.
Serve with rich sauce.

PLAIN PLUM PUDDING FOR CHILDREN.

One pound of flour, one pound of bread crumbs, three
quarters of a pound of stoned raisins, three quarters of a pound
of currants, three quarters of a pound of suet, four eggs, and

milk to moisten, say about one pint. Let the suet be finely chopped, the raisins stoned, the currants well washed, picked and dried. Mix them with the other dry ingredients, stir all well together; beat and strain in the eggs, and add just enough of the milk to make it mix properly. Tie it up in a well floured cloth, put it into boiling water, and boil for five hours. Serve with butter and sugar sauce, or wine sauce.

SWEET POTATO PUDDING.

Take one pound or a pint of hot boiled sweet potato, pass it hot through a sieve—the finer the better. To this add six eggs well beaten, three-fourths of a pound of butter, and a pound of sugar; flavor with grated lemon rind, and a little brandy. Make a paste around the dish, pour in the sweet potato mixture, and bake. Sprinkle finely pulverized sugar over the surface of the pudding. This is a Southern dish, and fit to grace the table of an epicure.

BAKED SUET PUDDING. ECONOMICAL AND WHOLESOME.

To a pound of flour, add by degrees six ounces of finely chopped suet, four eggs, together with as much milk as will make a firm batter. Beat all together hard, until the last moment before placing it in the oven. Pour it into a buttered dish, and bake. Serve as soon as done, with plain syrup, or butter and sugar sauce.

LEMON PUDDING. VERY NICE.

Six eggs, three lemons, six tablespoonfuls of corn starch, and one large spoonful of butter. Cook the corn starch in a pint and a half of water, and stir in the butter. Let it get cool, and then stir in the yolks of the eggs, the juice of the lemons, and the grated rind; also one cup of sugar. Bake this lightly in a pudding dish, and when cold pour it over a meringue, or icing, made with the whites of the eggs, and sufficient sugar to make a thick icing. Put it back into the oven, and let it brown lightly.

TEMPERANCE ICED CABINET PUDDING FOR SUMMER.

This is usually made in oval tin moulds, with a tight-fitting cover. Small moulds are the best. Cut some sponge cake about half an inch thick; shape it nearly to the mould; dilute a tablespoonful of any favorite extract, and pour it on to the cake. Then commence to fill up the mould in layers of currants, seedless raisins, sliced citron, and chopped almonds, then a layer of cake, until it is full. Make ready a custard of one pint of milk, the yolks of two eggs, a quarter of a pound of sugar, and half a teaspoonful of extract of lemon, rose, or almonds; let it simmer a little, but not enough to curdle, as it will certainly do if allowed to stay too long on the fire. When it simmers, take it off, and let it cool a little. When only lukewarm, pour it over the fruit and cake in the mould. Cover tightly, and bury it in ice and salt. It is, when well made, a most exquisite dessert.

SOUFFLÉE PUDDING.

Take a pint of milk, a cup of flour, one spoonful of sugar, and a piece of butter as large as an egg. Scald the milk, flour, and butter together. After the batter becomes cold, stir in the yolks of five eggs, and just before baking, stir in the whites. Bake in a quick oven, and serve with sauce.

OMELETTE SOUFFLÉE PUDDING.

Beat the whites of ten eggs to a stiff froth. Beat the yolks with three quarters of a pound of powdered sugar, and the juice and grated rind of a lemon. Mix all together lightly. Butter a thick-bottomed dish which will just hold the pudding; put it immediately in the oven, and bake it fifteen or twenty minutes. Serve it just as it comes from the oven. It should quiver like a golden jelly when served. If baked too long, it will be spoiled. The oven must not be too hot, or it will scorch; the heat should be as usual to bake pies.

VERY RICH PUDDING.

Line a deep pie dish with puff paste, having first buttered it thoroughly; place on this a layer of jam, then a layer of custard, then jam, then custard, until the dish is nearly full, leaving the custard layer at the top. Bake for twenty minutes in a moderate oven, let the pudding cool, beat up the whites of the eggs that were used for the custard into a stiff whip with a little powdered sugar, pile the whip on as high as possible, and serve.

PARISIAN PUDDING.

Lay slices of sponge cake at the bottom of a glass dish, spread over them a layer of preserve (red or black currant is very good for the purpose), place over that more slices of sponge cake, then another layer of jam. Do this until you have filled the dish. Pour over it sufficient sherry to soak the cake properly, then beat up the whites of four eggs with sufficient powdered loaf sugar to make it a very stiff froth, with which to cover the top of the cake completely, and bake.

BIRDS'-NEST PUDDING.

Take half a package of gelatine, using a little more than half the quantity of water given in the receipt for making jelly; in all other respects use the same proportions. When ready to strain put it into a large oval dish (a meat dish is nice); fill it nearly to the edge; then set it away to harden. Take some egg-shells that you have broken just the end off in getting out the egg; make a blanc-mange of corn starch; flavor it with vanilla, and sweeten; put this into the shells before it cools and hardens at all; set the eggs on end in a vegetable-dish so that they will stand top up, being careful not to let the blanc-mange run out. Cut some very thin yellow parings off the lemon rind, stew them in a little sugar and water; when cold lay each piece separately in a circle on the jelly, making two or three nests. Break open the egg-shells, take out the blanc-mange, and lay it in groups like eggs inside the nest. This makes a very pretty dish, and is very good. Ivy sprays or myrtle wound around the edge of the dish improves the appearance.

BIRD'S-NEST PUDDING.

Peel and core six mellow apples; line a pudding dish with pastry; lay the apples in the bottom of the dish, and stick long narrow strips of citron around them. Stir to a cream a pint of powdered sugar, and half a pint of butter. Beat separately the yolks and whites of eight eggs; mix them with the butter and sugar, season with nutmeg, place it on the fire, and stir until it is hot; then pour it over the apples, and bake immediately. It can be eaten warm or cold. Do not allow the top to brown too soon. It should be covered with a pan, when first put into the oven, to prevent this.

CROWS'-NEST WITH CINNAMON.

Cut nice sour cooking apples into a baking dish, small or large as you need; put sugar, cinnamon, and lemon over them; throw in a cup of water, and cover the dish with a crust of light pie crust. Put it in the oven, and bake it until the apples are tender. Be sure to cut air-holes in the crust before putting in to bake. Eat it with cream and sugar, or hard sauce of butter and sugar; beat together until firm enough to slice like butter. Grate a little nutmeg over the sauce, if cinnamon is not liked.

COTTAGE PUDDING.

One tablespoonful of butter, one cup of sugar, one cup of milk, two eggs, one teaspoonful of soda, one pint of sifted flour, two spoonfuls of cream of tartar; mix like cake; bake quickly in shallow tin pans; dredge the top with powdered sugar, which gives a nice crust to all puddings and cakes. Sauce to accompany this pudding : one tablespoonful of butter, one cup of powdered sugar, lemon extract for seasoning, or lemon juice, with half a pint of boiling water. All beaten together until it foams.

COUNTRY BATTER PUDDING WITH FRUIT, CHEAP AND NICE.

This is a pudding which requires no paste and is a nice way to use fruit, such as pie-plant, berries, strawberries, peaches, etc. To a quart of buttermilk add one egg, a large teaspoonful of soda, a little salt, and flour enough to make a thick

batter. Pour it over a quart of chopped fruit, such as mentioned, beat it a little, tie it tightly in a bag, drop it in a kettle
of hot water, and let it boil two hours. Serve with sugar and
cream. This pudding may be poured into a cake pan and
baked, if not convenient to boil it. Put in plenty of fruit.

RICE MERINGUE PUDDING.

Boil half a cup of rice in a quart of milk until it is thoroughly done. Sweeten to taste, and let it cool. Beat in
the yolks of four eggs. Flavor with lemon rind or essence
and nutmeg. Bake in a pudding-dish. When cool, pour
over it the whites of your eggs, beaten with a cup of white
sifted sugar. Bake light brown. Season to taste with lemon,
rose or vanilla.

APPLE MERINGUE.

Select handsome pippin apples if you can get them, pare
and core them whole, put them in the oven with a little water
in a deep dish, and let them cook a little but not enough to
break. When plumped, take them out and let them get
cold ; then fill the center of each apple with jelly. Make an
icing of the whites of eggs, beaten with sifted sugar, and
carefully cover each apple with it, wetting the knife while
smoothing the icing. Sift a little sugar over them and put
them in the oven to harden, but not to brown; too much heat
will cause the jelly to melt.

A CHEAP AND DELICATE PUDDING.

Take a tablespoonful of butter, a cup of sugar, a cup of
milk, two eggs, and a pint of sifted flour. Put into the
flour a small teaspoonful of soda and two teaspoonfuls of

cream of tartar; sift this in carefully, and set the flour aside.
Beat the eggs, yolks and whites together, briskly until they
foam; add to the eggs two tablespoonfuls of water; beat
them sharply again until the tissues of the eggs thoroughly
blend with the water, mix the sugar and butter together; add
the eggs, beat again, then pour in the flour which will make
a stiff batter; lastly, thin this with the small cup of milk
(sweet milk is the best), then bake in shallow pans and
serve with lemon sauce, or a rich wine sauce if that is
preferred.

A QUICKLY MADE PUDDING.

Split a few crackers, lay the surface over with raisins, and
place the halves together again; tie them closely in a cloth,
and boil them fifteen minutes. Serve with a rich sauce of
butter, wine, sugar and nutmeg.

ANOTHER QUICKLY-MADE PUDDING.

Get a light, square loaf of bread, split it in three or four
horizontal slices; strew in between the slices cut-up raisins or
currants; tie it up again; boil half an hour, and serve it with
a rich sauce. There are few better puddings made with so
little expense or trouble.

DELICIOUS BREAD PUDDING.

Butter some slices of bread, cut thin, and lay them in a
dish, with currants and citron between; pour over it a
quart of milk, with four well-beaten eggs, and sugar sufficient
to sweeten to taste, and bake. Serve with sauce. It is easily
made, and very nice. It is good hot or cold.

CHEAP GINGERBREAD PUDDING.

Take a half cup of butter, rub it up with three and a half cups of flour, one cup of milk, one cup of molasses, and one teaspoonful of saleratus. Steam three hours, and serve with a rich sauce.

A FRENCH FRIED PUDDING.

Beat four eggs to a quart of milk, sweeten and flavor to taste, cut slices of baker's bread and steep them until thoroughly saturated, then fry in hot butter and serve. Half this quantity for a small family.

MY OWN PUDDING.

Let a quart of milk be set on to boil; while it is getting hot, mix a cup of maizena or corn starch with enough cold water to form it into a thick batter; add to this a cup of white sugar and the yolks of four eggs; take the milk off and stir eggs, maizena, and sugar, into the milk; beat all together a few minutes, then pour the mixture into a baking dish and bake it lightly about ten minutes, or long enough only to cook the eggs; then take the pudding out, and while hot put over it a layer of jelly or jam; beat up the whites of the eggs with a cup of sugar, put this over the jelly and brown.

MARLBOROUGH PUDDING.

Take half a pound of grated apples, half a pound of fine white sugar, half a pound of butter, six eggs well beaten, the peel of one lemon grated, and the strained juice of two; line the dish with pie paste, put the pudding in, and bake in a quick oven.

MARLBOROUGH APPLE TARTS. VERY FINE.

Quarter, and stew a dozen tart apples. To each teacup of this pulp, rubbed through a sieve, add a teacup of sugar, half a cup of melted butter, the juice and grated rind of two lemons, a cup of milk, four eggs and half a nutmeg Beat all together and bake in pans lined with pastry, with a rim of puff paste around the edge. This is an old and always good recipe.

BAKED APPLE DUMPLINGS.

Make a nice pie crust, raised with yeast, or not, as you desire ; divide it into six parts, and roll each part thin ; have ready six good-sized tart apples, pared and cored ; fill up the cores with sugar and butter. Close the dough neatly around the apples, and turn that side down in a deep dish. If they are made with raised dough they should stand one hour ; if with unleavened paste, sprinkle some sugar over them, also a little ground cinnamon or other spice, and set them in the oven to bake. Spread a little batter over each of the dumplings as they go to the oven. Put plenty of spices, nutmegs, cinnamon and mace. Throw a little water in the dish, and bake three-quarters of an hour. Wine, or sugar and butter sauce is a great improvement, but it is very good without it.

PLAIN TAPIOCA CREAM.

Boil the pearl tapioca as you do rice ; when cool sweeten it to the taste, and grate nutmeg over it. Pour rich cream over it and serve.

TAPIOCA CREAM.

Soak two teaspoonfuls of tapioca for two hours in a little cold water. Boil a quart of milk, and to it add the tapioca, the yolks of three eggs, well beaten with a cup and a half of sugar; give it one boil, and set it away to cool; do not boil it long, or the eggs will curdle. Beat the whites of the eggs, and put them on top, or boil them in a little of the milk and put it on the cream. Set it on ice until wanted. This is a delicate and nourishing cream for convalescents, or invalids who require nourishing food.

A NICE SUPPER DISH.

Take one pint of cream, whip it until stiff, and one ounce of isinglass boiled and strained in about a pint of water. Boil it until reduced to half a pint. Boil in this water and isinglass, a vanilla bean, and when nearly cold, take out the bean, add four ounces of sugar, and when this is blood warm, stir in the cream. Eat with whipped cream.

RICE-MILK FOR CHILDREN.

To every quart of milk, allow two ounces of rice. Wash the rice and put it with the milk in a close-covered stew-pan, set it over a slow fire, and let it simmer gently for one hour and a half. It will scorch on a fierce fire.

NICE RICE CUSTARD.

Take two tablespoonfuls of boiled rice. If it is very dry, wash it with a little warm water. Put it in a pan, add a tablespoonful of butter, three or four eggs beaten light, a quart of sweet milk, sugar enough to make it quite sweet, and one cup of picked and seeded raisins. Flavor with nutmeg and essence of lemon or vanilla. Bake lightly. Do not allow it to remain in the oven long, as the milk will become watery and thus destroy the jelly-like consistency of the custard. It is a nice and cheap dessert for children. The raisins may be omitted if they are objectionable.

APPLE POT PIE.

First, the pastry : Rub into a pint of flour a heaping spoonful of lard. Strew in a little salt, and work it until the mass becomes numberless little globules and balls. Then moisten with cold water, and press them together until they adhere, and your pastry is made. It must not be kneaded or worked over at all. Let any cook try this method, and he will find it the best and easiest way to make fine leaf paste, and he will never again countenance the old rolling, larding, butter-spreading system.

Now for the fruit : Pare, core and quarter one dozen apples. Put them in a baking pan, with one large cup of sugar, one tablespoonful of spices, two of molasses and one of butter ; add water until the fruit is nearly covered, and put it in the oven to bake and stew, and brown. When the apples begin to soften, dredge in a little flour, for the juice, though plentiful, must not be watery. Roll out the pastry. Cut the cover to suit the pan, and make the trimmings into dumplings, which must be dropped at intervals among the fruit. Fold the pie cover in half, make several oblique incisions for openings, lay it on and brown it lightly. Serve on a dish like peach cobler. Like that substantial dessert, it may be eaten with cream.

SPANISH MOSS.

In goblin looms,
Depending from the many-elbowed arms
Of gnarled oaks, thou weavest Druid charms
Under weird moons!

Thy night-mare hug
Stifles the moaning of the dying pine;
The cedars know that strangler's cord of thine,
O vegetable Thug.

Thy robes of rags
The mightiest monarchs of the woods must wear,
And wreathe their crowns with locks of thy grey
hair
Like a Witch-hag's.

What ghostly foods
Sustain thy spectral sap, thy phantom breath?
Thou Succubus, thou eldritch Life-in-Death,
Thou Vampire of the Woods!

L. HEARN.

DEAD SEA FRUIT.

Item 1880

PRESERVES, SYRUPS AND FRUIT JELLIES.

HINTS ON PRESERVING.

Preserving kettles should be broad and shallow, with a handle on each side. If you wish to preserve in small quantities, use a small kettle. A charcoal furnace is most desirable in warm weather, as you can put it where you like, and thus avoid the heat of the kitchen. Slow, gentle boiling is absolutely necessary in preserving and pickling

Crushed or loaf sugar should be used for preserves, as it is less liable to ferment during the long hot summer.

Jelly bags may be made of cotton, linen, or flannel, and can be made like an old-fashioned reticule, with a string through the top, to close and suspend it while dripping.

It is a mistake to think dark fruits, like raspberries, strawberries, etc., can be preserved equally well with brown sugar, for the color of this sugar makes the preserves dark, or rather *dingy*, which is the proper word.

Glass is best for keeping preserves in, as they may be examined without opening the jars. When first put up they should be corked tightly, and dipped into coarse melted sealing-wax.

TO MAKE PRESERVES.

Most fruits are much easier preserved than jellied. Weigh the fruit, and to each pound of fruit the usual rule is a pound of sugar; make a syrup of the sugar with a half pint of water to each pound of fruit. Boil it clear, then put in the fruit and cook it well, and boil gently till the fruit is clear.

TO GREEN FRUIT FOR PICKLING OR PRESERVING.

Put vine leaves under, between, and over the fruit in a brass kettle, and over the leaves sprinkle a teaspoonful of beaten or ground alum; cover the fruit to be greened, with water, and boil it gently with the leaves and alum; if not a fine green, take more leaves and dust a little saleratus over them. Spread them out to cool when green, and proceed to preserve or pickle them as desired.

TO PRESERVE PEACHES.

Select white clings if you desire to preserve them whole. Yellow peaches make the most transparent preserve, but cannot always be procured. If white clings are convenient, peel and weigh them, and to each pound of fruit put one pound of sugar and half a pint of water. Put the syrup to boil, clarify it with an egg, and as it boils remove the scum. Keep the peaches in cold water all the time the syrup is boiling, as water keeps the fruit in good color, while leaving it exposed darkens it. When the syrup has boiled clear, put in the peaches; let them boil gently for half an hour, then take them out on a dish for two hours; put them back in the syrup and boil again until they are clear; they are then done, and you can put them in jars and pour the syrup over them, and cork and seal up for future use.

ANOTHER WAY TO PRESERVE PEACHES.

Peel, cut and weigh six pounds of peaches; take six pounds of fine white sugar, throw the sugar on the peaches until they are well covered, and let them stay all night. Early in the morning add three pints of water, and boil all together for one hour. Skim carefully, and then take the peaches out on a large dish, still keeping the syrup gently boiling, and skimming it as it boils. Lay the peaches in the sun on dishes for at least two hours, to harden. Taking the fruit out of the syrup a few times improves it, giving it firmness and transparency. Now replace the peaches in the syrup, and boil gently until they are clear. Cut peaches are much more easily kept than peaches preserved whole, but they are not so highly flavored. Cut fruit does not require so much boiling as whole fruit; this should be remembered in preserving.

PRESERVED CITRON.

Pare off the green skin and all the soft part of the rind, then cut the firm part in strips, or any shape you fancy. Allow a pound and a quarter of sugar to each pound of rind; line your porcelain kettle with grape-vine leaves and fill with the rind scattering a little pulverized alum over each layer. Cover with vine-leaves three thick, pour on water enough to reach and wet these and cover with a close lid. Let them heat together for three hours, but the water must not actually boil. Take out the rind, which will be well greened by this process, and throw at once into very cold water. Let it soak for four hours, changing the water for fresh every hour. Then make a syrup, allowing two cups of water to every pound and a quarter of syrup. Boil and skim until no more scum comes up; put in the rind and simmer gently nearly an hour. Take it out and spread on dishes in the sun until firm and almost cool. Simmer in the syrup for half an hour; spread out again, and when firm put into a large bowl and pour over it the scalding syrup. Next day put the syrup again over the fire, add the juice of a lemon and a tiny bit of ginger-root for every pound of rind. Boil down until thick, pack the rind in jars and pour over it the syrup. Tie up when cool.

TO PRESERVE PEARS.

Take small rich pears, and boil them gently in water until they will yield to the pressure of the finger. They must not be soft, or they will not preserve well. Take them out when a little boiled; let them cool, and pare them neatly, leaving a little of the stem on, as well as the blossom end. Make a syrup of a pound of sugar to a pound of fruit, and when it is boiling hot, pour it on the pears; next day boil them in the syrup till clear, and bottle them for use.

PINEAPPLE PRESERVES.

Take fine pineapples, cut off all the rough parts, and each apple in quarters, shaping each piece alike. Boil the pine-apples in just enough water to cover them, and put to this water all the cuttings, so as to make the syrup as rich in flavor as possible. When the pieces are tender, take them out, weigh them, and make a syrup of a pound of sugar to each pound of fruit, allowing a cup of the water the pineapples were boiled in, to each pound of fruit. Strain the water over the sugar, mix it, and let it boil fifteen minutes by itself ; skim it, and put in the pineapples, letting them boil until they are clear and perfectly tender. Pears done in this way make a delicious preserve. The usual way of putting them in the syrup without previous boiling, makes them little better than sweetened leather, as it makes them tough and stringy.

TO PRESERVE CRAB APPLES, GREEN.

Wash the apples and boil them in a very little water; cover them with vine leaves, while on the fire simmering, and they will then be very yellow. Take them out and spread them on a large dish to cool. Pare and core them, put them back in the kettle, with fresh leaves to cover them. Hang them over the fire, or on the stove in a preserving kettle until they are green ; then take them out of the pot, let them cool, weigh them, and allow a pound of sugar to a pound of fruit. Put only water sufficient to dissolve the sugar, as the fruit having been already boiled, will require very little water—a small cupful to each pound being quite enough. Boil this syrup, skim it, and put in your green apples, and boil them until they are clear and tender. Put the apples in jars, turn the juice on to them, and when cold tie them up or rather seal them in this Southern climate.

PEACH OR APPLE COMPOTE, FOR DESSERT.

Dissolve and boil a pound of loaf sugar in a pint of water; skim it, pare six or eight apples, or a dozen peaches, throw them into the boiling syrup, and cook until tender and transparent. Lemon improves the apples, but peaches are better without it.

PRESERVED HUCKLEBERRIES.

Take them just as they begin to ripen, pick and weigh them, allow a pound of fruit to a pound of sugar, then stew them until quite clear, and the syrup becomes thick. These make nice tarts when fruit is scarce.

PLUM PRESERVES.

Get plums before they are dead ripe; allow a pound of sugar to a pound of fruit, dissolve and boil the sugar and water (allowing half a pint of water to a pound). Boil the syrup until it is thick, then put in the plums and boil them until they are transparent; then put them in sealed jars.

FIG PRESERVES.

Boil the sugar and water syrup as directed in previous recipe. Let the figs be firm, not dead ripe, or they will boil to a mass. They should be laid in alum the day before they are to be preserved, then taken out, washed, and put into the boiling syrup. Boil for three hours, or until transparent; then bottle as usual and seal up with wax.

MYRTLE ORANGE PRESERVE, OR HOME-MADE LIMES.

Pluck the oranges before they turn yellow; they should be a rich dark green; cut a hole in the stem end and take out all the white pulp and seeds; scrape them carefully, grate the rind so as to break the oil cells, and allow the strong oil to escape. Wash them and throw them into strong salt and water; let them stay in it for three days, then soak them in fresh water three days. When you wish to preserve them you must boil them in clear water, slowly, in a brass kettle;

cover them with a few orange leaves while boiling, which will green them, and boil until they are tender, then set them up to cool. Weigh as much sugar as you have oranges, and allow pound for pound; boil the syrup clear and then put in the oranges; boil gently for half an hour, or until green and yellow. Use only a silver spoon in making this preserve.

TO MAKE WATERMELON PRESERVES.

Take the firm outside rind of a watermelon; scrape off the green and cut out the soft inside; cut the rind into any shapes you choose, stars, crescents, diamonds, etc. After they have been boiled in alum and leaves to green and harden, weigh them and make a syrup of a pound of sugar to a pound of fruit, with a cup of water to each pound. Boil the syrup clear, and put in the cut rinds, and boil them until transparent. Flavor with ginger for green color, and lemons for the yellow. If the rind is wanted yellow, you must boil it with fresh lemon skins and a little saffron before preserving it.

ANOTHER WATERMELON RIND PRESERVE.

In a bucket of cold water, put a handful of lime, stir it in, and when it settles clear, pour it over the watermelon rind you intend preserving; let it stay in the weak lime-water one day. Soak it a few hours, and get the taste of the lime from the rind, then put it in alum water and scald for ten minutes. Put grape-leaves in with the alum water while scalding; they will make the rind green. Take the rind from the alum, and put it in cold water for a few hours, and when cold, boil it in strong ginger tea until it is soft, and tastes of the ginger. Make the syrup of one and a half pounds of sugar, to each pound of rind, and a half pint of water to each pound of sugar. Let it cook slowly, skim it, and when it looks clear, put in the rind, and let it cook slowly until clear and transparent. The rind should be cut into beautiful shapes, and preserved with care. This is a little trouble; but the housekeeper is amply repaid by the beauty of the preserve.

TO MAKE ANY KIND OF FRUIT JELLY.

Wash and drain the fruit, put it in a stone jar, and put the jar into a kettle of water over the fire; let it boil, but see that none of the water gets into the fruit. When the fruit is tender, it will begin to break; pour it now into a flannel bag, but do not squeeze it—that will make the jelly cloudy. To each pint of juice strained, add one pound, or one pound and a quarter of white sugar, and the half of the beaten white of an egg. Boil this rapidly, skim, but do not stir the syrup, as stirring breaks its continuity and prevents its jelly-ing. Boil it twenty minutes, and try a little in some cold water, to find out if it jellies; if it does not, boil it a little longer. Too much boiling, or too slow boiling, injures jelly and makes it ropy. Too much sugar will cause jelly to grain; the quantity used must be in accordance with the requirements of the fruit, acid fruit requiring more sugar and dead ripe fruit less. Red currants take more sugar than black currants; they also take more time to boil to a jelly. A little practice *and a few mistakes* will make any one who takes pleasure in cooking a good jelly-maker and preserver.

CRAB APPLE JELLY.

This is the best of all apple jellies. Wash the apples, cut them up, remove all defects, remove the seeds and the blossom end, but do not pare them. Lay them in your preserving-kettle, and cover them with water; then boil them until they are soft, but do not let them mash up from too much boiling. Drain off all the water, and mash the apples with the back of a silver spoon. Put this in a jelly bag, and place a deep dish under it to collect the juice. To every pint of the juice allow a pint of loaf sugar; boil it and skim it. It will be ready to dip out into tumblers in half an hour, if you have complied with these directions. Always dip jelly out with a *silver* spoon, as any other kind darkens fruit. I have seen preserves rendered very dark by putting in them a new-tinned dipper. You must be careful of these things if you desire your confections to be elegant.

LEMON JELLY. A BEAUTIFUL DISH.

Set an ounce of isinglass in a pint of water on the stove in a stew-pan; stir the isinglass until it dissolves. Let it boil a few minutes, then add a pint of lemon juice sweetened with a pound and a half of sugar, or a little more, if it is wished very sweet. Stir this in with the rinds of six lemons, and boil all together. After boiling for about five minutes, put a teaspoonful of saffron in to color it yellow, and strain through a flannel bag. Fill your jelly-glasses with it; when cool, it is a most beautiful dish for a collation.

BLACKBERRY JELLY.

Cook the fruit till tender in a little water; throw off the water, bruise and strain the fruit, and to each pint of the juice add one pound of white sugar. Put it now in a preserving-pan, and boil it *rapidly*, but do not stir it while boiling, as that breaks the jelly; skim it carefully, and when it jellies, pour it into tumblers or small jars. I have made two pecks of berries into jelly in two hours. This is said for the benefit of young housekeepers who often boil their jelly too slowly and too long, which makes it ropy.

APPLE JELLY *WITHOUT WATER.*

Pare and core the fruit, which should be juicy and tart. Lay the apples in a vessel to cook without putting in any water; cover them closely, and cook until properly soft; strain the juice, and add three-fourths of a pound of sugar to a pint of apple juice. Beat in the white of an egg to clarify the jelly, and skim it as it boils; try it and, as soon as it jellies, take it from the fire and put it in glasses.

JAM.

This can be made from almost any kind of ripe fruit. Blackberries, strawberries or raspberries are specially suited for this form of preserve. You must weigh your fruit (say blackberries), and allow three quarters of a pound of good sugar to each pound of fruit. Crush the fruit and sugar, with a biscuit beater, until they are well mashed; add a gill of water to each pound of fruit; boil gently (not rapidly like jelly) until it becomes a jelly-like mass, and when done, put it into glasses, or small earthenware pots, and when cold, cover up like jelly. This is an excellent medicine in summer for dysentery; but if intended for invalids, you must spice it, and add a gill of brandy—fourth proof—to each pound of jam.

TOMATO JAM.

Take nice ripe tomatoes, skin them, take out all their seeds, but save the juice to put with the sugar. Weigh the fruit, and to each pound, add three-fourths of a pound of sugar; boil some lemons soft, take one for each pound of tomatoes, mash them fine, take out the pips, and put the lemons to the sugar and tomatoes; boil slowly and mash the jam smooth with a silver spoon. When smooth and jelly-like, it is done. Put it away in glasses carefully.

ORANGE MARMALADE. DELICIOUS.

Quarter the oranges and take out the seeds and white strings. To every pound of pulp, add a cup of cold water, and let it stand thus for twenty-four hours, Boil some of the peel in several waters until quite tender; then to each pound of pulp, add one-quarter of a pound of boiled peel, and one and a quarter pounds of white sugar. Boil this slowly until it jellies, and the bits of peel are quite transparent.

ORANGE MARMALADE *MADE WITH HONEY*.

Quarter a dozen large ripe oranges; remove the rind, seeds and filaments, but save all the juice. Put the juice and pulp into a porcelain kettle, with an equal quantity of strained honey, adding one-third as much sugar as honey. Boil until very thick, sweet and clear. When cold, put it in small jars.

MARMALADE.

This jam can be made of any ripe iruit, boiled to a pulp with a little water; the best are peaches, quinces, apples, oranges and cranberries. It is usual to crush the fruit. Put in three quarters of a pound of sugar to a pound of fruit, add a *little* water (half a cup to a pound), and boil until it is a jellied mass. When done, put it in glass or white earthenware.

TO CANDY FRUIT.

After peaches, quinces, plums, or citron, have been preserved, take them from the syrup, and drain them on a sieve. To a pound of loaf sugar, put a small cup of water, and when it is dissolved, set it over a moderate fire, and let it boil; when it boils, put in the fruit to be candied, and stir continually until the sugar granulates over the fruit; then take it up, and dry it in a warm oven. If not sufficiently candied, repeat the operation.

CANDIED PUMPKIN.

Peel a piece of pumpkin, and cut it in thin slices. Make a nice, thick syrup of brown sugar and water, and put the pumpkin into it, with a little of the juice of the lemon. Boil this until the pumpkin is nicely candied. Mace, or other spices, may be used for flavoring instead of lemon, if preferred. It may be eaten hot with meats at dinner, and is equally nice, when cold, for supper or lunch.

ORGEAT SYRUP WITHOUT ORANGE FLOWERS.

Make a syrup of a pound of sugar to every pint of water; boil this a few minutes, skim it clear, and when cold, to every four pounds of sugar used, allow a gill of orange water, or rose water, and two tablespoonfuls of pure essence of bitter almonds. Serve it in iced water.

ORANGE SYRUP.

This syrup is so easily made, and oranges are so abundant here, that it is advantageous to make this syrup in the season of orange harvest, in Louisiana. To make it, you must select ripe and thin-skinned fruit; squeeze the juice, and to every pint, add a pound and a quarter of white sugar; boil it slowly, and skim it as long as any scum rises; you may then take it off, let it grow cold, and bottle it. Be sure to secure the corks well. This is nice for a summer drink for delicate persons; it is also very convenient for pudding sauces, as half a cup of this syrup, mixed with melted butter, is admirable, where wine is not used. The flavor is so fine, it requires very little spicing to make it agreeable.

BRANDIED FRUITS, WINES AND CORDIALS.

PEACHES IN BRANDY.

Soak fine peaches in lye until you can remove the fuzzy outside; wipe them, and turn them into cold water. When you have prepared as many as you desire, weigh them, and to every pound of fruit, put three quarters of a pound of white sugar. Make a syrup like that for preserves, only using less water; boil the peaches in the syrup until they are tender; then take them out of the kettle, and place them in jars; fill up the jars with a brandy syrup, made of a pint of brandy, to a pint of the sugar syrup from the peaches. Cook them very carefully, and dip the mouths of the jars in rosin melted, and keep them in a cool dark place.

APRICOTS IN BRANDY.

Peaches and apricots are brandied the same way. Gather them as fresh as possible. Apricots should be taken from the tree as soon as ripe, as they soften so rapidly. Rub each one with a coarse towel, but do not peel it. Make a syrup of half the weight of the fruit in sugar, and just water enough to dissolve it. When the syrup is prepared and hot, put in the apricots, let them simmer until tender; then take the fruit out, and place it on dishes, then expose them to the sun, or in a warm oven to dry and harden. Boil the syrup again, after the fruit is out, until it is quite rich and thick. Skim it carefully. When the apricots are cold and firm, put them in white earthen preserve-jars, and fill up with syrup and brandy, half and half. Tie up with bladder skin.

PEACHES AND APRICOTS IN BRANDY.

Take nice smooth peaches not too ripe, put them in a vessel and cover them with weak lye; take them out in two hours, and wipe carefully to get off the down and outside skin, and lay them in cold water. Weigh the fruit, add their weight in sugar, and half a pint of water to each pound of sugar; boil and skim this syrup, put in the peaches; when the syrup is clear of scum, let them boil for twenty minutes or half an hour, then take them out and lay them on dishes to cool. Boil the syrup for an hour longer, or until reduced one-half and quite thick. When cold, put the peaches or apricots in jars, and cover them with equal quantities of the syrup and French brandy. If it is apricots, cook them very gently, or they will come to pieces in the syrup; ten minutes is long enough to stew them before bottling.

APRICOT AND PEACH WINE.

Mash the apricots or peaches in a mortar, remove the stones, and to eight pounds of the pulp, add one quart of water; let this stand twenty-four hours; then strain, and to each gallon of the juice, add two pounds of loaf sugar. Let it ferment, and when perfectly clear, bottle it. Peach wine is very nice, and may have a few of the kernels added for flavoring, if wished.

RAISIN WINE WITH ELDER FLOWERS.

Boil six pounds of raisins in six gallons of water. When soft, rub them to a pulp, and pass through a colander to get rid of the stones; add this pulp to the water it was boiled in, put to it twelve pounds of white sugar and a half-pint of yeast. When clear, suspend half a pound of elder flowers in it to flavor the wine; withdraw the flowers and bottle off the wine.

ORANGE AND LEMON WINE.

Take the outer rind of one hundred oranges pared, so that no white appears; pour upon them ten gallons of boiling water, let it stand ten hours and keep slightly warm. While still warm, add the juice of the oranges, mixed with twenty-five pounds of lump sugar, and a few tablespoonfuls of good yeast; let it ferment five days, or until the fermentation has ceased, and the wine is clear; then bottle. Lemon wine can be made in the same way.

SOUR ORANGE WINE.

Take one gallon juice of sour oranges, four gallons of water, and twenty pounds of sugar. Boil this mixture in a vessel large enough to hold it, and skim it as it boils until no more scum rises. Pour it into a flannel bag and strain; then put it in a cask, adding to it a quart of uncooked orange juice. Let it ferment, and when clear, bottle it. This will require about six months to finish. Keep in a cool closet or cellar during fermentation.

MIXED FRUIT WINE.

Cherries, black currants and raspberries, mixed together, make good wine. Dilute the juice and add the usual amount of sugar, and let it ferment; then bottle.

A SUPERIOR BLACKBERRY WINE.

Bruise your berries, measure them, and to every gallon, add a quart of boiling water. Let this stand twenty-four hours, stirring it three or four times during this time. The third day strain off the juice, and to every gallon of this strained liquor, put two pounds of refined sugar. Cork it tight, and let it stand until cool weather; when you will have a wine that you will never voluntarily be without.

BLACKBERRY WINE.

Mash the berries without boiling them; strain the juice, and to six pints of juice, add two pints of water and three pounds of sugar. Mix thoroughly and put it in a wide-mouthed stone jar to ferment. Cover it carefully with a cloth, to keep out all insects; open it and skim it every morning; then cover it up again carefully, for much of the bouquet of the wine depends on this. When it ceases to ferment, strain it and put it in a demijohn; do not cork it tightly, as it must have a little air, but cover the loose stopper with a piece of muslin or tarlatan, to keep out the insects. It will be ready to bottle in two months.

BLACKBERRY CORDIAL

Simmer nice ripe blackberries in water enough to cover them, and when they are tender take them out, mash them and strain them through a strong cloth; get all the juice out you can by squeezing, but do not let the pulp and seed come through the bag. Now add a little of the water they were boiled in, however not more than two tablespoonfuls to each pint of strained juice. To every pint of this liquor, add one pound of loaf sugar, one teaspoonful of mace, same of cloves and cinnamon. Boil all these together a few minutes, and strain it again to free it from the spice. When this syrup is cool, add to each pint a wineglass of good French brandy. If you cannot get brandy, substitute rum or whiskey, remembering to use twice as much as you would brandy. This is excellent for children during the prevalence of summer complaints, and an excellent tonic for all debilitated persons.

BLACKBERRY CORDIAL.

Select fine, ripe fruit. Squeeze the berries without boiling, and to a quart of the strained juice, put a pound of loaf sugar; boil it for half an hour, and add a quart of brandy, some cloves and cinnamon, when on the fire. If the fruit thickens too rapidly while boiling, throw in a cup of hot water.

RASPBERRY CORDIAL.

Squeeze the fruit through a flannel bag, and to every quart of juice add a pound of loaf sugar; put it in a stone jar and stir it constantly for half an hour; allow it to stand for three days, then strain it again and add to each quart of juice a quart of fine brandy.

TOMATO WINE.

Let the tomatoes be very ripe ; mash them well, let them stand twenty-four hours, strain, and to every quart of the tomato juice, add a pound of white sugar. This will ferment and should be allowed to do so, only keep it carefully covered from the flies. Skim off the foam as it rises, and when the liquor becomes clear, bottle it. This wine will be a pleasant acid, and should be served with sugar and water, in the tumbler with the wine.

ANOTHER TOMATO WINE.

Bruise your berries, or small tomatoes; measure the juice, and add two pounds of sugar to each gallon; put it in a cask, adding two gallons of water to each four gallons of juice. Let it ferment like blackberry wine.

A FINE TEMPERANCE BEVERAGE.

To the juice of a dozen lemons put one pound and a half of double refined sugar, and a picked quart of raspberries or strawberries; pare a ripe pineapple and slice it, put over it half a pound of sugar, stir the lemon juice with the sugar, crush in the berries, slightly bruise the pineapple and chop it up in small pieces., Put the lemon juice in a large punch bowl, add to it three quarts of ice water, then put in the strawberry and pineapple juice, stir it until all the sugar is dissolved, and then set it on ice. Serve in punch glasses.

CHAMPAGNE PUNCH.

Add to the above mixture a bottle of champagne, and a bottle of white wine, and you have a very delicious punch for festive occasions.

GHOSTESES.

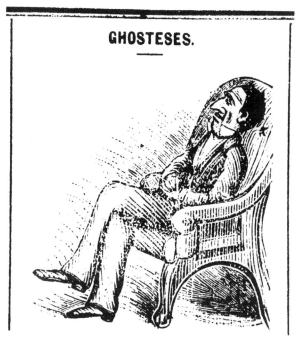

Item 1880

211. Moin pas ka prend dithé pou fièvre li. (Je ne veux pas prendre du thé
pour sa fièvre.)
"I don't propose to drink tea for his fever."[1]—[*Martinique.*]

[1] Or better still: "I don't intend to drink tea just because he has the fever." In
other words, "I don't intend to bother myself with other people's troubles." .... The
tea referred to is one of those old Creole preparations taken during fevers—the *tisànes*
of the black nurses: perhaps the cooling sassafras, or orange-leaf tea administered to
sufferers from *dengue* in New Orleans.

DELICATE PREPARATIONS FOR THE SICK AND CONVALESCENT.

BARLEY WATER.

Take four large tablespoonfuls of picked and washed pearl barley, and put it into a porcelain-lined kettle with two quarts of boiling water; let it boil slowly until the water is reduced one half, then strain it and season with salt, lemon, or sugar as may be agreeable to the sick.

TOAST WATER.

Cut two or three slices from a loaf of wheat bread, toast them very brown; while hot, put them in a small pitcher, and pour over them a pint and a half of water. Sugar may be added if liked, but when the stomach is affected it is better without it.

TO MAKE WATER GRUEL OF CORN MEAL OR OAT MEAL.

Put a quart of water on to boil in a stew-pan. Take a tablespoonful of sweet corn meal, or oatmeal, make it into a batter with milk and salt, stir it in the boiling water and let it boil gently for half an hour. When served it may be sweetened and nutmeg grated over it If wanted for a strengthening nourishment, a bit of butter and a glass of wine or brandy may be added. This is generally given after a dose of castor oil, or an emetic. Use very little salt.

BEEF TEA FOR INVALIDS.

Cut tender lean beef into small pieces, free it from fat and strings, fill a junk bottle with it, cork it tight and put it in a kettle of boiling water; let it boil three hours. In that way you obtain the juices of the meat undiluted. This is especially nourishing and good when the stomach can bear but little liquid.

MILK PUNCH AS A RESTORATIVE.

Take a large tumbler (it should hold a pint), half fill it with chopped ice, add to it a large tablespoonful of white sugar, beat it a little with the ice, then pour on it a wineglass of gin, rum or brandy, and fill up with fresh milk. It is generally very acceptable to an invalid who refuses other stimulants.

APPLE TEA, OR WATER, FOR INVALIDS.

Cut some ripe apples into thin pieces, add the peel of a fresh lemon; pour boiling water over them and let it stand till cold, then sweeten with loaf sugar. This is a grateful and cooling drink.

BAKED APPLES.

Bake them in a tin roaster, as iron discolors them; pour molasses over them and bake until soft. This is good for opening the bowels of patients who are a little constipated.

ARROW-ROOT BLANC MANGE FOR THE SICK.

Put a pint of new milk to boil; make a smooth batter with an ounce of Bermuda arrow-root and cold milk; add a little salt, and when the milk is boiling stir in the batter; let the fire be gentle or it will scorch, sweeten this with fine white sugar, and let it boil a few minutes; flavor with lemon, or orange water, or if lemon is objected to, boil a vanilla bean in the milk before the arrow-root is put in. Take it off the fire pour it in a mould and set it on ice; serve jelly or jam with the blanc mange, or eat it with cream if it agrees with the invalid.

ARROW-ROOT BLANC MANGE.

Mix in a little cold water, two tablespoons of arrow-root; sweeten a pint of milk with white sugar and put the arrow-root in the milk. Let it boil a few minutes, stirring it constantly; take it off, and if desired, you can let it cool and mould it in a bowl or jelly form; or it is nice to be eaten warm. Colored jelly over it is an improvement when moulded.

ARROW-ROOT GRUEL.

Mix a tablespoonful of arrow-root, or for an infant, half as much; when mixed with cold water, stir in it half a pint of boiling water. Season with salt, sugar or nutmeg.

MILK PORRIDGE.

Make a quart of milk boiling hot; make a tablespoonful of flour into a batter with cold milk, add a little salt and stir it in the boiling milk, stirring it constantly for five minutes while it boils; flavor with anything agreeable. Sweetened with loaf sugar, and nutmeg grated plentifully over it, it will make a most excellent remedy for looseness or dysentery.

TAPIOCA MILK.

Wash and soak a large tablespoonful of tapioca, put it to a quart of sweet milk, add a little salt, cover it, and set it over a gentle fire for an hour. Take it up, add sugar and nutmeg, or cinnamon to taste.

TAPIOCA PUDDING.

Put a coffee-cup of tapioca (soak it well first) into a pint and a half of milk, set it where it will get hot slowly, take it off when it boils, and when cool add four well-beaten eggs; flavor with lemon and peach, sweeten it to taste, and bake for an hour in a hot oven. If this is wanted for one person, take half the quantity of tapioca and milk.

WHITE WINE SYLLABUB.

Season a pint of milk with sugar and wine, but not enough wine to curdle the milk. Fill your glasses nearly full, and crown them with sweetened whipped cream. Season the cream with extract of lemon.

SYLLABUB.

Take the juice of a large lemon, and the yellow rind pared thin; one glass of brandy, two glasses of white wine, and a quarter of a pound of powdered sugar. Put these ingredients into a pan, and let them remain one night; the next day add a pint of thick cream, and the whites of two eggs beaten together; beat them all together to a fine froth, and serve in jelly glasses.

WINE SANGAREE OF PORT OR MADEIRA.

Take half a glass of water, sweeten it with a tablespoonful of white powdered sugar, and stir well until dissolved; add a gill of Madeira or port, some nutmeg grated and pounded ice. Serve with lady-cake or pound-cake, cut small.

STEWED PRUNES FOR SICKNESS.

Wash the prunes, put them in a stew pan, cover them with water, and to each pound of prunes put a cupful of clear brown sugar. Cover the stew pan and let them boil slowly, until the syrup is thick and rich.

WINE JELLY FOR THE SICK.

Take one pint of Madeira wine, one pint of water, and one ounce of isinglass dissolved in a teacupful of water. Let the wine and water be boiling hot, then stir into it the dissolved isinglass, and sugar to taste; make it quite sweet; let it come to a boil, try it by taking a little in a saucer, and if it is not a good jelly when cold, boil it until it is so; if lemon is allowed, use the juice of two to flavor this jelly.

JAUNE MANGE.

Break up and boil an ounce of isinglass in rather more than half a pint of water until it is melted; strain it; then add the juice of two large oranges, a gill of white wine, and the yolks of four eggs beaten and strained; sweeten to taste, and stir it over a gentle fire till it boils up; dip a mould into cold water and pour the preparation into it.

CARRIGEEN MOSS FOR INVALIDS.

Wash and pick a tablespoonful of Irish moss and put it into a tin cup; pour on it half a pint of boiling water, and set it on the coals for a short time; when it is all dissolved add sugar and nutmeg to taste. This may be made with milk, to resemble custard, and is very nourishing. Delicate infants may be fed on it when they will take no other nourishment.

TARTARIC ACID AS A SUBSTITUTE FOR LEMONS.

If lemons cannot be obtained to make either lemonade or jellies for the sick, tartaric acid is a good substitute, and if used in conjunction with the extract of lemon, is a very agreeable one.

LEMON JELLY WITHOUT LEMONS.

Take a box of Cox's gelatine, pour over it one quart of boiling water, and stir until it is dissolved. Add a teaspoonful of tartaric acid, and four cups of sugar; let it dissolve and bring it to a boil; while boiling, stir in the beaten whites of three eggs; let this boil up once again, and take it off the fire; when nearly cool, add to it a tablespoonful of good extract of lemon. Strain the mixture into moulds or cups, and set it in a cool place, or on ice, to become firm. It must be cool, or it will not jelly.

ORANGE SHERBET.

Squeeze the juice from a dozen oranges; pour boiling water on the peel, and cover it closely. Boil water and sugar (a pint to a pound) to a syrup; skim it clear; when all are cold, mix the syrup, juice and peel with as much water as may be necessary to make a rich orangeade; strain it, and set the vessel containing it on ice. Or it may be made the same as lemonade, using one lemon with half a dozen oranges.

STRAWBERRY SHERBET.

Take fifteen ounces of picked strawberries, crush them in a mortar, then add to them a quart of water; pour this into a basin, with a sliced lemon, and a teaspoonful of orange-flower water; let it remain for two or three hours. Put eighteen ounces of sugar into another basin, cover it with a cloth, through which pour the strawberry juice, after as much has run through as will; gather up the cloth, and squeeze out as much juice as possible from it; when the sugar is all dissolved, strain it again. Set the vessel containing it on ice, until ready to serve.

ALMOND CUSTARD.

Blanch and beat four ounces of almonds fine, with a spoonful of water; beat a pint of cream with two spoonfuls of rose water, add them to the yolks of four eggs, and as much sugar as will make it pretty sweet; stir it over a slow fire till it is of a proper thickness, but do not boil. Pour it into custard glasses.

SPONGE CAKE PUDDING.

Stale sponge or other plain cake may be made into a nice pudding by crumbling it into a little more than a pint of milk and two or three beaten eggs, and baking it. Sauce—sugar and butter beaten together.

GERMAN LADIES' FINGERS.

Beat one hour the yolks of five eggs with half a pound of sugar; add half a pound of blanched almonds pounded fine, the yellow part of one lemon grated. Mix well; add half a pound of flour very gradually. Roll out the paste, and cut it into strips the length and size of the forefinger; beat lightly the whites of two eggs, and wet the fingers.

DIMPLES.

Beat the whites of three eggs very stiff, add gradually three quarters of a pound of sugar, and beat till it is well mixed. Blanch almonds, and cut them into pieces as small as peas, and stir them into the egg and sugar—three quarters of a pound of almonds for three eggs. Drop the mixture in spots as large as a half penny on white paper upon a tin, and bake in a cool oven.

DELICATE RUSKS FOR CONVALESCENTS.

Half a pint of new milk, and one cup of hop yeast; add flour to make a batter, and set the sponge at night. In the morning add half a pint of milk, one cup of sugar, one of butter, one egg, one nutmeg, and flour to make it sufficiently stiff. Let it rise, then roll it, and cut it out; let it rise again, and then bake.

CHOCOLATE CARAMELS.

Half a pound of chocolate, three pounds of dark brown sugar, one-eighth pound of butter, a small teacup of milk; season with vanilla, or grated lemon or orange-peel. Boil it very quickly over a hot fire, stirring constantly. When it becomes hard on being dropped into water, take it off the fire and stir for a few moments before pouring into buttered dishes. Before it is quite cool, cut into little squares. Those who like the caramel very hard need not stir it, as this makes it "sugary." The grated peel should not be put in till the caramel is taken from the fire.

COFFEE, TEA, CHOCOLATE, ETC.

TO MAKE CHOCOLATE.

Scrape the best chocolate; allow for each square, or large spoonful of ground chocolate, half a pint of milk or milk and water; let it boil a few moments, then put it on the back part of the stove, and it is ready when wanted.

TO MAKE CHOCOLATE ANOTHER WAY.

Scrape or grate the chocolate, take a heaping tablespoonful for each cup to be served; allow half a pint of milk or milk and water to each heaping spoonful of chocolate. Make the milk hot, rub the chocolate to a smooth paste with the cold milk, then stir it in the boiling milk. Let it boil up once; cover it and set it back in a place where it will keep warm. It is now ready to serve. Toasted biscuit or rolls should be served with it. Sweeten the chocolate unless you use the prepared chocolate.

TEA—GREEN AND BLACK.

Scald your tea-pot *always* before putting in the tea; throw out the scalding water and allow a teaspoonful of tea to each person expected to drink it; turn on half a pint of boiling water at first, and let it steep—green tea requires about five minutes, black tea ten minutes. After this, pour on more boiling water, according to the number of persons. Mixed black and green tea is considered a more healthful drink than green tea alone.

COFFEE CREAM.

Take three cups of good clear coffee, sweeten it well and boil with it a pint of cream until reduced one-third.

COFFEE.

Old Java, and Mocha are the best coffees. A coffee roaster is the best thing to roast coffee in, but an iron pot is very good ; coffee should be dried gradually before being roasted. "Dripped" coffee is the French mode, but many make it in the old-time way by boiling. It is a matter of personal taste, not to be interfered with in this "land of the free." To make dripped coffee we grind a cupful for four persons, put this ground coffee in the top of the dripper and pour on half a pint of boiling water. It is served with boiling milk at breakfast.

CAKES AND CANDY.

Item 1880

157. *Lagniappe c'est bitin qui bon. (Lagniappe c'est du bon butin.)
 "Lagniappe is lawful booty."[1]—[*Louisiana.*]

[1] *Lagniappe,* a word familiar to every child in New Orleans, signifies the little present given to purchasers of groceries, provisions, fruit, or other goods sold at retail stores. Groceries, especially, seek to rival each other in the attractive qualities of their *lagniappe*; consisting of candies, fruits, biscuits, little fancy cakes, etc. The chief purpose is to attract children. The little one sent for a pound of butter, or "a dime's worth" of sugar, never fails to ask for its *lagniappe.*

Gombo Zhèbes 1885

CANDIES AND CREAM DROPS.

CREAM CANDY.

To make cream candy, take two pounds of light brown sugar, one teacup of water, two tablespoonfuls of butter, one of vinegar, and two of flavoring extract. Dissolve the sugar in the water, but do not stir it. Set it on to boil, let it boil briskly for twenty minutes, then try it by dropping a spoonful in a glass of cold water. If cooked enough to pull, butter some dishes and pour it into them; when cool enough to handle, pull it until it becomes as white as cream.

ANOTHER CREAM CANDY.

Three cups of sugar, half a cup of vinegar, and one-third of a cup of water. Boil together until it is thick and will harden when dropped into a cup of water. Butter some dishes, and just before filling them, add to the candy some flavoring essence; if you put this in earlier it will boil out. Pour the candy on the buttered dishes, and when a little cool prepare to pull it until it is white and light, which it will be if made by these directions.

POP-CORN CANDY.

Take a cup of molasses, one and a half cups of brown sugar, a tablespoonful of vinegar and a lump of butter the size of an egg. Boil until thick. Chop two cups of popped corn rather fine, put it into the boiling candy, and pour it all on the buttered plates. Cut in squares to be eaten without pulling.

CHOCOLATE PASTE FOR CAKE.

Boil one-half a cup of chocolate in one-half cup of milk, add a cup of sugar, and boil until it is a thick paste.

LOUISIANA ORANGE FLOWER MACCAROONS.

Take a coffee cup of the freshly gathered petals of the orange, cut them with a pair of scissors into two pounds of dry, sifted white sugar; this keeps their color fresh. Beat the whites of seven eggs to a stiff froth, and add to the orange flowers and sugar. Drop this mixture on white paper in small cakes, and bake in a slow oven; do not let them brown.

MOLASSES CANDY.

Take two quarts of molasses and one pound of brown sugar, and the juice of two lemons. Let the molasses and sugar boil moderately, without stirring it, for two hours; if not thick enough to pull then, let it boil a little longer; then put in your extract, for if this is put in earlier the flavor will boil away. When the candy is cool enough to handle, put into the pot a pint of parched pinders, or pecan meats, or almonds cut up. Butter two large dishes and pour out the candy.

MOLASSES CANDY OF OUR GRANDFATHERS' TIME.

One quart of molasses, and butter the size of an egg. Stew over a brisk fire till it will harden on being dropped into cold water. A teaspoonful of essence of wintergreen should be added when it is almost done. Pull it while warm, with buttered hands, and cut in sticks.

SUGAR CANDY.

Six cups of sugar, one of vinegar, one of water, one spoonful of butter, and one teaspoonful of soda dissolved in a little hot water. Boil all together without stirring, for half an hour. Flavor with lemon or vanilla. This is very good when "pulled" like the old-fashioned molasses candy, or it may be cooled on a buttered plate.

TO BLANCH ALMONDS.

Pour boiling water on them and let them remain in it a few minutes. Remove the skins, throw the almonds into cold water, drain them from the water, but do not wipe them.

EVERTON TOFFY.

In a shallow vessel, melt together one pound of brown sugar and one-quarter of a pound of butter. Stir well together for fifteen minutes, or until the mixture becomes brittle when dropped in water. Lemon or vanilla flavoring should be added before the cooking is complete. Butter a flat plate, pour the toffy on it to cool, and when partly cold, mark it off in squares with a knife ; it can then be easily broken.

LEMON DROPS.

Upon half a pound of finely powdered sugar pour just enough lemon juice to dissolve it, and boil to the consistency of thick syrup. Drop this in plates, and put in a warm place to harden. Or pour four ounces of lemon juice on one pound of loaf sugar, with four ounces of rose water. Boil to a syrup, add grated lemon peel and proceed as in the first recipe. By adding raspberry syrup, instead of lemon juice, you have raspberry drops.

POP-CORN BALLS.

To six quarts of pop corn boil one pint of molasses about fifteen minutes; then put the corn into a large pan, pour the boiled molasses over it, and stir it briskly until thoroughly mixed. Then with clean hands make into balls of the desired size.

COCOANUT CANDY.

Four cups of water, two and a half cups fine white sugar, four spoonfuls of vinegar, and a piece of butter as large as an egg; boil till thick, or about three quarters of an hour. Just before removing, stir in one cup of desiccated cocoanut, and lay in small, flat cakes on buttered plates, to cool and harden.

MARSH-MALLOW PASTE.

Dissolve one-half pound of gum arabic in one pint of water; strain it, add half a pound of fine sugar and place over the fire, stirring constantly till the sugar is dissolved and all is the consistency of honey, then add gradually the whites of four eggs, well beaten; stir the mixture till it becomes somewhat thin and does not adhere to the finger; pour all into a pan slightly dusted with powdered starch, and when cool divide into small souares. Flavor to the taste, just before pouring out to cool.

CHOCOLATE CREAM DROPS.

Mix one-half a cup of cream with two of white sugar, boil and stir fully five minutes; set the dish into another of cold water, and stir until it becomes hard ; then make into small balls about the size of marbles, and with a fork roll each one separately in the chocolate, which has in the meantime been put in a bowl over the boiling teakettle and melted. Put on brown paper to cool. Flavor with vanilla, if desired. This amount makes about fifty drops.

CHOCOLATE CARAMELS.

Two cups of sugar, one of molasses, one of milk, one spoonful of butter, one of flour, and half a pound of bakers' chocolate. Butter your saucepan, put in the sugar, molasses and milk, boil fifteen minutes; add butter and flour, stirred to a cream, and boil five minutes longer; then add the chocolate grated, and boil until quite thick. Butter tin flat pans, and pour in the mixture half an inch thick, and mark it in squares before it gets hard.

CHOCOLATE CARAMELS.

One pint of new milk, quarter of a pound of grated chocolate, and one cup and a half of white sugar. Boil all these together until it will pull like candy; try a little, and if stiff enough to pull, pour it on a buttered dish, and mark it off in squares with a knife as it cools. It will break easily when cold.

CHOCOLATE KISSES.

One-half pound of sugar, one ounce of finely-powdered chocolate. Mix the sugar and chocolate together, and then mix it with the whites of four eggs well beaten. Drop on buttered paper, and bake.

BOSTON CARAMELS.

One pint bowl of bakers' chocolate grated, two bowls of yellow sugar, one bowl of New Orleans molasses, one half a cup of milk, a piece of butter the size of a small egg and vanilla flavoring; boil about twenty-five minutes. It should not be so brittle as other candies. Pour in buttered tins, and mark deeply with a knife.

KISSES, OR SUGAR DROPS.

Rub to a cream half a cup of butter, with one cup of sugar. Add three well-beaten eggs, half a pound of sifted flour, and half a grated nutmeg. Drop this mixture on buttered tins, by the spoonful; let them be two or three inches apart; sprinkle sugar over them and bake quickly.

SUGAR KISSES.

Beat the whites of three eggs to a froth, then stir in powdered white sugar, a little at a time, till you have formed a very thick batter. Add two or three drops of essence of lemon. Wet a sheet of white paper, and lay it on a tin, and drop this mixture upon it in lumps about the size and shape of a walnut. Set them in a cool oven, and, as soon as their surface is hardened, take them out, and remove them from the paper with a broad-bladed knife. Let the oven cool still more, then place these little cakes, laying the flat part of two together, on a sieve, and return them to the oven, where they must remain for fifteen minutes before they are done.

HOW THEY DO IT.

Item 1888

THANKSGIVING.

Item 1880

DANDY-TRAPS.

Item 1880

249. Ptit lasoif ptit coco, grand lasoif grand coco. (Petite soif, petit coco;
grande soif, grand coco.)

   "Little thirst, a little cocoa-nut; big thirst, a big cocoa-nut."'—
[*Mauritius.*]

46. Ça qui fine goûté larac zamés perdi son goût. (Celui qui a goûté l'arac
n'en oublie jamais le goût.)

   "He who has once tasted arrack never forgets the taste."—
[*Mauritius.*]

CHEFS D'ŒUVRE.

THE SERVICE OF WINES.

Cosmopolite Louisiana is undoubtedly the wine-drinking section of the Union, and a word as to the manner of serving the wines which play no small part in the discussion of "La Cuisine Créole," will not be out of place.

The inherited French taste of the greater portion of the population, and the education by contact of the American element, makes claret the universal table wine. The climate, too, renders this wine particularly palatable, and during the long heated term it is seldom absent from the table of even the most economical. At the restaurant it is the exception to see a person dining without a bottle of *vin ordinaire*, while for breakfast, during hot weather, white wines of the lighter kinds are much used.

As to the manner of serving wines at dinner the following menu will convey the most adequate idea:

With Soup, ...	Sherry.
"　Fish, ...	White Wine.
"　Entrées, } . .	Claret, vin ordinaire.
"　Entremets, }	
"　Roast, } . . .	Champagne.
"　Salad, }	
"　Dessert, . .	Fine Claret or Burgundy.
"　Café Noir, ...	Cognac.

At large dinners in New Orleans a great deal of wine is
served, and you will be expected to drink with your raw
oysters, a light white wine ; with soup and hors d'œuvre, sherry
or Madeira ; with fish and entrées, a heavy white wine ; with
relevés and entremets, a good claret followed by a *Ponche
Romaine*, which is the turning point of the feast, or rest ;
after which will be served with the roast, champagne ; game
and salad, fine claret or burgundy, and with dessert, café noir
and liqueurs.

The most acceptable distribution of wines at a plain dinner—
which we think should never be over five, or six courses at
most—is given below. It is one which has the endorsement
of the best authorities :

With Oysters,	White Wine.
" Soup,	Sherry or Madeira.
" Fish,	Heavy White Wine (not absolutely necessary.)
" Entrées,	Champagne.
" Roast or Game, } " Salad, }	Fine Claret.

with the usual after-dinner wines as preferred.

GRAND BRULÉ A LA BOULANGER.

[*From a Gourmet.*]

The crowning of a grand dinner is a brûlé. It is the *piece
de résistance*, the grandest *pousse café* of all. After the coffee
has been served, the lights are turned down or extinguished,
brûlé is brought in and placed in the centre of the table upon
a pedestal surrounded by flowers. A match is lighted, and

after allowing the sulphur to burn entirely off is applied to the brandy, and as it burns it sheds its weird light upon the faces of the company, making them appear like ghouls in striking contrast to the gay surroundings. The stillness that follows gives an opportunity for thoughts that break out in ripples of laughter which pave the way for the exhilaration that ensues.

Pour into a large silver bowl two wineglasses of best French brandy, one half wineglass of kirsh, the same of maraschino, and a small quantity of cinnamon and allspice. Put in about ten cubes of white sugar; do not crush them, but let them become saturated with the liquor. Remove the lumps of sugar, place in a ladle and cover with brandy. Ignite it as before directed, then lift it with the contents from the bowl, but do not mix. After it has burned about fifteen minutes serve in wine glasses. The above is for five persons, and should the company be larger add in proportion. Green tea and champagne are sometimes added.

PETIT BRULÉ.

Take an ordinary-sized, thick-skinned orange; cut through the peel entirely around the orange like the line of the equator, then force off the peel by passing the handle of a spoon between it and the pulp. Into the cup thus formed put two lumps of sugar and some cinnamon, and fill with fine French brandy (cognac), and ignite it the same as the above and pour into glasses. The brûlé will be found to have a pleasant flavor given to it by the orange.

GIN FIZZ—No. 1.

One-half tablespoonful of sugar, a little lemon juice, two wineglassfuls of seltzwater, one wineglassful "Tom," or Holland gin, teaspoonful of white of an egg, and ice; shake well and strain into fancy glass.

CIN FIZZ—No. 2.

Use celestine vichy instead of seltzwater, and the yolk instead of the white of an egg.

JAMAICA RUM PUNCH.

Make same as whiskey or brandy punch. Santa Cruz, same.

PONCHE ROMAINE.

Two wineglassfuls of water, one wineglassful of whiskey, half wineglassful of Jamaica rum; sugar and lemon to taste. Shake, and use plenty of ice. Strain and serve in fancy glass.

PARLOR PUNCH (MORAN'S).

One tablespoonful of white sugar, a little lemon juice, two wineglassfuls of English black tea, one wineglassful of whiskey, one-half wineglassful of Jamaica rum, a little raspberry syrup, plenty of small ice. Shake well, and strain in fancy glass.

ROYAL COCKTAIL (MORAN'S OWN).

One lump sugar; two dashes of Boker's bitters, or Angostura bitters, two tablespoonfuls of Belfast ginger ale; one wineglassful of whiskey, or brandy; one lemon peel; plenty of ice. Shake well, and strain in fancy glass.

NEW ORLEANS TODDY.

One lump of sugar, one tablespoonful of water, one wine-glassful of whiskey or brandy, one lump of ice. Use small bar glass.

VIRGINIA TODDY.

Two lumps of sugar, two sherry or wineglassfuls of water, same of whiskey, plenty of ice; shake well and strain into small bar glass, with grated nutmeg on top.

WHISKEY, BRANDY, OR GIN COCKTAILS—New Orleans Style.

Two dashes of Boker's, Angostura or Peychaud bitters—either will make a fine cocktail. One lump of sugar, one piece of lemon peel, one tablespoonful of water, one wine-glassful of liquor, etc., with plenty of ice. Stir well and strain into a cocktail glass.

ANOTHER WAY—SPOON COCKTAIL.

One lump of sugar, two dashes Angostura bitters, one piece lemon peel, one lump of ice. Serve plain in small bar glass with spoon.

WHISKEY PUNCH, PLAIN—Use Regular Bar Glass.

Two wineglassfuls of lemon or lime juice, half a table-spoonful of sugar, one-half wine glass of whiskey, and plenty of ice; shake and strain into punch glasses.

FANCY PUNCH.

Half a tablespoonful of sugar, a little raspberry, a little lemon, lime, and pineapple juice. Two parts of water to one of whiskey or brandy, and plenty of ice. Shake and strain in punch glass; put fruits in season when serving; use regular bar glass.

CHAMPAGNE COCKTAIL.

One glass of wine, two dashes of Angostura bitters, and two bits of lemon peel. Put the bitters and lemon peel in the glass first, then pour in the wine, after which put in one small spoonful of sugar, and stir.

MINT JULEPS. MADE OF WHISKEY, BRANDY, GIN, ETC., ETC.

One-half tablespoonful of powdered sugar, one wineglass of water, one of whiskey, brandy or gin, etc., and one-half dozen sprigs of mint. Use plenty of fine ice, and decorate with strawberries and pineapples, or any fruit in season.

SQUIRTS. Use Large Glasses.

Whiskey, brandy, gin, white wine, claret or catawba makes good "squirts." Fill the glass half full of fine ice, put in one tablespoonful of white sugar, a little raspberry syrup, strawberries and pineapple; pour in your liquor, and fill up with seltzer water. Stir all rapidly.

HOW TO MIX ABSINTHE IN EVERY STYLE.

Plain absinthe: half a sherry glass of absinthe; plenty of fine ice, with about two wineglassfuls of water. Put in the water, drop by drop, on top of absinthe and ice; stir well, but slowly. It takes time to make it good.

ABSINTHE AND ANISETTE.

To half a wineglass of absinthe put two or three dashes of anisette. Mix same as above.

ABSINTHE AND SUGAR.

To half a wineglass of absinthe, put a teaspoonful of powdered sugar and mix same as above.

SUISSISSE.

To half a wineglass of absinthe, put half a tablespoonful of orgeat syrup, plenty of fine ice; add water, mix well and strain into a fancy glass.

POUSSE CAFÉ.—No. 1.

Maraschino, curaçoa, kirsh-wasser and brandy in equal parts of each; dash with Peychaud bitters serve in liquor glass.

POUSSE CAFÉ.—No. 2.

Bernardine, brandy and curaçoa, in equal parts of each; dash with Angostura bitters.

POUSSE CAFÉ.—No. 3.

Brandy, maraschino and cassis, in equal parts; dash with Boker's bitters.

POUSSE CAFÉ.—No. 4.

La grande chartreuse (yellow), brandy (French), and la grande chartreuse (green), in equal parts; dash with Peychaud bitters.

HOT SPICED RUM.

Two lumps sugar, two wineglasses boiling water, one wine-glass Jamaica rum, a little butter—about as much as you can put on a dime; cloves and allspice. Serve in small bar glass.

SOUPE LA REINE.

Boil two chickens in water with thyme, sweet-bay and pars-ley. When cooked (not to pieces), take them out of the water, cut up the breasts in small pieces the size of dice; fry a few pieces of onion without coloring them, add a little flour and the water that the chickens were boiled in, a little rice and the balance of the chickens, meat and bones, chopped fine. Boil all together, and when thoroughly cooked strain through a colander and put back to boil, stirring constantly. When it comes to a boil remove it from the fire and add the beaten yolks of a few eggs and a little cold milk, stirring continually. Keep the soup in "bain-marie." When ready to serve put the small pieces of the breasts in a soup-dish and pour the soup over them.

RED SNAPPER À LA CHAMBORD.

Clean your fish, and be careful not to damage it, and replace the roe. Take off the scales, and lightly raise the skin on one side, and lard it with bacon from fin to tail; put it in a pan, and moisten with white wine. Add salt, pepper, parsley, six laurel leaves, some thyme, sliced onions and three cloves; cover the head with strips of bacon, and put it into the oven, covering your fish-kettle with leaves of foolscap paper, and letting it simmer for an hour. When about to serve, drain it and put it on a platter, garnish it all round with forcemeat balls, or better, with pigeons à la Gautier, iced (glacés) sweetbreads, small glacés pope's eyes of a shoulder of veal, crabs, fowl livers, truffles, cock's combs and cock's kidneys. Strain the sauce through a silken sieve, and if not sufficiently seasoned, put into a pan two spoonfuls of Spanish sauce, and two spoonfuls of the dressing of your snapper; let it boil down one-half, put your small garnishes into it, and pour the sauce around the fish. Serve after having jellied and browned it.

CRAYFISH BISQUE A LA CRÉOLE.

Wash the cray-fishes, boil and drain them. Separate the heads from the tails. Clean out some of the heads, allowing two or three heads to each person. Peel the tails. Chop up a part of them, add to them some bread, onions, salt, black pepper and an egg or two. With this dressing, stuff the heads that you have cleaned out. Chop the claws and the parts adhering to them. Fry a little garlic, onions, ham, one turnip, one carrot, and a little flour; add some water, the chopped claws, a few tomatoes, thyme, sweet bay, parsley and a little rice, stirring often to avoid scorching. When well boiled, strain through a colander. After straining, put back to the fire and season to taste. Put the stuffed heads into the oven until brown. When ready to serve, put them and the tails aside in a soup dish and pour the soup over them. Before serving, add a little butter and nutmeg, stirring until the butter is melted.

BOUILLE-ABAISSE.

Chop some onions and garlic very fine, fry them in olive oil, and when slightly colored add some fish cut up in slices; also a few tomatoes scalded, peeled and sliced, some salt, black and red pepper, thyme, sweet-bay, parsley, and half a bottle of white wine, and enough water to cover the fish. Put it over a brisk fire and boil a quarter of an hour. Put slices of toasted bread in a deep dish, place the fish on a shallow dish with some of the broth, and pour the balance on the bread and serve hot.

BROWNED SNIPE A LA FAUVET.

Dress fourteen snipe, stuff them with a little browned stuffing, to which add two hashed truffles. Bend the skin back carefully while stuffing, and then replace it so the birds will retain as nearly as possible their natural appearance. Place the snipe so prepared and larded with bacon, into a frying pan; and to keep them sufficiently together in order that the skins may not shrink much while cooking, put some strips of bacon over them; moisten them with a little soup-stock, cover them with buttered paper and let them cook in the oven for forty minutes; then drain them, lightly trim the lower side, and lay them on a little mound of uncooked, but slightly browned stuffing, breast up, in the bottom of a dish, and ice them (glacez). Keep the dish hot in the oven for some minutes. Remove the skin and eyes from the heads of the snipe after cooking them and stick a small truffle in each bill, and lay between each two birds, one of the heads with the truffle up. Garnish the dish with stewed cock's combs, scallops, goose liver, and champignons; add a little Madeira sauce, boiled down and permeated with the flavor of the game. Ice (glacez) the snipe and truffles, and serve with a separate sauce. Let everything be very hot.

SALADE À LA RUSSE.

Cut up all kinds of vegetables, such as carrots, turnips, snap beans, etc., boil them in water with salt and butter, then drain and season lightly with salt, black pepper and vinegar; add a few cooked green peas, mashed and well drained. Put all in a salad dish in the form of a pyramid, and lightly cover it over with mayonnaise. If you have the hearts of artichokes put them around the dish, as a wreath, with a little asparagus mixed in. Keep as cool as possible until served.

BISCUIT GLACÉ FOR TWENTY.

Ten yolks of eggs, one and a half pound pulverized sugar, half a gallon of cream, vanilla extract, white of eggs well beaten if the cream is too light. To be frozen in a square box and cut in small pieces. A coat of strawberry sherbet on top of cream, before cutting, to give nice appearance. A tin box three inches wide and six inches long, which is enclosed in a box three inches larger all around. The inside box has a tight fitting top, and is packed in the outside box, which has a perforated bottom to allow water or melted ice to escape. Place inside box within the outer, and stuff with ice and salt and let it freeze; when frozen, place red sherbet on top of biscuit to give pretty appearance.

CHAR-COAL.

Item 1880

Black-coalee-coaly!
Coaly-coaly; coaly-coaly; coal-coal-coal!
Coaly-coaly!
Coal-eee! Nice!
Coaly-cc-o-oal!
Cha'coal!
Twenty-five! Whew!
O charcc-oh-oh-oh-oh-oh-lee!
Oh-lee!
Oh-lee-e!

[You get some coal in your mout'
young fellow if you don't keep it sheet.]
  Pretty coalee-oh-ee!
  Char-coal!
  Cha-ah-ah-ahr-coal.
  Coaly-coaly!
  Charbon! du charbon, Madame? Bon
charbon? Point! Ai-ai! *Tonnerre de
Dieu!*
  Char-r-r-r-r-r-r-rbon!
  A-a-a-a-a-w! High-ya-a-ah! High-yah!
  Vingt-cinq! Nice coalee! Coalee!
Coaly-coal coal!
  Pretty coaly!
  Charbon de Paris!
  De Paris, madame; de Paris!

Item 1880

HINTS ON COOKING.

When salt hams or tongues are cooked they should be instantly thrown into cold water, as the change from the boiling water they were cooked in, to the cold water, instantly loosens the skin from the flesh, and it peels off without trouble.

Fresh vinegar should be added to chopped capers, because it brings out their flavor, and makes the sauce more appetizing.

Butter sauce should never be boiled, as it becomes oily if boiled in making. The whites and yolks of eggs should be beaten separately, because the tissues of both can be better separated; and a tablespoonful of water beaten with each is an improvement, and should never be omitted.

Onions, turnips and carrots should be cut across the fibre, as it makes them more tender when cooked.

Plenty of fast-boiling water should be used in cooking vegetables, as the greater the volume of water the greater the heat. If only a little water is used the whole affair soon cools, the vegetables become tough, and no length of time will render them tender.

In boiling greens, it is best to throw into them soda with the salt, as the soda extracts the oil in them which is injurious to the digestion; from one-half to a whole teaspoonful of soda for a pot of greens is the right quantity.

Parsley should never be boiled in soda, but in boiling water and salt; boil from one to two minutes, and then chop fine. Use plenty of water to boil parsley, as a little water toughens it, and turns it brown.

Never soak dried beans in cold water as it extracts the nutritious portion of the bean. They should be washed first in warm water, then in cold, tied in a cloth and dropped into boiling water, with a little salt in it and be kept boiling for four hours. Then they are nice baked around pork, or served with gravy. To make a purée of them you throw them when boiled, into cold water, when the skins will drop off easily, and you can mash them through a sieve or colander, and season with butter, pepper, and salt.

Open the oven door, when baking meat, to let off the burnt, scorched air. The oven should be very hot, and the meat well larded, or covered with fat, or dripping, then well floured; this keeps in the juices and renders the meat tender.

TAXES

Item 1880

WASHERWOMEN.

Item 188(

16. Balié nef, balié prope. (Un balai neuf, un balai propre.)
    "A new broom's a clean broom."—This is a Creolization of our household phrase: "A new broom sweeps clean."—[*Mauritius.*]

32. Bon lilit, bon ménaze. (Bon lit, bon ménage.)
    "Where there's a good bed, there's good housekeeping."—[*Mauritius.*]

Gombo Zhèbes 1885

HINTS ON HOUSECLEANING.

SOAP BOILING, ETC.

House cleaning should commence at the top of the house and work downwards. In this case it may be undertaken by spells, with intervening rests.

After the floors are cleaned, the walls and ceilings claim attention.

A very beautiful whitening for walls and ceilings may be made by slaking the best lime in hot water, covering up to keep in the steam, and straining the milk of lime through a fine sieve; add to a pailful half a pound of common alum, two pounds of sugar, three pints of rice-flour made into a thin, well-boiled paste, and one pound of white glue dissolved slowly over the fire. It should be applied with a paint-brush when warm.

Paint should be cleaned by using only a little water at a time and changing often; a soft flannel cloth or sponge is better than cotton or a brush; a piece of pine wood with a sharp point should be used for the corners. Where the paint is stained with smoke, some ashes or potash lye may be used. A soft linen towel should be used for wiping dry. Glass should not be cleaned with soap; a little paste of whiting and water should be rubbed over, and with another cloth it should be rinsed off, and the glass polished with a soft linen or old silk

handkerchief. Alcohol or benzine is a good thing to clean
glass, and clean paper is probably better than any cloth,
sponge or towel; dry paper leaves an excellent polish. Marble
may be cleaned with a mixture of two parts of common soda,
one part of pumice stone, and one of chalk, finely powdered
and tied up in a fine muslin rag; the marble is wetted with
water, the powder shaken over it, and it is rubbed with a soft
cloth until clean, then washed in clean water and dried with
a soft linen or silk handkerchief. No soap or potash should
be allowed on marble. A good furniture polish is made by
melting two ounces of beeswax, one ounce of turpentine, and
one dram of powdered rosin together, with a gentle heat, and
rubbing on when cold, with a soft flannel cloth, and polishing
with a soft linen or silk cloth. If for mahogany, a little
Indian red may be used. Cracks in furniture may be filled
with putty, mixed with Indian-red or burnt umber, to get the
desired shade. When dry it will take an equal polish with
the wood.

HARD SOAP FOR HOUSEHOLD PURPOSES. AGREEABLE AND CLEAN.

To seven pounds of tallow, or other clean grease, use three
pounds of rosin, add six gallons of water to this, and stir in
two pounds of potash; boil this together for five hours, then
turn the soap, while hot, into a wash-tub and let it stay all
night; when cool cut into bars, and lay on a board to harden.
This quantity should be sufficient for a family of four persons
for one year.

WASHING MIXTURE.

An excellent and harmless washing mixture may be made
by cutting up a large bar of soap and dissolving it with two

ounces of borax in a half gallon of water. Boil the mixture till the soap is soft, and put it away to be used when required. There is nothing in it to take the color out of goods, and it saves labor.and soap.

FRUIT STAINS.

Fruit stains may often be removed from clothing by plunging the latter into boiling water, letting it remain immersed for a few minutes, and then washing it out in the ordinary way.

TO PREVENT GOODS FROM FADING.

Drop into a pail of water a teaspoonful of sugar of lead,, and let it dissolve. Soak the goods in this mixture for half an hour before washing them in the ordinary manner.

IVIES FOR INSIDE DECORATIONS.

It is not generally known that the various evergreen ivies will grow and flourish to perfection in the shade, and that, therefore, any room may be most charmingly decorated with them. Such is the fact, however. Put the plants in large pots, filled with rich and mellow garden soil kept at a suitable regulation of moisture, and you will have no trouble about the matter. The vines may be trained on wire trellises fastened to the wall or ceiling; or upon any other convenient arrangement. In a treatise on this subject the *Rural New Yorker* says :

"It may also be stated that the room decorated with ivy should not be kept too warm, but at a moderate temperature; such as is most healthful for a person is the best. No one need to fear to make the room unhealthy by introducing the ivy in abundance; for plants purify the air, and it is only when we introduce those emitting strong odors that anything but beneficial effects result. As all ivies succeed well in the shade, they are more suitable for the purpose herein designated than almost any other kind of plant.

"There is also another plant largely used for this purpose, which is not a true ivy, although known as German ivy (*Senecio scandens.*) It grows even more rapidly than any of the true ivies (*Hedera*), and we have seen a small plant grow so fast that it encircled quite a large room in a few weeks. It thrives well in the shade, and the leaves resemble somewhat the common English ivy, but are of a lighter and more cheerful green color. This, and a great variety of ivies are grown for sale by our florists."

DES PERCHES.

Item 1880

Pitis sans papa, pitis sans maman,
  Qui ça ou z'aut' fé pou' gagnin l'arzan!
N'a couri dans bois ramasse caucos,
Avé non la caze n'a trapé zozos,
  Et v'la comme ça n'a te fé pou' l'arzan.

Pitis sans papa, pitis sans maman,
  Qui ça ou z'aut' fé pou' gagnin l'arzan!
N'a couri a soir chez Mamzell Maroto,
Dans la rie Ste Anne, ça n'a té sous leto,
  Et v'la comme ça n'a te fé pou' l'arzan.

Item, July 7, 1880.

INDEX.

266   *INDEX.*